ENGLISH

AS A FOREIGN LANGUAGE

Sandra Stevens

Assistant author: Bismarck Vallecillo
Language consultant: John Shepheard

TEACH YOURSELF BOOKS

For UK order queries: please contact Bookpoint Ltd, 39 Milton Park, Abingdon, Oxon OX14 4TD. Telephone: (44) 01235 400414, Fax: (44) 01235 400454. Lines are open from 9.00–6.00, Monday to Saturday, with a 24 hour message answering service.
Email address: orders@bookpoint.co.uk

For U.S.A. & Canada order queries: please contact NTC/Contemporary Publishing, 4255 West Touhy Avenue, Lincolnwood, Illinois 60646–1975, U.S.A.
Telephone: (847) 679 5500, Fax: (847) 679 2494.

Long renowned as the authoritative source for self-guided learning – with more than 30 million copies sold worldwide – the *Teach Yourself* series includes over 200 titles in the fields of languages, crafts, hobbies, sports, and other leisure activities.

British Library Cataloguing in Publication Data

Library of Congress Catalog Card Number: On file

First published in UK 2001 as *Teach Yourself English* by Hodder Headline Plc, 338 Euston Road, London, NW1 3BH.

First published in US 2001 as *Teach Yourself British English* by NTC/Contemporary Publishing, 4255 West Touhy Avenue, Lincolnwood (Chicago), Illinois 60646 – 1975 U.S.A.

Typeset by Transet Limited, Coventry, England.
Printed in Great Britain for Hodder & Stoughton Educational, a division of Hodder Headline Plc, 338 Euston Road, London NW1 3BH by Cox & Wyman Ltd, Reading, Berkshire.

Impression number	9 8 7 6 5 4 3 2 1
Year	2005 2004 2003 2002 2001

CONTENTS

ABOUT THE AUTHOR

Sandra Stevens has worked in English as a foreign language for the last 30 years, as a teacher, teacher trainer, trainer of trainers and materials writer. She has worked in the UK, France, Spain and Nicaragua with the British Council, Ministries of Education and private language schools. She has also made working trips to other countries, including Argentina, Hong Kong, Italy, Kuwait, Mexico, Poland and Uruguay.

Before becoming a teacher of English as a foreign language, Sandra was an interpreter/translator (English/French) and a teacher of French. She also speaks German and has taught herself Spanish.

In addition to teaching and training, Sandra is a Joint Chief Assessor of the Cambridge Certificate in English Language Teaching to Adults (UCLES, CELTA) and a committee member for the development of Certificates and Diplomas in English Language Teaching to Young Learners. She has been Examiner and Assistant Chief Examiner of the written paper of the Cambridge Diploma. Sandra is co-author of *Basic Listening*.

Acknowledgements

The author and Publisher would like to thank the following for their kind permission to use their copyrighted material in this book:

Thistle Hotels plc (p. 324)
London Underground (p. 216–7)

INTRODUCTION

What is 'Teach Yourself English'?

A complete self-access course to learn English without a teacher.

Who is 'Teach Yourself English' for?

This course is for adult learners who want to understand and speak English with confidence.

How much English do I need to use this book?

You can follow this course with very basic English.

If you know a lot of English, this book teaches you how to use the language in real, everyday situations.

What is different about this book?

It is a real self-access course. We use a new method, devised especially for learners without a teacher.

How does this new method work?

The 'learn alone method' is carefully organised, step by step to help you *understand* and *use* new language.

- First, you listen to a conversation. The course follows a story, so you know the characters and the situation. Questions help you understand the conversation.
- Then you listen for some of the words and expressions they use in the conversation.
- Next we look at this new language (grammar, functions, vocabulary and pronunciation). The explanations are in clear, simple English.
- Finally, you practise the new language in lots of different situations.

What is special about this course?

- You learn English in English.
- The course is flexible. You decide where, when and how long you study. Each exercise has a complete title, so you can stop and start at any time. We recommend that you study little and often. Some people find it fun and helpful to work with a friend.
- The focus of the course is communication. You learn some grammar and you also learn how to do things in English, for example, *ask for information*, *offer to do something*, *accept or reject an invitation*, *make a suggestion* etc. This book also teaches 'the little things', for example how to attract attention. These 'little things' help learners feel more confident with their English.
- It teaches you how British people communicate their feelings and attitudes through language, stress and intonation.
- It teaches you about British life, habits and customs.
- It prepares you to talk about yourself, your life, your family, your work or studies and your country.
- After every practice exercise, we give you the answers. You can check your progress immediately.

What is the structure of this course?

The complete course consists of this course book and two CDs or 2 × 60-minute cassettes, with all the listening and pronunciation material.

It is important to have the CDs or cassettes, if possible:

- They give you practice in listening and understanding.
- They are also a model for pronunciation.
- They include the guided pronunciation exercises.

All the material on the CDs or cassettes is in grey .

What is in this book?

This course book contains ten **topic areas** and a **reference section**.

Each **topic area** starts with a box which lists the important new language in that topic. There are four main sections in each topic:

1 Understanding new language

Understanding the important information Listening to a conversation and understanding the key points.

Understanding more Listening again and understanding more details.

What do they say? Listening for some of the words and phrases they use. These are the important grammar points.

Find the words and phrases Listening/reading for useful words and expressions.

How do you pronounce it? Listening (for pronunciation) and practice.

What's the right word? Vocabulary and dictionary exercises on the topic.

2 Using the new language

Using these words and phrases Practising some words and expressions from 'Find the words and phrases' above.

Grammar and communication Explanations and lots of practice from 'What do they say?' above. These are the main language points in the topic.

British culture Information about British life, customs and habits.

Question and answer Questions learners of English often ask, with answers.

Common mistake Advice on problem spots for learners.

About you, your family and your country You talk about the topic in relation to you, your life and your country.

What would you say? We give you some practice in unusual situations.

Sections with a * These give you extra information about the language.

3 Revision

Join the conversation Another look at the first conversation in the topic. This time you participate.

Translation You translate into your language some examples of the main language points.

4 Test

The **reference section** at the back of the book has three sections:

1 A **glossary** The first time we use a grammar term it is in *italics*, with a short definition in brackets ( ).

In the glossary we give full definitions, with more examples, of these grammar terms.

2 A **quick reference section of phrases for communication**. This is in alphabetical order, to help you find words and expressions quickly.

3 A complete **index** With the help of the index, you can find a specific exercise quickly. This is particularly useful for teachers.

I study English in a school. Is this book useful for me?

Yes, you can use this course at the same time as other books, for extra practice.

I'm a business person. Can this book help me?

Yes. This book emphasises social competence in English in a variety of situations.

I want to travel. Is this book useful?

Yes. This book gives lots of practice in the language you need, for example, to order food and drink, find a hotel and use public transport.

I'm an English teacher. How can I use this book?

- For reference
- As a course book
- As supplementary material.
- The recorded material as a listening course.
- For homework
- The grammar / functions / pronunciation / vocabulary } syllabus and exercises can be used alone or in the combination you choose
- The **Common mistake** exercises can help with persistent problem areas
- The **You, Your family and Your country** sections can be used for personalisation
- The **British culture** sections can be starting points for comparisons with customs and habits in students' own countries/fluency work
- The **tests** can be used independently

1 SAYING 'HELLO'

Grammar and communication	**Vocabulary**
◆ Starting a conversation – question tags ◆ Continuing a conversation – short answers ◆ Continuing a conversation – saying more ◆ Invitations and offers – *Would you like…?* ◆ *A/Some* – countables and uncountables ◆ Offering more – food and drink ◆ Saying *yes* and *no* to offers	◆ Food and drink **Pronunciation** ◆ Introduction to intonation

Our story begins on a plane …

The first conversation

→ If you have the cassette or CD, cover the text of Recording 1, *The Story*.
→ Read the sentences below.
→ Listen to the conversation 1, 2 or 3 times.
→ If you don't have the cassette or CD, read the text of the recording.
→ Choose the correct answer **a**, **b** or **c**.

1 It's **a** cold / **b** sunny / **c** hot } in the plane.

2 The conversation is about
a London.
b a drink.
c dinner.

3 The woman would like
a some Coke.
b to sleep.
c to eat.

Recording 1 (and 8) – The Story

Man	It's hot, isn't it?
Woman	Yes, it is – very hot.
Man	Would you like a drink?
Woman	M'm, yes, please.
Man	What would you like?
Woman	Some Coke, please.

Check your answers

1c **2**b **3**a

What do they say?

→ Cover the text of Recording 1 again.
→ Read the sentences below.
→ First listen and complete the words.
→ Then read the text of the recording to help you.

1 a The man starts the conversation.
He says, 'I _' s/h _ _ /, i _ n' _ /i _ ?'

b The woman answers,
'Y _ _, i _ / i _ / – / v _ _ _ / h _ _ .'

2 a The man offers a drink.
He says, 'W _ _ _ d / y _ _ / l _ k _ / a / d _ _ _ k ?'

b The woman accepts.
She says, 'Y _ _ / p _ _ _ s _.'

3 a The man asks what drinks she wants.
He says, 'W _ _ _ / w _ _ _ _ / you / l _ _ _ ?'

b The woman answers,
'So _ e / C _ k _ /, p _ _ _ _ e.'

Check your answers

1a It's hot, isn't it? b Yes, it is – very hot.
2a Would you like a drink? b Yes, please.
3a What would you like? b Some Coke, please.

English pronunciation

Intonation

★ Intonation is very important in English. What is intonation? The *music* or movement of our voice. Sometimes our voice goes up ↗ (a rise) – sometimes our voice goes down ↘ (a fall). This is **intonation**.

★ Different languages express things in different ways. English uses intonation a lot for communication. A different intonation gives a different message. Is intonation important in your language? This book explains and gives practice in understanding and using intonation in English.

Intonation and Grammar – questions

Listen to Recording 2, part 1 and repeat the words. (**a** rises and **b** falls)

Recording 2, part 1

1a	Yes?	b	Yes.	4a	O.K.?	b	O.K.
2a	This?	b	This.	5a	Alright?	b	Alright.
3a	No?	b	No.	6a	Sorry?	b	Sorry.

Q ***Is there a pattern here?***

A Yes. In general, a rise is a question. (Some questions go down. See Topic 3.)

Q ***Where exactly is this rise or fall?***

A On the **syllable** with **stress** or emphasis. (A **syllable** is a word or part of a word with a vowel sound.)

Intonation and feelings – voice movement

★ In English we use intonation to express **attitude** (our feelings).

★ In general, big voice movements express strong feelings.

★ Flat intonation expresses that you are not interested or that your attitude is **negative**.

Listen to Recording 2, part 2, and repeat the words. (**a** big movements = positive and interested, **b** small movements = not very positive, not interested, negative).

Recording 2, part 2

1a	Yes	b	Yes	4a	O.K.?	b	O.K.?
2a	This?	b	This?	5a	Alright	b	Alright
3a	No	b	No	6a	Sorry	b	Sorry

Find the right word

Drinks

→Find seven drinks in this word search. The words go across → and down ↓.

→Use the pictures and your dictionary if necessary.

o	w	r	m	c	s	z
s	i	j	b	o	g	w
v	n	e	n	f	o	a
y	e	m	w	f	a	t
j	u	i	c	e	t	e
l	a	l	b	e	e	r
c	o	k	e	r	a	p

Check your answers

o	w	r	m	c	s	z
s	i	j	b	o	g	w
v	n	e	n	f	o	a
y	e	m	w	f	a	t
j	u	i	c	e	t	e
l	a	l	b	e	e	r
c	o	k	e	r	a	p

Grammar and communication 1

Starting a conversation – question tags

Example from *The Story*:

The man starts the conversation. He says, 'It's hot, **isn't it**?'

Q ***What is 'isn't it?'***

A It's a **question tag**.

★ Question tags are very common in English.

Q ***What are question tags?***

A Question tags are short questions at the end of a sentence.

Meaning

Q ***Is this a real question?***

A No. The man knows it's hot. The falling intonation also tells us it's not a real question. Here, the question tag starts a conversation.

Form

★ We use the same tense in the main verb and the question tag.
★ With a **positive main verb**, we use a **negative question tag**.
With a **negative main verb**, we use a **positive question tag**.

Grammar summary – Question tags with verb *be*			
Positive verb + negative tag		**Negative verb + positive tag**	
I am right,	aren't I?	I'm not wrong,	am I?
He / She / It is English,	isn't he? / she? / it?	He / She / It isn't English,	is he? / she? / it?
We / You / They are happy,	aren't we? / you? / they?	We / You / They aren't happy,	are we? / you? / they?

Q ***And if there isn't a verb?***

A That depends. Here are some examples.

Positive	Negative
'It's good, isn't it? OR 'Good, isn't it? (Informal)	It's not very good, is it? OR Not very good, is it? (Informal)

With an **adjective** we use a **negative question tag**.
With ***'not'* + adjective**, we use a **positive question tag**.

★ In informal spoken English, it is possible to start with the adjective. For example, 'It's interesting, isn't it?' is correct and always appropriate. 'Interesting, isn't it?' is correct and informal.

British culture – the weather

- In Britain it is very common to talk about the weather. Why? Because the weather can change a lot.
- People often use the weather to start a conversation.

Question tags with falling intonation

→ Complete with the correct question tag.

1 It's really cold today, _______/___?
2 Nice and warm this morning, ______/__?
3 The weather's not bad today, ____/__?
4 Lovely day, ____/___?

Check your answers *(Recording 3)*

1 It's really cold today, isn't it?
2 Nice and warm this morning, isn't it?
3 The weather's not bad today, is it?
4 Lovely day, isn't it?

How do you pronounce it?

Starting a conversation

→ Listen to Recording 3 above and start these conversations. Pay special attention to the falling intonation on the question tag.

Question tags with falling intonation

→ Match the pictures (**1–9**) below with the correct sentence **a–i** and complete the question tags.

a It's a very good film, ________ ?

b You're David, ________ ? My name's Sam.

c The food's very nice, ________ ?

d This programme's not very interesting, ________ ?

e She's beautiful, ________ ?

f This isn't right, ________ ?

g It's not very warm in here, ________ ?

h They're lovely, ________ ?

i He's a good singer, ________ ?

Check your answers *(Recording 4)*

1 d This programme's not very interesting, is it?
2 g It's not very warm in here, is it?
3 a It's a very good film, isn't it?
4 b You're David, aren't you? My name's Sam.
5 h They're lovely, aren't they?
6 i He's a good singer, isn't he?
7 e She's beautiful, isn't she?
8 c The food's very nice, isn't it?
9 f This isn't right, is it?

More pronunciation practice

→ Listen to Recording 4 above and start these conversations. Pay special attention to the falling intonation on the question tags.

Grammar and communication 2

Continuing a conversation – short answers

Example from *The Story*:

Man: '**It's** hot, **isn't it**?' Woman: '**Yes, it is** – very hot.'

Yes, it is is a short answer.

Meaning

The woman wants to continue the conversation.

Form

Man: '**It's** hot, **isn't it**?' Woman: 'Yes, **it is** – very hot.'

Here's a different example:

Man: '**It's not** very nice, **is it**?' Woman: 'No, **it isn't**.'

Short answers

Q ***Can I just say 'Yes'?***

A *Yes* and *No* alone can sound impolite. ☹

It can mean you are not interested in the conversation.

Q ***The negative has two forms 'No, it isn't' and 'No, it's not'. Are they different?***

A No, they are the same.

! Common mistake – short answers

'It's hot, isn't it?'

'Yes, it is.' (Not: '~~Yes, it's~~')

'It's' is the **contraction** (short form) of 'it is'. It is not possible to end a sentence with a positive contraction.

And in the negative?

'It isn't very hot, is it?'

'No, it isn't.'

This is correct. It is possible to end a sentence with a negative contraction.

Short answers

→ Complete the short answers with expressions from the box below.

Example: They aren't here, are they? ***No, they aren't.***

1 He's not there, is he? No, ____________

2 She's pretty, isn't she? Yes, ____________

3 This isn't difficult, is it? No, ____________

4 We're ready, aren't we? Yes, ____________

5 You're Paul, aren't you? Yes, ____________

6 They're in France, aren't they? No, ____________

I am	***he isn't***	***it isn't***	***they aren't***	***she is***	***we are***

Grammar and communication 3

Continuing a conversation – saying more

★ It is very common to say more after short answers.

→ Look at these responses:

A Nice weather, isn't it?
B Yes it is, OR Yes, lovely.
OR Yes, it's lovely.
OR Yes, it is. It's lovely.
OR Yes, it is, isn't it.

→ Here are the sentences from Recording 4 (page 9) again.
→ This time match sentences **1–9** with responses **a–i** and complete the responses.

				Response
1	It's a very good film, isn't it?	**f**	**a**	Yes _______. They're beautiful.
2	You're David, aren't you?		**b**	Yes,______. It's delicious.
3	The food's very nice, isn't it?		**c**	No,_______ Not at all.
4	This programme's not very interesting, is it?		**d**	Yes,_____ I like him a lot.
5	She's beautiful, isn't she?		**e**	Yes, _____. She's wonderful.
6	This isn't right, is it?		**f**	Yes, ***it is***. It's excellent.
7	It's not very warm in here, is it?		**g**	No,_____. You're not too good at maths, are you?
8	They're lovely, aren't they?		**h**	Yes, that's right______. And your name is ...?
9	He's a good singer, isn't he?		**i**	No, _____. The window's open.

Check your answers

1f Yes, it is. **2**h I am. **3**b Yes, it is. **4**c No, it isn't. **5**e Yes, she is. **6**g No, it isn't. OR No, it's not. **7**i No, it isn't. OR No, it's not. **8**a Yes, they are. **9**d Yes he is.

Grammar and communication 4

Invitations and offers – food and drink

Example from *The Story*:

The man suggests a drink.
He says, 'Would you like a drink?'

→ Listen to Recording 5 and practise your pronunciation and intonation.

Recording 5

Would you like a drink?

W…

Would…

Would you…

Would you like…

Would you like a…

Would you like a drink?

What's the right word?

Food

→ Label these pictures. Use your dictionary if necessary.

Check your answers

rice

crisps

sandwich

bread

biscuits

grapes

soup

hamburger

Grammar and communication 5

'*A*'/'*Some*'

The man offers a drink. He says, 'Would you like **a** drink?'

The woman wants Coke. She says, 'Yes, **some** Coke please.'

→Look at these examples:

Would you like **a** sandwich?	**a** sandwich	*singular* (one)
Would you like **some** crisps?	**some** crisps	*plural* (more than one)
Would you like **some** bread?	**some** bread	*uncountable* (can't count it)

★ '*A*' is for singular things, for example, a hamburger, a biscuit.
★ '*Some*' is for plural things, for example, some grapes, some biscuits, and things we can't count, for example, some soup, some rice.

A or *some*?

→Write 1–10 next to the correct picture.

1 an ice cream
2 some ice cream
3 some ice creams
4 a cake
5 some cake

6 some cakes
7 a chocolate
8 some chocolate
9 some chocolates
10 a pizza
11 some pizza
12 a Coke
13 some Coke

Check your answers

→ Now write invitations for these pictures.

1 Example:  ***Would you like a hamburger?***

2 

3 

4 

5 

6 

7 

8 

☑ Check your answers *(Recording 6)*

1 Would you like a hamburger?
2 Would you like some bread?
3 Would you like some soup?
4 Would you like a sandwich?
5 Would you like some grapes?
6 Would you like a biscuit?
7 Would you like some crisps?
8 Would you like some rice?

→ Listen to the exercise above on Recording 6 and repeat the questions.

Invitations and offers – food and drink

Q *Can I say, 'Do you want a drink?'*

A *Do you want ...?*

★ The grammar is correct.
★ It is very informal.
★ You can sound rude. ☹

Tip: Use *Would you like ...?*.
Say *Do you want...?* only with people you know very well.

Q *Can I say 'Do you like...' for offers and invitations?*

A No.

Do you like...? is a general question about likes.

For example: '**Do you like** ice cream?' – **a general question**.
'**Would you like** an ice cream?' – **an invitation or offer**.

Grammar and communication 6

Offering more – food and drink

→ Look at the table below.

First offer	Second offer	
A sandwich?	**another** sandwich?	*singular*
Some crisps ?	**(Some) more** crisps?	*plural*
Some water?	**(Some) more** water?	*uncountable*

→ Complete these offers with '*another*' or '*more*' or '*some more*'.

1 _______ drink?
2 Would you like _______/_______ crisps?
3 _______ wine?
4 Would you like _______ biscuit?
5 _______/_______ milk?

Check your answers

1 Another drink? **2** Would you like some more crisps? **3** More wine? **4** Would you like another biscuit? **5** Some more milk?

British culture – saying *yes* and *no* to offers

- People say *please* and *thank you* a lot in English.
- It is the norm to say *Yes, please* or *No, thank you* (or *thanks*) to offers.
- *Yes* or *no* alone can sound rude.
- *Thanks* is a little more informal than *thank you.*

Grammar and communication 7

Saying *yes* and *no* to offers

→ Look at these examples.

Saying *yes*

1 Would you like some water? — Yes, please. ☺

2 Another cake? — Yes, please, that would be nice. ☺☺

3 Would you like a cup of tea? — Yes, please, I'd love one. ☺☺☺

4 Juice? — Yes, please, I'd love some. ☺☺☺

Saying *no*

1 Would you like some ice cream? — No, thank you.

2 Some more coffee? — No, thanks. I'm fine.

Q ***In an offer, for example, 'Would you like some tea?' can I answer, 'Yes, I would' or 'No, I wouldn't'?***

A The grammar is correct but they are not appropriate answers to offers. ☹ Say, 'Yes, please' and 'No, thank you' with offers.

How do you pronounce it?

Offers – rising intonation
Saying *yes* and *no*

→ Listen to Recording 7 and repeat the offers and answers.

Recording 7

1 A Coffee?
B Yes, please.

2 A Some more tea?
B No, thanks.

3 A Would you like another drink?
B Yes, please.

4 A More orange-juice?
B No, no more thank you. I'm fine.

5 A Would you like some more bread?
B Yes, please, I'd love some.

About you – food and drink. Answer these questions.

Are you hungry? Would you like something to eat?________________

What would you like?________________________________

Are you thirsty? Would you like something to drink?_______________

What would you like?________________________________

What would you say?

Situation 1: You are in the street.
A person says to you, 'Hello Chris.' You are not Chris.
You say:____________________________

Situation 2: You are in a coffee shop.
You want tea, your friend wants coffee.

The waiter says to you: 'Here's your coffee and tea for your friend.
You say: ______________________________

Possible answers

1 Sorry, I'm not Chris. **2** Thanks, but the coffee's for my friend and the tea's for me.

Revision

What is it in your language?

→ Here are some examples of the important points in this topic.
→ Translate the sentences below into your language in the spaces.
→ Remember – translate the idea, not the words.

1 It's hot, isn't it?

____

2 Yes, it is – very hot.

____

3 Would you like a drink?

____

4 Yes, please.

____

5 What would you like?

____

6 Some Coke, please.

____

Join the conversation

→ Look at Recording 1 on page 1 again.
→ Listen to Recording 8.
→ Say the **man's** words in the spaces.

That's the end of Topic 1.
Well done!
Now try the test.
There's one at the end of each topic.

TEST 1

Which one is right?

→ Choose the correct sentence, **a** or **b**.

1 Starting a conversation	**a** Nice day, is it? **b** Nice day, isn't it?
2 Offering	**a** Would you like a drink? **b** Do you like a drink?
Saying *yes*	**a** Yes, I do. **b** Yes, please.
3 Starting a conversation	**a** This topic's not very difficult, isn't it? **b** This topic's not very difficult, is it?
4 Starting a conversation	**a** This soup are delicious. **b** This soup's delicious.
Responding	**a** Yes, it is, isn't it? **b** Yes, it's.
5 Offering more	**a** Another bread? **b** Some more bread?
Saying *no*	**a** No thanks, I'm fine. **b** No.

Write a dialogue

Situation: You are in the street with a friend. It's cold.

You | **Your friend**

1 Start the conversation

2 Respond

3 Invite your friend for a drink

4 Say yes

O.K. Let's go then

Check your answers

Which one is right?

1 Starting a conversation	**b** Nice day, isn't it?
2 Offering	**a** Would you like a drink?
Saying *yes*	**b** Yes, please.
3 Starting a conversation	**b** This topic's not very difficult, is it?
4 Starting a Conversation	**b** This soup's delicious.
Responding	**a** Yes, it is, isn't it?
5 Offering more	**b** Some more bread?
Saying *no*	**a** No, thanks. I'm fine.

Dialogue: model answers

1 You	Cold, isn't it?
2 Your friend	Yes, it is – very cold.
3 You	Would you like a hot drink?
4 Your friend	Yes, please.
	Yes please, that would be nice!
	Yes please, I'd love one.

2 ASKING FOR THINGS

Grammar and communication

- Responding to offers
- Making decisions – *I'll*
- Asking for things, *Could I have…?*
- Ordering drinks
- Talking about availability – *have got, there is + some/any, any*
- Opinions and comparisons, *What's… like?*, *smaller*, etc.
- Asking for permission, *Is it alright if I…?*

Vocabulary

- Food and drink (2)

Pronunciation

- Introduction to stress
- Intonation and communication

The two passengers would like a drink …

Understanding the important information

→ Cover the text of Recording 1.
→ Read the sentences below.
→ Listen and answer 'Yes' or 'No'.

1 The woman wants Coke Yes/No
2 The man wants water Yes/No
3 The woman wants ice Yes/No
4 The woman wants lemon Yes/No
5 The man wants ice Yes/No
6 The man wants lemon Yes/No

Recording 1 (and 11) – The Story

Man	Excuse me.
Flight attendant	Yes, sir?
Man	Could I have a Coke and some orange juice, please?
Flight attendant	Of course. Would you like the Coke with ice and lemon?
Woman	Yes please.
Flight attendant	Ice for you, sir?
Man	No thanks.
Flight attendant	Here you are. One Coke with ice and lemon and one orange juice.
Man and woman	Thank you/Thanks.

Check your answers

1 Yes **2** No He wants orange juice **3** Yes **4** Yes **5** No **6** No

What do they say?

→ Cover the text of Recording 1 again.
→ Read the sentences on page 24.
→ First, listen to the recording and try to complete the words.
→ Then read the text to help you if necessary.

1 The man wants the attention of the flight attendant.
He says, 'E _ _ _ _ _ / m _ .'

2 The man asks for the drinks.
He says, 'C _ _ _ _ / I / h _ _ _ / _ / Coke and / s _ _ _ / o _ a _ _ _ j _ i c _ /, please?'

3 The flight attendant gives them the drinks.
He says, 'H_ _ _ / y _ _ / a _ _ /.
O _ _ /Coke with ice and lemon and / _ _ _ / orange juice.'

Check your answers

1 Excuse me. **2** Could I have a Coke and some orange juice, please? **3** Here you are. One Coke with ice and lemon and one orange juice.

British culture – attracting attention

- In English, we say, *Excuse me* to attract attention.
- Other ways, for example, a sound like 'ts,ts,ts', are impolite.

English pronunciation

Stress

Q ***What is stress?***

A Emphasis or accent. English has no written accents. It has stress on some words and syllables. This book explains and gives practice in stress.

Word stress

Q ***Where's the stress in words?***

A In words with two syllables or more, one syllable has stress.

(*Q* What's a syllable? *A* Part of a word with a vowel sound.)

Examples from the conversation above are, 'excuse', 'orange', 'lemon'.

→ Listen to the words below and underline the syllable with stress.

Recording 2, part 1

1 syllables
2 examples
3 conversation
4 above
5 important
6 information

Check your answers

1 syllables **2** examples **3** conversation **4** above **5** important **6** information

Q ***Where's the stress on a word? How do I know?***

A In some dictionaries, they show stress (ˈ) at the beginning of the syllable. For example, *above* / əˈb ʌ v /

Stress in phrases and sentences

Q ***Where's the stress in phrases and sentences?***

A On the important or new information.
For example, in *My name's Tom*, the stress is on Tom.

→ Listen to the phrases below and underline the syllable with stress.

Recording 2, part 2

1 Some Coke
2 To London
3 From David
4 Are they here?
5 Does it change?
6 Ask them

Check your answers

1 Some Coke. **2** To London. **3** From David. **4** Are they here?
5 Does it change? **6** Ask them.

Q ***What about the other syllables – the syllables without stress?***

A In these little words (for example, *some, to, from, are, does, them*), sometimes the vowel sound changes to the first sound in the word *above*. It's the only sound with a name. It's called *schwa*. We write it like this / ə /. *Schwa* means 'weak'.

→ Listen to Recording 2, part 2 again.

How many / ə / sounds are there: 4, 5, 6, 7 or 8? Where are they?

Check your answer

Seven. **1** Some (/ə/) Coke. **2** To (/ə/) London (/ə/). **3** From (/ə/) David.

4 Are (/ə/) they here? **5** Does (/ə/) it change? **6** Ask them (/ə/).

Weak forms

Q ***Is the pronunciation of the words above, for example 'some' 'to', always the same?***

A No. Without stress the vowel sound is weak (*schwa*).
When the word is important, the vowel sound is strong.

Q ***So, one word has two different pronunciations?***

A Yes, that's right.

→ Listen to Recording 2, part 3 and repeat the phrases with these words. In **a** the vowel is weak, in **b** the vowel is strong.

Recording 2, part 3

1 Some	weak	**a**	Some (/ə/) Coke
	strong	**b**	Would you like some?
2 To	weak	**a**	to (/ə/) London
	strong	**b**	Where to?
3 From	weak	**a**	from (/ə/) David
	strong	**b**	Who from?

4 Are	weak	**a**	/ə/ Are they here?
	strong	**b**	Yes, they are.
5 Does	weak	**a**	/ə/ Does it change?
	strong	**b**	Yes, it does.
6 Them	weak	**a**	Ask /ə/ them.
	strong	**b**	Ask them, not me.

Q ***Is there a name for this, when one vowel has two different pronunciations?***

A Yes, the weak pronunciation, / ə /, is called a *weak form.*

Q ***Why are weak forms important for learners of English?***

A Learners often say 'I can't understand English people – they speak very fast and swallow their words'. One reason for this is weak forms. This book explains and gives practice in understanding and using weak forms.

What's the right word?

Food

→ Label the pictures with the food names.
→ Use your dictionary if necessary.

fish
chicken
beef
lamb
vegetarian
pork

Check your answers

a beef **b** pork **c** chicken **d** fish **e** lamb **f** vegetarian

Our story continues... the flight attendant serves dinner

Understanding the important information

→ On Recording 3 the flight attendant serves eight passengers.
→ Listen and tick the right answer

Passenger 1	**a**	chicken	**b**	beef		
Passenger 2	**a**	beef	**b**	vegetarian		
Passenger 3	**a**	fish	**b**	pork		
Passenger 4	**a**	lamb	**b**	fish		
Passenger 5	**a**	fish	**b**	beef		
Passenger 6	**a**	fish	**b**	beef		
Passenger 7	**a**	vegetarian	**b**	chicken		
Passenger 8	**a**	fish	**b**	chicken	**c**	a sandwich

Recording 3 – The Story

1	**Attendant**	Chicken or beef, sir?
	Passenger	Chicken, please.
2	**Attendant**	Beef or vegetarian, madam?
	Passenger	Beef for me, please.
3	**Attendant**	Would you like fish or pork, sir?
	Passenger	I'd like fish, please.
4	**Attendant**	What would you like to eat, madam, fish or lamb?
	Passenger	Could I have the lamb, please?

5	**Attendant**	Is it fish or beef for you, madam?
	Passenger	I'll have beef, please.
6	**Attendant**	And for you, sir?
	Passenger	The same for me too, please.
7	**Attendant**	Would you like vegetarian or chicken, sir?
	Passenger	I don't mind. I like both.
8	**Attendant**	Would you like fish or chicken, madam?
	Passenger	Nothing for me thanks. I'm not very hungry. Could I have a sandwich instead?
	Attendant	Of course.

Check your answers

1 a chicken **2 a** beef **3 a** fish **4 b** lamb **5 b** beef **6 b** beef **7 a** or **b** we don't know **8 c** a sandwich

What do they say?

Responding to offers – food and drink

→ Cover the text of Recording 3, *The Story* again.
→ Read the questions and responses below.
→ Listen and try to complete the responses.
→ Then read the text of Recording 3 to help you if necessary.

1	**Attendant**	Chicken or beef, sir?
	Passenger	Chicken, / p _ _ _ _ _/.
2	**Attendant**	Beef or vegetarian, madam?
	Passenger	Beef / f _ _ / m _/ please.
3	**Attendant**	Would you like fish or pork, sir?
	Passenger	I' _ / l _ _ _ / fish, please.
4	**Attendant**	What would you like to eat, madam, fish or lamb?
	Passenger	C _ _ _ _ / I / h _ _ _ / the lamb, please?
5	**Attendant**	Is it fish or beef for you, madam?
	Passenger	I' _ _ / h _ _ _ / beef, please.

Check your answers

1 Chicken, please. **b** Beef for me, please. **3** I'd like fish please. **4** Could I have the lamb, please? **5** I'll have beef, please.

→ Now listen to Recording 3, Passengers 1–5, and repeat the responses.

Grammar and communication 1

Responding to offers

→ Look at the text of Recording 3 on pages 28–9.
→ Complete the sentences below and answer the questions.

1 Asking for the same

In the mini-dialogues on pages 28–9, Passenger 5 wants fish.
Passenger 6 wants fish, too.

Passenger 5 says 'Could I have fish please?'
Passenger 6 says, ' T_ _ / s _ _ _ / f _ _ / m _ / t _ _ , please.'

2 Verb *mind*

The flight attendant asks Passenger 7, 'Would you like vegetarian or chicken, sir?'
He says, 'I don't mind…'

→ Choose the correct meaning below, **a**, **b** or **c**.

a He wants vegetarian.
b He wants chicken.
c It isn't important. He likes vegetarian and chicken.

3 Saying *no*; talking about alternatives

The flight attendant asks Passenger 8, 'Would you like fish or chicken, madam?' She isn't hungry. She says, 'N _ _ _ _ _ _ / f _ _ / m _, thanks. I'm not very hungry. Could I have a sandwich i _ _ _ _ _ _ , please?'

Check your answers

1 Passenger 6 The same for me too, please. **2 c** **3** Nothing for me, thanks. I'm not very hungry. Could I have a sandwich instead, please?

Grammar and communication 2

Making decisions – *I'll*

Example from the listening exercise on pages 28–9:

The flight attendant asks Passenger 5, 'Is it fish or beef for you, madam? The passenger says, '**I'll** have beef, please.'

Tip: When you decide and speak, say *I'll...* .

→ Make decisions in these situations.

1 Would you like Coke or fruit juice?
__'__/ _______ fruit juice, please.

2 Which cake would you like, fruit or chocolate?
__'__/ ____ a slice of the chocolate one, please.

3 It's lunch time…I think__'__ / _____ some bread and cheese.

4 Are you tired?
Yes, I think __'__ go to bed.

5 The supermarket is closed now. __'__ / ___ tomorrow.

Check your answers

1 I'll have fruit juice, please. **2** I'll have a slice of the chocolate one, please. **3** I think I'll have some bread and cheese. **4** I think I'll go to bed. **5** I'll go tomorrow.

! Common mistake – negative decisions

It's time to go to work but you feel terrible. You decide to stay at home.

I **don't think** **I'll** go to work. ✓
(**don't think**: Negative; **I'll**: Positive)

Not: **I think** **I won't** go to work. ✗
(**I think**: Positive; **I won't**: Negative)

> **Tip:** Put the negative with *think*, not with *I'll*.

Grammar and communication 3

Asking for things (requests)

Example from *The Story*:

Oliver asks for the drinks. He says, 'Could I have a Coke and some orange juice, please?'

In Topic 1 we look at *a/an* and *some* with offers.
For example, 'Would you like some coffee?'

★ *Please* is very common when you ask for something.

→ Look at the examples below:

Singular

Offer	Would you like **a cup** of coffee?
Request	Could / Can } I have **a cup** of coffee, please?

Plural

Offer	Would you like **some biscuits**?
Request	Could / Can } I have **some biscuits**, please?

Uncountables

Offer	Would you like **some fruit juice**?
Request	Could / Can } I have **some fruit juice**, please?

> **Tip:** The use of *a/an* and *some* is the same in offers and requests.

→ Complete the requests below. Put the words in the right order.

1 **A** Would you like a drink?
B Yes,__________________, please?
have/I/coffee/some/could

2 **A** Would you like something to eat?
B Yes, ______________, please?
sandwich/have/can/I/a

3 **A** What would you like to drink?
B ________________________, please?
have/something/we/can/cold

4 **A** Would you like some pizza?
B Yes, __________________, please?
slice/have/I/could/small/a

5 Excuse me, _________________, please?
a/water/I/glass/could/have/of

6 **A** Would you like some grapes or some strawberries?
B ________________________, please?
grapes/could/have/I/some

☑ Check your answers

1 Could I have some coffee, please? **2** Yes, can I have a sandwich, please? **3** Can we have something cold, please? **4** Could I have a small slice, please? **5** Excuse me, could I have a glass of water, please? **6** Could I have some grapes, please?

> **Tip:** Flight attendants and other people who work with food and drink don't always say *some*. They say 'Tea?', 'Chicken?, 'Fish or beef?', etc. for offers. This is practical and short.

How do you pronounce it?

Requests – intonation

★ Intonation is important with requests.
★ A big fall sounds polite.
★ Flat intonation can sound rude.

- → Listen to the requests on Recording 4. You will hear each one twice.
- → Listen to the fall on the syllable with stress. One is rude (flat intonation) and one is polite (big fall).
- → Circle 'R' for rude (flat intonation) or 'P' for polite (big fall)

Recording 4

A Could I have some coffee, please?
1 R/P **2** R/P

B Yes, can I have a sandwich, please?
1 R/P **2** R/P

C Can we have something cold, please?
1 R/P **2** R/P

D Could I have a small piece, please?
1 R/P **2** R/P

E Excuse me, could I have a glass of water, please?
1 R/P **2** R/P

F Could I have some grapes, please?
1 R/P **2** R/P

Check your answers

A	**1** Polite	**2** Rude
B	**1** Rude	**2** Polite
C	**1** Rude	**2** Polite
D	**1** Polite	**2** Rude
E	**1** Rude	**2** Polite
F	**1** Polite	**2** Rude

- → Now listen to Recording 5 and repeat the request.
- → Pay special attention to the big fall on **Coke**.

Recording 5

Could…
Could I…
Could I have…
Could I have some…
Could I have some Coke…
Could I have some Coke, please?

More requests

→ Ask for the things in the pictures.

1 Could ______________, please?

2 ______________________________

3 ______________________________

4 ______________________________

5 ______________________________

Check your answers (*Recording 6*)

1	Could I have some water, please?	(uncountable)
2	Could I have some bread, please?	(uncountable)
3	Could I have an ice cream, please?	(countable)
4	Could I have another sandwich, please?	(countable)
5	Could I have some more coffee, please?	(uncountable)
OR		
	Could I have another cup of coffee, please?	(countable)

→ Now listen to Recording 6 and repeat the requests.
→ Pay special attention to the big fall on the syllables with stress.

Grammar and communication 4

Ordering drinks

Situation You work in a coffee shop.

→ On Recording 7 on page 36, three customers are ordering drinks. What would they like?
→ Listen and write their orders.

Customer 1	Customer 2	Customer 3
__________	__________	__________
__________	__________	__________
	__________	

Check your answers *(Recording 7)*

1 Three coffees and one tea, please.
2 Could I have four Cokes, two orange juices and one hot chocolate?
3 We'd like two lemon teas, please.

Tip: It is common to omit *cup* and *glass* when you order drinks.

Asking for things

Q *What's the difference between 'Could I have...?' and 'Can I have...?'*

A
- ★ The grammar in both is correct.
- ★ *Could I...?* is always appropriate.
- ★ *Can I...?* is a little informal.

'Give me...' The imperative can be impolite. Use it only in informal situations and with people you know well. (See Topic 9.)

Our story continues... the flight attendant serves drinks

Understanding the important information

What drinks would these three passengers like?

- → Cover the text of Recording 8.
- → Listen and:
- → Write the drink they would like
- → Is it possible? Choose *Yes* or *No*.

Passenger 1__________ Yes/No
Passenger 2__________ Yes/No
Passenger 3__________ Yes/No

Recording 8

Passenger 1
Would you like a drink with your dinner? I've got some apple juice.
Yes, please.

Passenger 2
What would you like to drink with your dinner, sir?
Have you got any cold beer?
Of course… Here you are.

Passenger 3
Could I have some white wine, please?
I'm sorry, madam. I haven't got any more white wine. Would you like red instead?

Check your answers

1 Apple juice – possible. **2** Beer – possible. **3** White wine – impossible.

Grammar and communication 5

Talking about availability – *have got*

→ Cover the text of Recording 8 again.
→ Listen and try to complete the words below.
→ Then read the text of the recording to help you if necessary.

Passenger 1
Flight attendant: I'_ _ / g _ _ / some apple juice.
Passenger 2
H _ _ _ / y _ _ / g _ _ / any cold beer?
Passenger 3
Flight attendant: I h _ _ _ _ ' _ / g _ _ / any more white wine.

Check your answers

1 I've got some apple juice. **2** Have you got any cold beer? **3** I haven't got any more white wine.

Meaning

★ *Have got* is about availability.

Form

Grammar summary – *have got*

Affirmative			
I/you/we/they	have 've	got	a drink.
He/she/it	has 's		
Negative			
I/you/we/they He/she/it	haven't hasn't	got	
Questions			
Have Has	I/you/we/they he/she/it	got	a drink?

Question tags				**Short answers**		
I you we they	've got…	haven't	I? we? you? they?	Yes,	I you we they	have
he she it	's got …	hasn't	he? she? it?	Yes,	he she it	has
I you we they	haven't got…	have	I? you? we? they?	No,	I you we they	haven't
he she it	hasn't got…	has	he? she? it?	No,	he she it	hasn't

→ Complete the sentences below with the correct parts of *have got*.
→ Use the table above to help you.

1 **A** What sort of drinks ***have you got?***
B I' _ _ / g _ _ / water, juice, beer or wine.

2 **A** Could I have chicken, please?
B I'm sorry, we _ _ _ _ _ ' _ / _ _ _ / any more chicken.

3 **A** If you’re hungry, I’ _ _ / g _ _ / a pizza.
B H _ _ _ / y _ _ ? Could I have some now, please?

4 **A** _ _ _ he _ _ _ any milk for the coffee?
B Yes, he _ _ _. Here it is.

5 **A** We _ _ _ _ _ _ ’ _ / _ _ _ any bread.
B H _ _ _ _ _ ’ _ / _ _ ? O.K. I’ll go and buy some.

6 **A** I _ _ _ _ _ _ ’ t / _ _ _ chicken but I’ _ _ / _ _ _ lamb.
B No, thanks. Can I have a sandwich, instead, please?

7 **A** They’ _ _ / g _ _ / Coke, h _ _ _ _ _ ’ t / they?
B Yes, I’ll ask for some.

8 **A** Why _ _ _ _ _ ’ _ he / _ _ _ / any rice?
B I don’t know.

Check your answers

1 I’ve got water, juice, beer or wine.
2 We haven’t got any more chicken.
3 **A** If you’re hungry, I’ve got a pizza.
B Have you? Could I have some now, please?
4 **A** Has he got some milk for the coffee?
B Yes, he has. Here it is.
5 **A** We haven’t got any bread.
B Haven’t we? O.K. I’ll go and buy some.
6 **A** I haven’t got chicken but I’ve got lamb.
7 **A** They’ve got Coke, haven’t they?
8 Why hasn’t he got any rice?

Talking about availability – *there is/ there are*

What food or drink is it – tea, lemonade, etc.?
Have they got it?

→ Cover the text of Recording 9 on page 40.
→ Listen to these six mini-dialogues.
→ **a** Write the food or drink, and **b** choose Yes/No/We don’t know.

	Name of food/drink	Have they got it?
1	________	Yes/No/We don't know
2	________	Yes/No/We don't know
3	________	Yes/No/We don't know
4	________	Yes/No/We don't know
5	________	Yes/No/We don't know
6	________	Yes/No/We don't know

Recording 9

1 A What is there to drink?
B There's some beer, if you like.
2 A Is there any bread?
B Yes, it's in the cupboard.
3 A There isn't any cheese!
B Yes, I know. I'll get some later.
4 A There are some biscuits in the tin, aren't there?
B I'm not sure.
5 A Are there any crisps?
B Sorry.
6 A There aren't any grapes.
B Yes, there are. They're in the fridge.

Check your answers

1 Beer – yes. **2** Bread – yes. **3** Cheese – no. **4** Biscuits – we don't know. **5** Crisps – no. **6** Grapes – yes.

Grammar summary – Availability – *there is, there are*	
Affirmative There is + *singular/uncountables* 's	There are + *plurals*
Negative There isn't + *singular/uncountables*	There aren't + *plurals*

Questions Is there? + *singular/uncountables*	Are there? + *plurals*
Question Tags There's…, isn't there? There isn't…, is there?	**Short answers** Is there…? Yes, there is No, there isn't Are there…? Yes there are No, there aren't

'Some'/'any' with plurals and uncountables

→ Look at these examples with *there is* and *have got.*

→ Pay special attention to the words *some* and *any.*

Yes	There's **some** beer	I've got **some** apple juice
No	There isn't **any** cheese	I haven't got **any** wine
Question	Is there **any** bread?	Have you got **any** cold beer?

★ We use *some* to say yes.

★ We use *any* to say no.

★ We use *any* to ask questions.

→ Complete these sentences with *some* or *any.*

1 I've got _____ wine but there isn't _____ beer.

2 **A** Is there ______ more pizza?
B No, but there's _____ bread.

3 **A** Are there ______ hamburgers?
B No, but there are ______ sandwiches.

4 **A** Have you got ______ biscuits?
B No, and there isn't ____ chocolate either.

5 **A** Is there ______ soup?
B Sorry, I haven't got ____ more.

Check your answers

1 I've got some wine but there isn't any beer. **2 A** Is there any more pizza? **B** No, but there's some bread. **3 A** Are there any hamburgers? **B** No, but there are some sandwiches. **4 A** Have you got any biscuits? **B** No, and there isn't any chocolate either. **5 A** Is there any soup? **B** Sorry, I haven't got any more.

Summary – Offering, choosing and asking for an alternative

Situation You're at home with a friend. It's time to eat.

→ Put this dialogue in the correct order.
→ Use your dictionary if necessary

_____	**A**	Actually, I don't drink alcohol, so could I have some Coke, fruit juice or something like that instead, please?
_____	**B**	I really don't mind. I like all vegetables.
__1__	**C**	What would you like to eat? There's chicken or I've got some beef, too.
_____	**D**	We've got some apple juice in the fridge. Could you get it for me?
_____	**E**	And would you like something to drink? I've got some wine if you'd like some.
_____	**F**	I'd like some chicken, please.
_____	**G**	Of course. Here you are.
_____	**H**	With peas or carrots?

Check your answers

1 C What would you like to eat? There's chicken or I've got some beef too.
2 F I'd like some chicken, please.
3 H With peas or carrots?
4 B I really don't mind. I like all vegetables.
5 E And would you like something to drink? I've got some wine if you'd like some.
6 A Actually, I don't drink alcohol, so could I have some Coke, fruit juice or something like that instead, please?
7 D We've got some apple juice in the fridge. Could you get it for me?
8 G Of course. Here you are.

... and the story continues... the passengers have dinner. The flight attendant talks to a passenger

→ Cover the text of Recording 10.
→ Read the questions below.
→ Listen and choose True or False.

1	The chicken isn't good.	True/False
2	More passengers eat beef.	True/False
3	More passengers eat chicken.	True/False
4	The passenger wants to try the beef.	True/False
5	The passenger wants to try the chicken.	True/False

Recording 10 – The Story

Passenger	This fish isn't very nice at all. What's the chicken like?
Attendant	I think it's very good.
Passenger	Nicer than the beef?
Attendant	I think so, but the beef is more popular. In fact, beef is always the most popular dish on the plane.
Passenger	Could I change this fish then, please? Is it alright if I have a different dinner?
Attendant	Of course. What would you like instead?
Passenger	Can I try the chicken, please, if that's O.K.?

Check your answers

1 False **2** True **3** False **4** False **5** True

What do they say?

→ Cover the text of Recording 10 again.
→ Read the sentences below.
→ Listen and try to complete the words.
→ Then read the text to help you, if necessary.

1 The passenger isn't happy with the fish.
She says, 'This fish / i _ _ ' _ / very nice/ a _ / a _ _ .'

2 She wants an opinion about the chicken.
She says 'W _ _ _ ' s / the chicken / l _ _ _ ?'

3 The flight attendant thinks it's very good.
The passenger asks for a comparison with the beef.
She says, 'N _ _ _ _ / t _ _ _ / the beef?'

4 The flight attendant thinks yes
She says, 'I think / s _ .'

5 But the passengers eat more beef.
'Beef is m _ _ _ / p _ _ _ _ _ _ than chicken. In fact beef is t _ _ / m _ _ _/ p _ _ _ _ _ _ dish on the plane.'

6 **a** The passenger wants to change the fish.
He says, 'C _ _ _ _ / I / change this fish then, please?'
b He wants to have another dinner.
He says, 'I _ / i _ / a _ _ _ _ _ t / i _ / I have a different dinner?'
c He would like to try the chicken.
He says, 'C _ _ / I / try the chicken, please, if that's O.K.'

Check your answers

1 This fish isn't very nice at all.
2 What's the chicken like?
3 Nicer than the beef?
4 I think so.
5 Beef is more popular than chicken. In fact beef is the most popular dish on the plane.
6 **a** Could I change this fish then, please?
b Is it alright if I have a different dinner?
c Can I try the chicken, please, if that's O.K.?

Grammar and communication 6

Opinions and comparisons

Example from *The Story* above:

The passenger asks for an opinion about the chicken.
She says, 'What's the chicken like?'
The attendant thinks the chicken is **nicer than** the beef, but beef is **more popular** than chicken. In fact, beef is **the most popular** dish on the plane.

Grammar summary – comparisons
Comparing two Short adjectives → *adjective* + er + than → nicer than Long adjectives → more + *adjective* + than → more popular than
Comparing three or more Short adjective → the + *adjective* + 'est' → the nicest Long adjectives → the + most + *adjective* → the most popular

→ Complete these sentences.
→ Use the table above to help you, if necessary.

1 **A** How big is London?
B Well, it's b _ gg _ _ / t _ _ _ New York.

2 **A** Which is the t _ _ _ _ _ _ building in the world?
B The Empire State Building, isn't it?

3 Which is m _ _ _ / difficult, understanding English or speaking it?

4 He's t _ _ / m _ _ _ / interesting person I know!

Check your answers

1 It's bigger than New York. **2** Which is the tallest building in the world? **3** Which is more difficult, understanding English or speaking it? **4** He's the most interesting person I know.

Common mistake

'Tea is the most popular drink in Britain.'
Not, 'Tea is the ~~more~~ popular drink in Britain.'

> **Tip:** To compare three or more, say *the most* OR *the ...est.*

i

British culture – Food

- The most popular drinks in Britain are tea and coffee.
- Traditional English food is meat, potatoes and vegetables, but nowadays there's a lot of international food from all over the world in the supermarkets and markets.
- There are normally two courses, a meat dish and a dessert.
- People usually eat a light lunch and a big meal in the evening.
- The most traditional dish is roast beef with roast potatoes (cooked in the oven) and vegetables. One of the most traditional desserts is called trifle.
- Beer is very popular. People often go to pubs for a drink and to talk. Pubs are typical British bars.

About your country: Food and drink

→ Write answers to the questions below or prepare to tell a friend.
→ Use the text above and your dictionary to help you.

1 What is the most common drink in your country?

____

2 What is the most common food? Is it with rice, potatoes, pasta, etc.?

____

3 Talk/write about the traditional drinks and dishes in your country.

____

4 When is the biggest meal of the day – in the middle of the day or in the evening?

____

Grammar and communication 7

Asking for permission

Examples from *The Story*:

The passenger wants to change the fish, have a different dinner and try the chicken.
He says, '**Could I** change this fish then, please?'
'**Is it alright if I** have a different dinner?'
'**Can I** try the chicken instead?'
The flight attendant responds: '**Of course**.'

Ask for permission in these situations. You are in a friend's house.

1 You want to use the phone ______________________________
2 You want to use the toilet ______________________________
3 You want to smoke____________________________________
4 You want to have some more bread_______________________
5 You want to watch T.V.________________________________

Check your answers

1		use the phone?
2	Can I	use the toilet?
3	Could I	smoke?
4	Is it alright if I	have some more bread?
5		watch T.V.?

Saying *yes* and *no* to requests

The attendant says, 'Of course.'
Another response: 'Yes, go ahead.'

Negative responses: *I'm sorry but* + reason, for example,
'I'm sorry but my mother's on the phone at the moment.'

→ Complete these mini-dialogues.

1 **A** Is it alright if we go later?
B Yes, o _ / c _ _ _ _ _ .

2 **A** Can I invite my friend?
B I'm s _ _ _ _ . We've only got three tickets.

3 **A** Could I read your magazine?
B Yes, g _ / a _ _ _ _.

4 **A** Is it alright if I borrow your car?
B I'_ / _ _ _ _ _ _ . I don't think that's possible.

Check your answers

1 Yes, of course. **2** I'm sorry. We've only got three tickets. **3** Yes, go ahead. **4** I'm sorry, I don't think that's possible.

What would you say?

Situation 1 You are a customer in a coffee shop
Another customer says to you, 'Excuse me, could I have two teas, please?'

Situation 2 In a restaurant
You ask the waiter for chicken. Then your friend says, 'Oh the chicken here isn't very nice at all but the beef's wonderful.' Now you want beef. Talk to the waiter.

Possible answers

1 'I'm sorry, I'm a customer here too.'
Advanced alternative: 'I'm sorry but I don't work here.'

2 'Excuse me, could I have beef and not chicken, please?
Advanced alternative: 'Excuse me, would it be possible for me to have beef instead of chicken, please?'

Revision

What is it in your language?

→ Here are some examples of the important points in this topic.
→ Translate the sentences below into your language.
→ Remember – translate the idea, not the words.

1 **A** Excuse me, could I have some bread, please?
B Of course, here you are.

2 **A** Beer or wine? **B** I don't mind. I like both.

3 **A** I've got some coffee but I haven't got any milk.

B There's some milk in the fridge, isn't there?

---

4 **A** Is it alright if I use your toilet, please?
B Yes, go ahead.

---

5 One tea and two coffees, please.

Join the conversation

→ Look at Recording 1 (page 23) again.
→ Listen to Recording 11.
→ Say the **man's** words in the spaces.

TEST 2

Which one is right?

→ Choose **a** or **b**.

1 **In a restaurant** **a** Please, please, a Coke.
b Excuse me, could I have a Coke, please?

2 **I'll make you a cup of tea**
a Is it alright if I have water instead, please?
b Is it possible I have water in the place of tea?

3 **Would you like some white wine or red?**
a Red for me, please.
b Red to me, please.

4 **Fruit juice or lemonade?**
a I don't mind.
b I'm not mind.

5 **a** I think I go to the supermarket later.
b I think I'll go to the supermarket later.

6 **a** Could I have some biscuits, please?
b Could I have any biscuits, please?

7 **a** I haven't got some beer.
b I haven't got any beer.

8 **a** There isn't any more cake, is there?
b There isn't any more cake, isn't it?

9 **a** Would you like something for drink?
b Would you like something to drink?

10 **a** Which test is the more difficult in the book?
b Which test is the most difficult in the book?

Write a dialogue

Situation You are in a restaurant with a friend. It is the end of the meal.

1 **You**
Offer your friend tea or coffee

2 Your friend wants coffee

3 You would like coffee too.
Call the waiter and order.
You'd like some ice cream
But it's not on the menu. Ask

4 The waiter hasn't got any ice cream

5 He gives you the coffee

[10 minutes later]

6 Offer your friend more coffee

7 Your friend says no

8 Call the waiter and ask for the bill

[The waiter brings the bill]

9 Check if it's possible to pay by card

10 The waiter says yes

Check your answers

Which one is right?

1 b 2 a 3 a 4 a 5 b 6 a 7 b 8 a 9 b 10 b

Dialogue: model answers

1	**You**	Would you like tea or coffee?
2	**Friend**	Coffee for me, please.
3	**You**	Excuse me, (Can/Could I have) two coffees, please? Have you got any ice cream?
4	**Waiter**	No, I'm sorry, we haven't.
5	**Waiter**	Two coffees.
6	**You**	Would you like some more coffee?
7	**Friend**	No thanks, I'm fine.
8	**You**	Excuse me, can/could I have the bill, please?
9	**You**	Is it alright if I pay by card?
10	**Waiter**	Yes, of course.

3 MAKING CONVERSATION

Grammar and communication	Pronunciation
◆ Everyday activities – present simple ◆ Ability – *can* ◆ Expressing interest – echo questions **Vocabulary** ◆ Countries, nationalities, languages	◆ Intonation – 'wh' questions – expressing interest with echo questions ◆ Plurals with an extra syllable ◆ Stress and weak forms – *can/can't*

The conversation on the plane continues...

Understanding the important information

→ Cover the text of Recording 1, *The Story*.
→ Read the sentence below.
→ Listen to the recording and circle ( ) ALL the correct answers.

They talk about **a** countries
b their families
c nationalities
d their names
e languages

Recording 1 (and 10) – The Story

Woman	Where are you from?
Man	I'm English. And you?
Woman	I'm from England too.
Man	Oh, really? But your book isn't in English.
Woman	Well, actually, I live in South America, in Uruguay and so I speak Spanish.
Man	Do you? That's interesting!
Woman	Yes, I like it there. How about you? Do you speak any foreign languages?
Man	I can speak a bit of French.
Woman	Can you?
Man	Yes, I use it in my job sometimes – but I'm not really very good at it.
Woman	Oh, aren't you? I really like languages.

Check your answers

a countries **c** nationalities **e** languages

Understanding more

→ Cover the text of Recording 1 again.
→ Read the sentences on page 54.
→ Listen to the recording and choose the correct answer.

1	The woman's English.	Yes/No/We don't know
2	The man's English.	Yes/No/We don't know
3	She speaks Spanish.	Yes/No/We don't know
4	She uses her foreign language in her job.	Yes/No/We don't know
5	She lives in London.	Yes/No/We don't know
6	He lives in London.	Yes/No/We don't know
7	He can speak a little French.	Yes/No/We don't know
8	He uses his foreign language in his job.	Yes/No/We don't know
9	Languages are easy for him.	Yes/No/We don't know
10	She's interested in languages.	Yes/No/We don't know

Check your answers

1 Yes **2** Yes **3** Yes **4** We don't know. **5** No – she lives in South America. **6** We don't know. **7** Yes **8** Yes **9** No **10** Yes

What do they say?

→ Read the sentences below.
→ Listen to Recording 1 again and try to complete the words.
→ Read the text of the recording to help you, if necessary.

1 Nationalities

a The woman asks, 'W _ _ _ _ / a _ _ / y _ _ / f _ _ _?'
b The man answers, 'I'_ / E _ _ _ _ _ _.'
c The woman says 'I'_ / f _ _ _ / E _ _ _ _ _ _ / t _ _.'

2 Asking questions; expressing interest

a The woman says, 'I'm from England.'
The man is interested. He says, ' Oh, r_ _ _ _ _?'
b The woman says, 'Actually, I /l _ _ _ / in South America, in Uruguay.'
The man is interested. He says, 'D_ / y _ _?'
c The woman asks about languages.
She says, ' D_ / y _ _ / s _ _ _ _ / any / f _ r _ i _ n / l _ n g _ a _ e s?'
The man answers.
'I / c _ _ / s _ _ _ _ / a / b _ _ / o _ / F _ _ _ _ h.'
The woman is interested. She says, 'C _ _ / y _ _ ?'

Check your answers

1 **a** Where are you from?
b I'm English.
c I'm from England too.

2 **a** Oh! Really?
b Actually, I live in South America, in Uruguay.
Do you?
c Do you speak any foreign languages?
I can speak a bit of French.
Can you?

Find the words and phrases

→ Read the questions below.
→ Read the text of Recording 1 (page 53) and find the answers.

1 Asking the same question

a The woman asks: 'Where are you from?'
The man doesn't ask, 'Where are you from?' He asks, 'A _ _ / y _ _ ?'

b The woman says, 'I speak Spanish.'
She doesn't ask the man, 'Do you speak Spanish?' She asks, 'H_ _ / a _ _ _ _ / y _ _ ?'

2 Making conversation

The woman says, 'I speak Spanish.'
Then she says, 'A _ _ _ _ _ _ y, I live in South America.'

3 The man doesn't speak French very well.
He says, ' I speak a bit of French…but I'm not very good /_ _/ it.'

Check your answers

1 **a** And you?
b How about you?
★ These two questions mean the same.
★ You can use both questions with all tenses.
★ The structure of the questions is always the same.

2 Actually, I live in South America.

3 I speak a bit of French… but I'm not very good at it.

Using these words and phrases

1 Asking about the same topic – *And you? How about you?*

→ Complete these dialogues.

1 **A** What's your name?
B I'm Sam. __________?
A My name's...

2 **A** I'm cold. __________?
B I'm alright, actually.

3 **A** Here's the coffee bar. I'd like something cold to drink. ______________?
B I think I'll have the same.

✓ Check your answers

1, 2, 3 'And you?' or 'How about you?'.

2 Making conversation – *actually*

★ *Actually* makes the sentence less direct.

→ Make mini-dialogues. Match **1–5** below with **a–e**.

1 Terrible weather, isn't it?	**a** Yes, actually the food here is always good.
2 Are you Japanese?	**b** I don't mind, actually. I like both.
3 Tea or coffee?	**c** Yes, I'm from Tokyo, actually.
4 Where is he?	**d** Yes, it is actually, isn't it?
5 This is really delicious!	**e** Actually, I'm not sure.

✓ Check your answers

1 d **2** c **3** b **4** e **5** a

! Common mistake – *actually*

Situation A tourist in Europe.
'~~Actually, I'm in Paris~~. Tomorrow it's Madrid.'

★ In some languages *actually* means *now, at the moment*.
★ In English *actually* does not refer to time.

Grammar and communication 1

Everyday activities – Present simple

Examples from *The Story*:

1 The woman says, 'I **live** in South America.'
2 The man says, 'I **use** my French in my job sometimes.'

Meanings

★ In sentence **1** above the present simple is for permanent situations.
★ In sentence **2** the present simple is for repeated actions.

Form – present simple

Affirmative (*yes*)				
	I You We They	live	He/she/it	lives
Questions				
Do	I you we they	live?	Does he/she/it live?	
Negatives (*no*)				
	I You We They	don't live (do not)	He/she/it	doesn't live
Short answers				
Yes,	**Positive** I you we they	do	**Negative** No, I you we they	don't
	he/she/it	does	he/she/it	doesn't

Question Tags					
I		I?	He	lives, doesn't	he?
You	live, don't	you?	She	doesn't live, does	she?
We	don't live, do	we?	It		it?
They		they?			

→ Complete the sentences about the two passengers.
→ Use the grammar summary to help you, if necessary.

	She says	Talking about the woman:
1	'I speak Spanish.'	She ________ Spanish.
2	'I live in South America.'	She ________ in South America.
3	'I like it there.'	She ________ it there.
	He says	Talking about the man
4	'I use French in my job sometimes.'	He ______ French in his job sometimes.

Check your answers

1 She speaks Spanish. **2** She lives in South America. **3** She likes it there.
4 He uses French in his job sometimes.

Present simple – questions and answers

→ Look at the table above and complete the questions and answers about the two passengers. Use the information from *The Story* on page 53.

Example: Does she speak Spanish? ***Yes, she does.***

1 ______ she live in South America? ________________
2 ______ she like it there? ________________
3 ______ the man speak Spanish? ________________
4 ______ he speak French? ________________
5 ______ he live in South America? ________________
6 ______ they work together?

About you

7 Do you speak Spanish? ________________
8 Do you speak French? ________________

Check your answers

1	Does she live in South America?	Yes, she does.
2	Does she like it there?	Yes, she does.
3	Does the man speak Spanish?	No, he doesn't.
4	Does he speak French?	Yes, he does.
5	Does he live in South America?	No, he doesn't.
6	Do they work together?	No, they don't.

7 and 8 Yes, I do, OR No, I don't.

How do you pronounce it?

Intonation of questions with *what?*, *where?* etc.

Example from *The Story*:

The woman asks 'Where are you from?'

→ Read the questions below.

→ Listen to these mini-dialogues on Recording 2, part 1. Pay special attention to the important word in the question – the syllable with stress.

In questions with *what? where?* etc. the voice:

a goes **up** on the syllable with stress or ↗

b goes **down** on the syllable with stress. ↘

→ Choose **a** or **b**. The answer is the same for all the questions.

Recording 2, part 1

1	What's your name?	Monica.
2	Where are you from?	New York.
3	Where does he work?	In a school.
4	When do they arrive?	At 5 o'clock.
5	Who can drive?	I can.
6	Which one's yours?	That one.
7	Why aren't they here?	Their train's late.
8	How's your Mother?	She's fine.
9	Whose is this?	I don't know. It's not mine.

Check your answer

b The voice goes down. ➘
Many learners of English go up with questions.
Questions with question words (*what*, *when*, etc.) go down. ➘

→ Now listen again and repeat the questions.
→ Pay special attention to the fall on the syllable with stress.

Plurals with an extra syllable – *languages*

Example from *The Story*:

The woman says 'Do you speak any foreign languages?'
And 'I really like languages.'

★ Sometimes plural nouns have an extra syllable.

For example, *language* has two syllables (lang-uage) and *languages* has three syllables (lang-uag-es). (A syllable is part of a word with a vowel sound.)

★ The pronunciation of the extra syllable is 'is' / ɪz /.

→ Look at the pictures below and opposite and listen to Recording 2, part 2.
→ Write the number of syllables you hear in the boxes.

Recording 2, part 2

1 page ☐ 2 pages ☐
1 box ☐ 2 boxes ☐
1 bus ☐ 2 buses ☐
1 house ☐ 2 houses ☐
1 bridge ☐ 2 bridges ☐
1 sandwich ☐
2 sandwiches ☐
1 slice ☐ 2 slices ☐

1 piece ☐ 2 pieces ☐
1 dishes ☐ 2 dishes ☐
1 glass ☐ 2 glasses ☐
1 orange juice ☐ 2 orange juices ☐
1 kiss ☐ 2 kisses ☐

☑ Check your answers

1 page (1) pages (2) **2** box (1) boxes (2) **3** bus (1) buses (2) **4** house (1) houses (2) **5** bridge (1) bridges (2) **6** sandwich (2) sandwiches (3) 7 slice (1) slices (2) **8** piece (1) pieces (2) **9** dish (1) dishes (2) **10** glass (1) glasses (2) **11** orange juice (3) orange juices (4) **12** kiss (1) kisses (2)

Q ***How do I know when there's an extra syllable?***

A After the letters 's', 'ss', 'sh', 'ch', 'ge', 'se', 'ce', 'x' there's an extra syllable.

Q ***Why these letters?***

A Because after these letters it's difficult to pronounce the 's' without an extra vowel in the middle. An extra vowel = an extra syllable.

→ Now listen to Recording 2, part 2 again and repeat the words.

Grammar and communication 2

Ability – *can*

Examples from *The Story*:

The woman asks about languages. He says, 'I can speak a bit of French.' She's interested. She says, 'Can you?'

Meaning

★ Here, *can* is for ability.

Form – *can*

Affirmative		
I You He/she/it We They	can	eat fish
Negative		
I You He/she/it We they	can't	eat fish

Questions, short answers and question tags						
Can	I you he/she/it we they	eat fish?	Yes, No,	I you he/she/it we they	can, can't can't, can	I? you? he/she/it? we? they?

! Common mistakes – *can*

'He can speak French.'
Not '~~He can to speak French~~.'

'Can you speak English?'
Not '~~Can you to speak English?~~'
Or '~~Do you can speak English?~~'

Ability, *can*

→ Complete the questions and short answers.

1 The man ______/ ______ French but he ______/______ Spanish.
2 _____the woman _______ Spanish? Yes, _____/_____.
3 _____they both_______ English? Yes, they're English.
4 About you: I _____ /______ some English.

Check your answers *(Recording 3)*

1 The man can speak French but he can't speak Spanish.
2 Can the woman speak Spanish? Yes, she can.
3 Can they both speak English? Yes, they're English.
4 I can speak some English.

How do you pronounce it?

Can

★ The vowel 'a' in *can* has two different pronunciations, one strong / æ / and one weak / ə /.

★ The vowel 'a' in *can't* / a: / is different from the two pronunciations of 'a' in *can*.

→ Listen to Recording 3 above. Can you hear three different vowel sounds?

→ Then read **1, 2, 3** below to check your answers.

1 weak *can* / ə / (*can* is not the important word in the sentence):
 a The man can speak <u>French</u>.
 b Can the woman speak <u>Spa</u>nish?
 c Can they both speak <u>Eng</u>lish?
 d I can speak some <u>Eng</u>lish.

2 strong *can* / ɑe / (*can* is the important word):
 a Yes, she <u>can</u>.

3 Negative *can't* / ɑ: / (The negative doesn't change. The vowel is the same as in 'car')
 a He can't speak Spanish.

Q ***Why is this pronunciation important?***

A Because if you say strong 'can' instead of weak *can*, sometimes people hear *can't*.

→ Now listen to Recording 3 again and repeat the sentences.

→ Pay special attention to *can/can't*.

Grammar and communication 3

Expressing interest – echo questions

→ Look at these examples from *The Story* and answer the questions.

1 The woman says, 'I'm from England too.'
The man is interested. He says, 'Really?'

2 The woman says, 'I live in South America.'
The man is interested. He says, 'Oh, do you?'

3 The man says, 'I can speak a bit of French.'
The woman is interested. She says, 'Oh, can you?'

Another possibility for **2** and **3** above:
'I live in South America.'
'Oh, really?'
'I can speak a bit of French.'
'Oh, really?'

→ Answer these questions.

1 It is always possible to use *really*. Yes/No
2 We use short question forms to express interest. Yes/No

Check your answers

1 Yes. You can use *really* with all tenses. It doesn't change.
2 Yes. Use **auxiliary** (*do*, *can* etc.) + subject. These are **echo questions**.

How do you pronounce it?

Intonation – expressing interest, echo questions

★ To express interest, intonation is important.
★ A big fall and a little rise in the voice expresses interest.
★ A small fall and no rise in the voice expresses little or no interest.

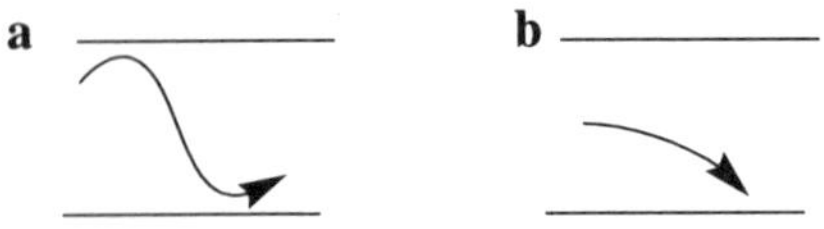

a very interested **b** not interested

→ Listen to Recording 4.
→ Write 'I' for 'interested or 'NI' for 'not interested' in the boxes.

Recording 4

Examples:

1	**a**	Really? **NI**	**b**	Really? **I**	
2	**a**	Do you? ☐	**b**	Do you? ☐	
3	**a**	Can't she? ☐	**b**	Can't she? ☐	
4	**a**	Is it? ☐	**b**	Is it? ☐	
5	**a**	Does he? ☐	**b**	Does he? ☐	
6	**a**	Aren't you? ☐	**b**	Aren't you? ☐	

Check your answers

2	**a**	Interested	**b**	Not interested
3	**a**	Interested	**b**	Not interested
4	**a**	Not interested	**b**	Interested
5	**a**	Interested	**b**	Not interested
6	**a**	Not interested	**b**	Interested

Expressing interest, making conversation – echo questions

→ Express interest. Choose the correct question from box 1 on page 66.
→ Continue the conversation. Choose from box 2.

Example: His new song is really good. *Is it?* *What's it called?*

1 I can play the guitar. ______ ______
2 My brother's new job's very interesting. ______ ______
3 My father lives in the States. ______ ______
4 My children don't like ice cream. ______ ______
5 I'm thirsty. ______ ______
6 Sue's not here today. ______ ______
7 I like this cold weather. ______ ______
8 Jessica can't drive. ______ ______
9 I don't drink tea. ______ ______
10 I'm not very well. ______ ______

Box 1

Are you?	Oh, can you?
Don't you?	Isn't she?
Do you?	Does he?
Can't she?	Aren't you?
Don't they?	Is it?

Box 2

What's the matter?
So, how does she get to work?
What does he do?
I prefer the summer myself.
What sort of music do you play?
Isn't that her, over there?
I have about five cups a day.
Whereabouts?
Would you like something to drink?
It's very popular in my house.

Check your answers *(Recording 5)*

1 A I can play the guitar.
B Oh, can you? What sort of music do you play?
2 A My brother's new job's very interesting.
B Is it? What does he do?
3 A My father lives in the States.
B Does he? Whereabouts?
4 A My children don't like ice-cream.
B Don't they? It's very popular in my house.
5 A I'm thirsty.
B Are you? Would you like something to drink?
6 A Sue's not here today.
B Isn't she? Look, isn't that her over there?
7 A I like this cold weather.
B Do you? I prefer the summer myself.
8 A Jessica can't drive.
B Can't she? So, how does she get to work?
9 A I don't drink tea.
B Don't you? I have about five cups a day.
10 A I'm not very well.
B Aren't you? What's the matter?

→ Now listen to these mini-dialogues on Recording 5 and respond. Remember to show your interest with your intonation.

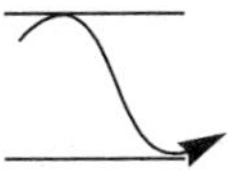 Very interested

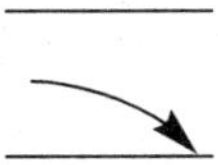 Not very interested

Example: Can you? Can you?

How do you pronounce it?

Countries – stress

→ Look at the names of the countries in the box.
→ Look at the stress patterns below the box, for example, (●o).
→ Listen to Recording 6.
→ Write the countries under the correct stress pattern.

Recording 6

the United States		Italy	Portugal	Egypt
China	Australia	Mexico	England	Poland
Brazil	Germany	Japan		

a ● o
Example: ***Egypt***
____
____
____

b o ●
____
____

c ● o o
____
____
____
____

d o ● o o
____

e o o o o ●
____

Check your answers

a ● o
Egypt
China
England
Poland

b o ●
Brazil
Japan

c ● o o
Mexico
Italy
Portugal
Germany

d o ● o o
Australia

e o o o o ●
The United States

What's the right word?

Countries, nationalities and languages

→ Match these countries, nationalities and languages.
→ Write your answers in the spaces below.
→ Use your dictionary to help you, if necessary.

Example: a

Country	**a**	Spain
Nationality	**2**	Spanish
Language	**B**	Spanish

Country	Nationality	Language
a Spain	**1** Polish	**A** English
b Japan	**2** Spanish	**B** Spanish
c the United States	**3** Mexican	**C** Polish
d Italy	**4** Portuguese	**D** German
e Portugal	**5** Australian	**E** Chinese
f Egypt	**6** Brazilian	**F** Portuguese
g China	**7** American	**G** Japanese
h Australia	**8** English	**H** Arabic
i Mexico	**9** Italian	**I** French
j England	**10** Egyptian	**J** Italian
k Poland	**11** Japanese	
l Brazil	**12** Chinese	
m Germany	**13** French	
n France	**14** German	

a _2B___ **b** _____ **c** _____ **d** _____ **e** _____
f _____ **g** _____ **h** _____ **i** _____ **j** _____
k _____ **l** _____ **m** _____ **n** _____

Check your answers

a 2 B **b** 11 G **c** 7 A **d** 9 J **e** 4 F **f** 10 H **g** 12 E **h** 5 A **i** 3 B
j 8 A **k** 1 C **l** 6 F **m** 14 D **n** 13 I

How do you pronounce it?

Languages – stress

→ Look at the groups of languages in Recording 7 on page 69.
→ Listen to the recording.
→ Underline the syllable with stress.

Recording 7

English	Japanese	Italian	Arabic
Spanish	Chinese		
Polish	Portuguese		
German			

Check your answers

English	Japanese	Italian	Arabic
Spanish	Chinese		
Polish	Portuguese		
German			

Nationalities and languages

→ Write the name of your country and three more – not those on the list above.
→ Write the nationality and language for each one.
→ Underline the stress on all the words.
→ Use your dictionary if necessary.

	Country	Nationality	Language
1			
2			
3			
4			

→ Check your answers in a dictionary.

Stress is marked (ˈ) at the beginning of the stressed syllable in the phonetics in dictionaries. For example, *Swedish* in the dictionary is

Swedish / ˈswi:dɪʃ /.

Countries and languages

Q ***In Recording 1 the woman says, 'Where are you from?' Can I say 'Where do you come from?'***

A Yes, both are correct and common. The meaning is the same.

***Q** Can I say 'Do you speak English?'*
and 'Can you speak English?'

A Yes, both are correct and common.

British culture – ability, responses

- The British don't usually say *I can... very well.* More common expressions are: *I can... but not very well* and *I can... not too badly.*

→ Look at the symbols in Recording 8, for example (+) and the expressions below.
→ Listen and repeat the answers.

Recording 8

1	**A**	Do you speak Polish?	(–)	**B**	No, not at all.
2	**A**	Do you speak Japanese?	(+)	**B**	Yes, but not very well.
3	**A**	Can you speak Russian?	(++)	**B**	Yes, not too badly.
4	**A**	Do you speak Italian?	(+++)	**B**	Yes, actually it's my native language.

Ability, can, responses

Situation You can speak two foreign languages.

→ Read the questions below and look at the response symbols.
→ Copy the right response phrase from the exercise above.
→ Listen to Recording 9.
→ **a** Write the language you hear.
b Read your response.

1 Can you speak__________? **You** (-)__________________
2 And do you speak__________? **You** (++)__________________
3 How about __________? **You** (+)__________________
4 And what is your native language? **You** __________________.

Check your answers *(Recording 9)*

1	Can you speak Arabic?	No, not at all.
2	And do you speak Italian?	Yes, not too badly.
3	How about Japanese?	Yes, but not very well.
4	And what's your native language?	Yours ________

What can you do? How well? A little? Not too badly?

→ Write about the topics below or prepare to tell a friend.
→ Use your dictionary to help you if necessary.

1 Transport – for example, can you ride a bike, drive a car, drive a bus

2 In the house – for example, cook

3 Sport – for example, swim

4 Hobbies – for example, play chess

5 Music – for example, play the guitar, sing

6 Languages

What would you say?

Situation 1 In the street

Someone speaks to you in a language you can't speak.

Situation 2 You are in a language class

At the end of the class another student takes your dictionary by mistake.

Possible answers

1 I'm sorry but I don't understand. **2** Excuse me, that's my dictionary. Advanced alternative: Excuse me, I think that dictionary's mine.

Revision

How do you say it in your language?

→ Here are some examples of the important points in this topic.
→ Translate the sentences into your language.
→ Remember – translate the idea, not the words.

1 Where are you from?

____

2 I'm from…

____

3 Oh, really?

____

4 How about you?

____

5 **A** Can you speak German? **B** Yes, but not very well.

____

6 **A** Do you like it here? **B** Not very much, actually.

____

7 He lives in Paris. **B** Does he? That's interesting.

____

Join the conversation

→ Look at the text of Recording 1, *The Story*, again.
→ Listen to Recording 10.
→ Say the **woman's** words in the spaces.

TEST 3

Which one is right?

→ Choose the correct sentence **a** or **b**.

1 Ability
- **a** He can swim.
- **b** He can to swim.

2
- **a** I'm not very good in maths.
- **b** I'm not very good at maths.

3 Present simple – everyday activities.
  a Do he drive to work?
  b Does he drive to work?

4 Echo questions – making conversation.
  I'm not an English student.
  a Are you?
  b Aren't you?

5 He lives next door.
  a Does he?
  b Is he?

Write a dialogue

Situation You are at a friend's house. You meet Claudia there. She isn't from your country.

You

1 Ask Claudia where she's from

Claudia

2 Respond. Ask the same question

3 Reply

4 Express interest and make conversation

5 Ask about languages – which?

6 Respond

7 Express interest and make conversation.

Check your answers

Which one is right?

1 a **2** b **3** b **4** b **5** a

Dialogue: model answers

1 You Where are you from?
2 Claudia I'm from Italy. And you?
3 You I'm [your nationality]
4 Claudia Are you? That's interesting.
5 You Which languages do you speak?
6 Claudia Italian, of course, some English and a little Chinese.
7 You Chinese? Really? Isn't it difficult? Can you write it too?

4 TALKING ABOUT YOUR DAILY LIFE

Grammar and communication
- Jobs and *a/an* – the article
- Using prepositions *in*, *for*, *to*
- Asking *Do you like it?* – saying *yes* and *no*
- Likes and dislikes – verbs + *ing* – the gerund

Vocabulary
- Jobs and work

Pronunciation
- Stress and weak forms – *do/don't, does/doesn't*
- Stress for emphasis
- Intonation
  – Single words/short phrases

The two passengers continue their conversation. They talk about their work ...

Understanding the important information

→ Cover the text of Recording 1, *The Story*.
→ Read the questions below.
→ Listen to the recording and answer the questions.

1 What's the man's job?

2 What does the woman do?

Recording 1 (and 6) – The Story

Woman	What do you do?
Man	I work in computers. And you? – what's your job?
Woman	I'm a teacher.
Man	You're not an English teacher by any chance, are you?
Woman	Yes, I am, actually. I teach in a school in Uruguay.
Man	Really? Whereabouts?
Woman	In a town about 75 miles from the capital. I teach in an International School.
Man	Do you? Do you like your job?
Woman	Yes, I really enjoy teaching and the students are lovely. What about you? What sort of work do you do in computers?
Man	Well, I'm in marketing. I work for a big company, so I travel a lot for my job. In fact, I'm on my way home now from a Computer Fair in Argentina.
Woman	And do you enjoy working in marketing?
Man	It's O.K., but I'm not very keen on all the travelling.

Check your answers

1 He works in marketing computers. **2** She teaches English.

Understanding more

→ Cover the text of Recording 1 again.
→ Read the sentences on page 76.
→ Listen to the recording and tick ✓ all the correct answers.

1 The woman

- ☐ **a** lives in London.
- ☐ **b** works in South America.
- ☐ **c** teaches in an International School.
- ☐ **d** doesn't like her job.

2 The man

- ☐ **a** lives in Argentina.
- ☐ **b** is on a business trip.
- ☐ **c** works for a small company.
- ☐ **d** likes his job.
- ☐ **e** really enjoys the travelling.

Check your answers

1 The woman
b works in South America.
c teaches in an International School.

2 The man
b is on a business trip.
d likes his job.

What do they say?

→ Read the sentences below.
→ Listen to Recording 1 again and try to complete the words.
→ Then read the text of the recording to help you, if necessary.

1 Talking about jobs

a The woman asks, 'What / _ _ / you / _ _?'
The man answers, ' I / w _ _ _ / _ _ / computers.'

b The man asks, 'W _ _ _ ' s / y _ _ _ / j _ _?'
The woman answers, 'I' _ / _ / teacher.'

c The woman asks for more information. She says,
'W _ _ _ / s _ _ _ / of / w _ _ _ / do you do in computers?'
The man answers,
'I ' _ / _ _ / m _ _ _ _ _ _ _ g.'

d The man talks about his company.
He says, ' I work / _ _ _ / a big company.'

2 Likes and dislikes

a The man asks, 'D _ / y _ _ / like / your / _ _ _ ?'
She answers, 'Yes, I / really/ e _ _ _ y / t _ _ ch _ _ g.

b She asks,
'D _ / you / e _ _ _ y / w _ _ k _ _ g / _ n / marketing?
He answers, '_ _ ' _ / O.K.'

c He doesn't like the travelling very much. He says,
I'm n _ _ / v _ _ _ / k _ _ n / _ n / all the travelling.'

Check your answers

1 Talking about jobs

a 'What do you do?'
'I work in computers.'

b 'What's your job?'
'I'm a teacher.'

c 'What sort of work do you do in computers?'
'I'm in marketing.'

d 'I work for a big company.'

2 Likes and dislikes

a 'Do you like your job?'
'Yes, I really enjoy teaching.'

b 'Do you enjoy working in marketing?'
'It's O.K.'

c 'I'm not very keen on all the travelling'.

Find the words and phrases

→ Read the questions below.
→ Read the text of Recording 1 again and find the answers.

1 The man thinks the woman is an English teacher. He wants to check and make conversation.
He says, 'You're / _ _ _ / an English teacher, b _ / _ _ _ / c _ _ _ _ _ _ /, / _ _ _ / you?

2 The woman says she teaches in an International School.
He asks where. He says 'W _ _ _ _ _ _ _ _ _ _ s?'

3 The woman talks about her job. Then she asks the man about his job.
She doesn't ask, 'How about you?'
Instead she asks, ' _ _ _ _ about you?'

4 It's the end of the computer fair in Argentina. Where is the man going?
He says, 'I_/ f _ _ _,/ I'm / o _ / m _ / w _ _ / h _ _ _ / now/ f _ _ _ / a fair in Argentina.'

Check your answers

1 You're not an English teacher, by any chance, are you?
★ The phrase 'by any chance' makes the question less direct.

2 Whereabouts?

3 What about you?
★ 'What about you?' and 'How about you?' mean the same.

4 In fact, I'm on my way home now from a fair in Argentina.
★ 'In fact' is very similar to 'actually'. (See Topic 3.) 'In fact' can be more formal.

Using these words and phrases

1 *Where?* and *whereabouts?*

Q ***What's the difference between 'where?' and 'whereabouts?'.***

A The meaning is the same.

Where is more direct and specific.
Example: 'I can't find my keys? Where are they?'

Whereabouts is common because it is less *direct.*

It is especially common when it is the only word in the question.
Example: A 'Paul works in the States.'
B 'Does he? Whereabouts?'

Whereabouts

→ Complete these conversations.
→ Choose **a–f** from the box on page 79.

1 **A** I live in London.
B ________________ ?

2 **A** We go to Italy for our holidays.
B ________________ ?

3 **A** My parents are in Australia.
B ________________ ?

4 **A** I travel to Cadaques a lot.
B ________________ ?

5 **A** This is the name of the hotel.
B ________________ ?

6 **A** Whereabouts do you work?
B ________________ .

a	Really? Whereabouts are they?
b	Do you? Whereabouts?
c	I know what it's called but whereabouts is it?
d	In the centre of town, actually.
e	That's nice. Whereabouts do you go?
f	That's interesting but whereabouts is it?

Check your answers

1 b **2** e **3** a **4** f **5** c **6** d

2 On the way ...

→ Look at the pictures below and complete the sentences.

1

2

They'___/___/___/ ___ to school.

___'s / on / ___ / ___ / home.

3

4

He'___ / ___ / ___ / ___ / to work.

We'__ / on ___ / way / ___ / the / ___ .

5

___ / ___ my / ___ / there right now.

6

Check your answers

1 No, I'm on my way back. **2** They're on their way to school. **3** She's on her way home. **4** He's on his way to work. **5** We're on our way to the airport. **6** I'm on my way there right now.

Grammar summary – *on the way…*		
On the way	there back	No *to* with these words
	to school to work	No *the* with these places
	to the aiport	

How do you pronounce it?

Do/don't

★ The vowel in *do* has two pronunciations, one strong / u: /and one weak / ə /.

★ The vowel 'o' in *don't* / əʊ / is different from the two pronunciations of 'o' in *do*.

→ Listen to Recording 2, part 1. Can you hear three different vowel sounds?

Recording 2, part 1, do/don't

A Do you drive?	Weak *do* / ə / (*do* is not the important word)
B Yes, I do.	Strong *do* / u: / (*do* is the important word)
C Oh! I don't.	Negative *don't* / əʊ / (The negative doesn't change.)

★ The vowel in *does* has two pronunciations, one strong / ʌ /, one weak / ə /.

★ The vowel in *doesn't* / ʌ / is the same as in strong *does* / ʌ /.

→ Listen to Recording 2, part 2. Can you hear two different vowel sounds?

Recording 2, part 2, does/doesn't

A Does David drive?	Weak *does* / ə / (*does* is not the important word)
B Yes, he does.	Strong *does* / ʌ / (*does* is the important word)
C No, David doesn't drive.	Negative *doesn't* / ʌ / (The same vowel as strong *does*.

→ Listen to Recording 2, part 3 below and repeat.
→ Pay special attention to the vowels in *do*, *don't*, *does*, *doesn't*.

Recording 2, part 3, do/don't, does/doesn't

1 What do you do?	weak / ə / strong, / u: /
2 Where do you live?	weak / ə /
3 How do you know?	weak / ə /
4 I don't know.	negative / əʊ /
5 Yes, you do.	strong / u: /
6 **A** Does your father like golf?	weak / ə /
7 **B** Yes, he does **C** No, he doesn't.	strong and negative / ʌ /

Q *Why are these differences important?*

A If you know that some words can be very short, with weak vowels, you can understand more when people speak.

If you use stress and weak vowels when you speak, people can understand you better.

Stress for emphasis

In *The Story*, the woman asks the man about his job.
She says, 'What do you do?'
The man answers. Then he asks 'What's <u>your</u> job?'

★ Stress is on the important information words in a sentence.
For example, A asks: 'What's your name?'
The important information word is '<u>name</u>'.
B answers and asks the same question. 'What's <u>your</u> name?' This time, 'name' isn't important – we know the conversation is about 'names'. This time 'your' is important.

→ Read the seven half-dialogues below. The person answers a question and then asks the same question. <u>Underline</u> the stressed word in the questions.

1 I'm <u>fine</u> thanks. How are you?
2 I'm <u>Ca</u>rol. And you? What's your name?
3 I live in <u>Lon</u>don. Where do you live?
4 My birthday's in <u>Ap</u>ril. When's yours?
5 I <u>don't smoke</u>. Do you?
6 I'd like some <u>co</u>ffee. How about you? Would you like a drink?
7 I <u>live</u> with my <u>par</u>ents. Do you live with yours?

Check your answers *(Recording 2, part 4)*

1 I'm fine, thanks. How are <u>you</u>?
2 I'm Carol. And <u>you</u>? What's <u>your</u> name?
3 I live in London. Where do <u>you</u> live?
4 My birthday's in April. When's <u>yours</u>?
5 I don't smoke. Do <u>you</u>?
6 I'd like some coffee. Would <u>you</u> like a drink?
7 I live with my parents. Do you live with <u>yours</u>?

→ Listen again and repeat the answers and questions.
→ Pay special attention to the stress in the questions.

Intonation and meaning – single words and short phrases

★ One way to express feelings in English is through intonation.

Example from *The Story*:

'It's **O.K.**' is positive. 'It's O.K.' is not very positive.

★ To sound positive, start high and finish low.
★ Flat intonation expresses that you are not very happy or interested.

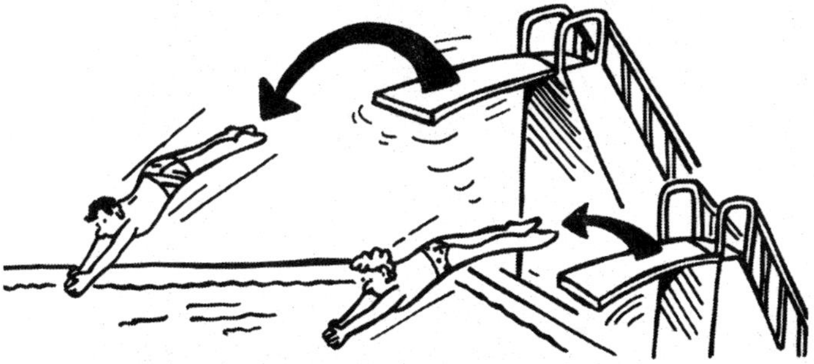

Intonation summary

POSITIVE	= HIGH START	+ BIG FALL
NOT VERY POSITIVIE	= LOW START	+ SMALL FALL

→ Listen to Recording 2, part 5 on page 84.
→ For each question, one response is positive and one response is not very positive.
→ Write 'P' for 'positive' or 'NP' for 'not very positive' in the boxes.

Recording 2, part 5

1 Can you help me?
- a O.K. ☐
- b O.K. ☐

2 How are things?
- a Alright. ☐
- b Alright. ☐

3 Is that nice?
- a It's not bad. ☐
- b It's not bad. ☐

4 Are you happy about it?
- a Yeah. ☐
- b Yeah. ☐

5 Is this alright?
- a Yes, it's fine. ☐
- b Yes, it's fine. ☐

6 Do you agree?
- a Of course. ☐
- b Of course. ☐

7 Do you like it?
- a Yes. ☐
- b Yes. ☐

Check your answers

1 a P
b NP

2 a P
b NP

3 a NP
b P

4 a NP
b P

5 a P
b NP

6 a NP
b P

7 a NP
b P

★ *Yeah* is informal for *Yes*.

→ This time listen and repeat the responses. Can you hear the difference? Can you use intonation to sound positive?

What's the right word?

Jobs

→ Look at the pictures and the letters.
→ Write the correct word for each job.
→ Use your dictionary if necessary.

1 ITAX VREDIR

2 TAWREI

3 ROTCOD

4 TPSIERECONTI

5 CIMECAHN

6 STEDNIT

7 TACRO

8 OPSH SSTANISAT

9 UROT DUEGI

10 REDSSREAIHR

11 AVRTEL GTAEN

12 EIRSHCA

13 TDUSENT

Check your answers

1 Taxi driver **2** Waiter **3** Doctor **4** Receptionist **5** Mechanic **6** Dentist **7** Actor **8** Shop assistant **9** Tour guide **10** Hairdresser **11** Travel agent **12** Cashier **13** Student

Grammar and communication 1

Jobs – *a, an*

Example from *The Story*:

The man asks, 'What's your job?'
The woman says, 'I'm a teacher.'

Common mistake

'She's a teacher.'✓
(Not '~~She's teacher~~.')

Grammar summary – Jobs			
	She's He's	a an	travel agent actor
	Subject + verb *be*	**indefinite article**	**job**
Plurals Compare	 He's They're	 a **X**	 doctor (+ article *a*) doctors (no article)

Jobs

→ Look again at the pictures on page 85. Some people have name labels, for example, the waiter is Dan.

→ Complete the answers and questions below and on page 87.

Example: 'What does Dan do?' **You *'He's a waiter.'***

1 What does Dan do? ______________________

2 What's Pat's job? ______________________

3 What does Carl do? ____________________

4 What's Kate's job? ____________________

5 Now you ask: Jo ?______________ She's a tour guide.

6 You ask again: Jim? ______________ He's a travel agent.

Check your answers *(Recording 3)*

1 What does Dan do? He's a waiter.
2 What's Pat's job? He's a hotel receptionist.
3 What does Carl do? He's a mechanic.
4 What's Kate's job? She's a shop assistant.
5 What does Jo do? OR What's Jo's job? She's a tour guide.
6 What's Jim's job? OR What does Jim do? He's a travel agent.

→ Listen to Recording 3 and repeat the questions and answers.

Grammar and communication 2

Using prepositions

work in

Example from *The Story*: 'I'm **in** marketing.'

→ Correct A in the conversations below. Use the words in the box at the end.
→ Use your dictionary if necessary.

Example: David makes planes.
A You're a dentist, aren't you, David?
B No, ***I'm in engineering***, actually.

1 Jack is a Member of Parliament.
A Jack works in publishing.
B No, he's __________

2 Brenda works for Barclay's Bank.
A Brenda's in education.
B No, she's __________

3 Paul is the director of a language school.
A Paul works in banking.
B No, not Paul. He's________

4 Matt draws pictures for books.

A Matt works in administration.

B Are you sure? I think he works _______

publishing ***education*** ***banking*** ***engineering*** ***politics***

Check you answers

1 in politics. **2** in banking. **3** in education. **4** in publishing.

work for

Example from *The Story*: 'I work **for** a big company.'

→ Write the words in the correct order.

1 for/Sue/Kodak/works.

____

2 does/for/brother/which/your/company/work?

____

3 who/know/she/for/works/do/you?

____

Check your answers

1 Sue works for Kodak.
2 Which company does your brother work for?
3 Do you know who she works for?

★ In spoken English you can finish a question or sentence with a preposition.
★ In written English we sometimes avoid this.

Grammar and communication 3

Asking *Do you like it?*

Examples from *The Story*:

The woman says: 'I really enjoy teaching.'

Then she asks: 'Do you enjoy working in marketing?'
The man says: 'It's O.K. but I'm not very keen on all the travelling.'

→ Read the phrases and look at the symbols below.
→ Listen to Recording 4 and repeat the phrases.

★ To answer only *yes* or *no* to the question *Do you like…?* can sound rude. Use one of these phrases instead.

Recording 4

'I really enjoy it.' (++)

'I quite like it.' (+)

'I don't mind it.' (+/-)

'I'm not very keen on it, actually.' (-)

'Actually, I don't like it at all.'(- -)

★ With *actually*, the negative isn't so direct.
★ This is the other common use of the word *actually*.

Do you like it? – responses

→ Look at the questions and symbols (for example ++) below.
→ Listen to Recording 5 and respond.

Example: You are the woman in *The Story*.
Question: Do you like being a teacher?
You answer: (++) ***Yes, I really enjoy it.***

These are from the vocabulary exercise earlier in this topic (page 87).

1 Dan, do you enjoy being a waiter? (+) Yes,____________________
2 Pat, do you like working in reception? (-) No,____________________
3 Carl, how do you like your job? (++) ____________________
4 Kate, do you enjoy working in a shop? (+/-) ____________________
5 Jo, what's it like being a tour guide? (- -)____________________
6 Do you like working in travel. Jim? (+) Yes, ____________________

Check your answers *(Recording 5)*

1 'Yes, I quite like it.'
2 'No, I'm not very keen on it, actually.'
3 'I really enjoy it.'
4 'I don't mind it.'
5 'Actually, I don't like it at all.'
6 'Yes, I quite like it.'

Grammar and communication 4

Likes and dislikes – verb + *ing*/gerund

Examples from *The Story*:

'I really enjoy teaching.'
'I'm not very keen on all the travelling.'

After *enjoy*, *like*, *not mind* and *be keen on* the verb ends in *ing*. This is the **gerund**.

enjoy + verb/'*ing*' *like* + verb/'*ing*',
mind + verb/'*ing*' *be keen on* + verb/'*ing*'

→ Read this interview with a schoolgirl, Sophie.
→ Underline all the verbs + gerunds.

Interviewer So, tell us about what you like doing and don't like doing, Sophie.

Sophie Well, I really enjoy going out with my friends at the weekend. I like inviting them home, too. I don't mind doing my homework – I know that's important, but I'm not very keen on helping my Mum with the housework.

Check your answers

Interviewer Like doing… don't like doing…
Sophie enjoy going out… like inviting… don't mind doing… not very keen on helping

Likes and dislikes

→ Complete these mini-dialogues using *enjoy*, *like*, *don't mind*, *not keen on*.

→ Use the verbs in the box below.

1 A What sort of thing do you like ______ in the evening?

B Well, actually, I enjoy ________  and I like ______  too.

2 A Jack, can you help us with some housework on Saturday?

B O.K. I don't mind ___________  but I'm not very keen on ____________ 

3 A Do you like _______ ? 

B Yes I really enjoy__________ 

4 A That new film is on at the cinema.

B Actually, 'I'm ____________ out tonight. I'm very tired.'

5 A I'm sorry but the dentist can't see you for another half an hour.

B That's O.K. I ____________________

hoover	*cook*	*go*	*do*	*watch T.V.*	*make*
	wait	*iron*	*read*		

Check your answers

1 A doing.

B watching T.V, reading

2 B hoovering, ironing

3 A cooking

B making cakes

4 B not very keen on going

5 B don't mind waiting

What's the right word or phrase?

Work

→ Match **1–12** with **a–l**.
→ First try without a dictionary. Then use your dictionary if necessary.

1 Hannah works in the house for her family.
2 Kate is 70.
3 Dawn hasn't got a job.
4 Sue works from 10–2.
5 Twenty people work for Julie.
6 May works 50 hours a week.
7 Denise works from 9–5.
8 Moyra is a student doctor at the hospital.
9 Chris's office is in her house.
10 Sheila works in the same office. as her sister.
11 Lena works on short contracts for different companies.
12 Lucy goes to University.

☐ **a** She works full-time.
☐ **b** She's unemployed.
☐ **c** She's a colleague.
☐ **d** She does a lot of overtime.
☐ **e** She's a housewife.
☐ **f** She's a manager.
☐ **g** She works part-time.
☐ **h** She works freelance.
☐ **i** She's retired.
☐ **j** She works shifts.
☐ **k** She works from home.
☐ **l** She's a student.

Check your answers

1 e, **2** i **3** b **4** g **5** f **6** d **7** a **8** j **9** k **10** c **11** h **12** l

How about you? – work

→ Write or prepare to tell a friend about your job/studies. What do you do/study?
→ Give some extra information about your job/studies.
→ Use some of the expressions in the vocabulary exercise above. How much do you enjoy your job/studies?

British culture – work

- In Britain, usual office hours are 9.00 or 9.30 a.m.–5.00 or 5.30 p.m., Monday to Friday.
- The average working week is 35 hours.
- People usually have one hour for lunch between 12 and 2 o'clock.
- Four weeks per year is the average holiday.
- The company deducts some money from the salary before they pay it:
  - about 22% income tax on an average salary.
  - about 10% national insurance (N.I.). This is for medical services.
- The current average salary is about £15,000.
- It is not usual to ask people their salary.

→ Write or prepare to tell a friend about work in your country. Give information on the points above.
Use the phrases in the text to help you.

____

____

____

What would you say?

1 You and John work for the same company. John leaves and goes to work for another company. Someone telephones and asks you, 'Can I speak to John, please?'

____

2 You work in a shop that is open seven days a week. You work on Saturdays and Wednesdays. It's the end of the day on Saturday. A colleague asks you, 'Are you in tomorrow?'

Possible answers

1 'I'm sorry but John doesn't work here any more.'
2 'No, I'm not in again until Wednesday.'
★ Here 'to be in' means 'to be here, at work'.

Revision

How do you say it in your language?

→ Here are some examples of the important points in this topic.
→ Translate the sentences into your language in the spaces.
→ Remember – translate the idea, not the words.

1 What do you do? I'm a... ______________________

2 Do you like cooking? ______________________
Yes, I really enjoy it. ______________________
Yes, I quite like it. ______________________
It's O.K. ______________________
I'm not very keen on it, actually. ______________________
Actually, I don't like it at all. ______________________

3 I don't mind waiting. ______________________

4 I'm on my way home. ______________________

Join the conversation

→ Look at the text of Recording 1 (page 75) – *The Story*, again.
→ Listen to Recording 6.
→ Read the **man's** words.

TEST 4

Which one is right?

Choose **a** or **b**.

1 **a** What work does your brother?
b What does your brother do?

2 **a** Like you your job?
b Do you like your job?

3 **a** We're on our way there now.
b We go to there now.

4 **a** Are you enjoy to travel?
b Do you enjoy travelling?

5 **a** What sort of company does he work for?
b For which sort of company he works?

6 **a** We can't use the car but I don't mind to walk.
b We can't use the car but I don't mind walking.

Choose the correct stress

7 My brother's a mechanic.
a What does your brother do?
b What does your brother do?

Write your part of the dialogue

Situation You are at a party. You are in the middle of a conversation with a person you don't know.

You

1 Say what you do.
Ask his job

The other person

I work in television

2 Ask for details

I read the news

3 You think you know him.
You think his name is David
West. Check

Yes, I am, actually

4 Ask if he likes working in television

Yes, it's very interesting.
The only thing I'm not too keen on is working late at night.
What sort of work do you do exactly?

5 Respond

Do you enjoy your job?

6 Respond

His wine glass is empty. Offer more

7

Yes, please. That would be nice

☑ Check your answers

Which one is right?

1 b **2** b **3** a **4** b **5** a **6** b **7** a

Dialogue: model answers

1 I'm a… What do you do? OR What's your job?
2 What sort of work do you do in television?
3 I think I know you. You're David West, aren't you?
4 Do you like working in television?
5 I … [details about you]
6 I really enjoy it OR I quite like it OR I don't mind it OR I'm not very keen on it actually OR Actually I don't like it at all.
7 Would you like some more wine? OR Would you like another glass of wine?

5 GIVING EXPLANATIONS

Grammar and communication	Vocabulary
◆ Possessive pronouns – *mine*, etc.	◆ First names
◆ Present progressive	◆ The family
– temporary actions in the present	
– present progressive and present simple	**Pronunciation**
◆ Present progressive	◆ Extra syllable, 3rd
– future arrangements	person singular,
◆ Saying why – *to*, *so that*, *because*	present simple
	◆ Weak form *to*

The conversation on the plane continues... They exchange names, talk about their families and the reasons for their trips

Understanding the important information

→Read the sentences below.
→Listen to Recording 1, *The Story*.
→Circle *Yes* for the things they talk about.
→Circle *No* for the things they don't talk about.

They talk about

a	their names	Yes/No
b	where he lives	Yes/No
c	his family	Yes/No
d	the reason for her trip	Yes/No
e	her mother	Yes/No
f	her father	Yes/No

Recording 1 (and 5) – The Story

Woman What's your name?
Man Oliver. And yours?
Woman My name's Tasha. It's short for Natasha, a Russian name. My mother's Russian. So, whereabouts in England do you live, Oliver?
Man I live in Scotland, actually, in Edinburgh, but I'm staying in London for a couple of weeks, because of my job. And you? Are you on holiday?
Woman Yes, I'm going to England to see some friends of mine. They live near London.
Man Oh, right. And your family?
Woman My father's working in the States at the moment – until next June. He works abroad quite a lot. It's nice because my mother organises her work so that she can travel with him. Even if they aren't at home, I go to England every year because I need to see other relatives and friends.

Check your answers

a yes **b** yes **c** no **d** yes **e** yes **f** yes

Understanding more

→ Cover the text of Recording 1, *The Story*.
→ Read the questions below.
→ Listen to the recording and circle the right answer.

1 His name is Oliver/Leo.
2 Her name is Sasha/Tasha.
3 Her name is from Greece/Russia.
4 Her mother/father is from the same country.
5 The man lives in Edinburgh/Glasgow.
6 But for the next 2/3 weeks his work is in Oxford/London.
7 She's on her way to visit her family/some friends.
8 They live in/near London.
9 Her parents are in South Africa/America, for another 2 years/6 months.
10 When her parents aren't in England she goes/doesn't go home.

11 When she goes to England she visits her friends and museums/ her family.

Check your answers

1 Oliver **2** Tasha **3** Russia **4** mother **5** Edinburgh **6** 2 weeks … London **7** some friends **8** near **9** America… 6 months **10** goes **11** her family

What do they say?

→ Cover the text of Recording 1, *The Story* again.
→ Read the sentences below.
→ Listen to the recording and try to complete the words.
→ Then read the text of the recording to help you, if necessary.

1 The woman asks the man his name.
He says, 'Oliver.' Then he asks the same question 'A _ _ / y _ _ _ _ ?'

2 **a** Oliver has work in London for two weeks.
He says, 'I'_ / s _ _ _ _ _ _ _ / in London for a couple of weeks.'
b He says why.
'B _ _ _ _ _ _ / o _ / my job.'

3 Oliver asks Tasha, 'Are you on holiday?'
She says, 'Yes,/ I' _ / g _ _ _ _ _ / t _ / England/ t _ / see some friends / o _ / m _ _ _ .'

4 Tasha's parents aren't in England now.
She says, ' My / f _ _ _ _ _ 's / w _ _ _ _ _ _ g / in the States at the moment.'

5 Tasha's mother likes travelling with her father but she works.
Tasha says, 'My mother organises her work s_ / t _ _ t / s _ _ / c _ _ travel with him.'

6 Why does Tasha go to England every year? She says,
'B _ _ _ _ _ e / I / n _ _ _ / t _ / see other relatives and friends.'

Check your answers

1 And yours? **2** **a** I'm staying in London for a couple of weeks. **b** Because of my job. **3** Yes, I'm going to England to see some friends (of mine). **4** My father's working in the States at the moment. **5** My mother organises her work so that she can travel with him. **6** Because I need to see other relatives and friends.

Find the words and phrases

→ Read the sentences below.
→ Read the text of Recording 1 on page 98 and complete the words.

1 Tasha is the short name. Natasha is the long name.
Tasha is s _ _ _ t / f _ _ Natasha.

2 Tasha says, 'My mother's Russian.' Then she starts a new topic.
She says, ' _ _ / whereabouts in England do you live, Oliver?'

3 Tasha asks, 'Whereabouts in England do you live, Oliver?'
Oliver doesn't live in England, he lives in Scotland.
He says, 'I live in Scotland /, a _ _ _ _ _ _ _ _ /.'

4 Oliver's going to London. How long for? Two weeks.
He says, 'f_ _ / a / c _ _ _ _ e / o _ / weeks.'

5 Is Tasha working? No, she's _ _ holiday.

6 Tasha says, 'I'm going to England to see some friends. They live near London.'
Oliver responds with another question.
He says, 'O _, / r _ _ _ t. And your family?'

7 Tasha's father works in other countries. He works a _ _ _ _ _ _.

8 Does Tasha's father work in other countries all the time?
Not all the time but q _ _ _ e / _ / l _ _ of the time.

9 Tasha goes to England when her parents are there and when her parents aren't there. She goes to England e _ _ _ / i _ her parents aren't there.

10 How often does Tasha go to England? E _ _ _ _ / y _ _ r.

Check your answers

1 Tasha is short **for** Natasha. (preposition!)
2 So, whereabouts in England do you live, Oliver?
3 I live in Scotland, actually.
4 I'm staying in London **for** a couple of weeks. (preposition!)
5 She's **on** holiday. (Not: '~~in~~ holidays'). (preposition!)
6 Oh, right.
7 He works abroad.
8 Not all the time but quite a lot of the time.

9 She goes to England even if her parents aren't there.
10 Every year. (Not: every ~~years~~).

British culture – first names

- In Britain, it is common to have one first name, one middle name and one family name.
  Example:

Victoria	Ann	Smith
First	Middle	Family name or surname

- Some people have more than one middle name. It is not common to use your middle name(s).
- First names and middle names often come from other members of the family.
- It is very common to shorten first names, e.g. Victoria → Vicky.
- If a first name has a short form, it can be more formal to use the long form. e.g. Michael can be more formal than Mike.
- When we write a name, we usually start with the first name, e.g. Collette Dickenson. 'Collette' is the first name, 'Dickenson' is the family name. On official papers and documents, the family name usually comes first.
- At work it is very common to use first names.
- You can give your child the name you like. There is no official list.

Find the right first name

Example from *The Story*:
'Tasha is short for Natasha.'

→ Look at the names on page 102 and in the box.
→ Match the short and long names.

Girls		Boys	
1 Jo	_____	**1** Pat	_____
2 Alex	_____	**2** Chris	_____
3 Liz	_____	**3** Nick	_____
4 Sam	_____	**4** Ricky	_____
5 Kate	_____	**5** Sam	_____
6 Ros	_____	**6** Joey	_____
7 Chris	_____	**7** Mike	_____
8 Nicky	_____	**8** Alex	_____
9 Pat	_____	**9** Tom	_____
10 Di	_____	**10** Dan	_____

Girls		**Boys**	
Patricia	Christine	Nicholas	Samuel
Joanna	Rosalyn	Michael	Daniel
Alexandra	Elizabeth	Richard	Thomas
Nicola	Catherine	Alexander	Christopher
Samantha	Diana	Patrick	Joseph

Check your answers

Girls		Boys
1	Jo/Joanna	Pat/Patrick
2	Alex/Alexandra	Chris/Christopher
3	Liz/Elizabeth	Nick/Nicholas
4	Sam/Samantha	Ricky/Richard
5	Kate/Catherine	Sam/Samuel
6	Ros/Rosalyn	Joey/Joseph
7	Chris/Christine	Mike/Michael
8	Nicky/Nicola	Alex/Alexander
9	Pat/Patricia	Tom/Thomas
10	Di/Diana	Dan/Daniel

As you can see, some short names are the same for both men and women.
→ How many examples can you find in the lists? Write them here.

____

Asking someone about their name

→ Put these words in the right order:

for/name/what/your/'s/short? ________________

Check your answers

Four. Alex, Sam, Chris and Pat are short names for both boys and girls. What's your name short for?

About you: first names

→ Write answers to these questions or prepare to tell a friend.

Is your first name short for another name?____________________
Does another member of the family have the same name?__________
Where does your name come from?___________________________
Is it common or unusual in your country?____________________
What does your first name mean?___________________________

Using these words and phrases

1 *So*

Example from *The Story*:

Tasha My mother's Russian. So, whereabouts in England do you live, Oliver?

★ We can use *so* to change the topic
In the conversation above, Tasha talks about her mother. Then she asks Oliver where he lives. *So* starts the new topic
★ *So* is not essential.

So, to start a new topic

Situation John and Jean live in Miami. They have a party. Two guests have a conversation.

→ Read the conversation on page 104. The topic changes three times.
→ Write *so* where the topic changes.

Jo My name's Jo and yours?
Sam Sam.
Jo Where do you come from Sam?
Sam I'm from New York. I work in a bookshop there.
Jo Do you like it?
Sam Yes, I really enjoy it, actually. I love books. Do you know this town well?
Jo Quite well. I come for a holiday from time to time. How about you? Where do you go on holiday?
Sam I like going to Europe for my holidays – I love London and I know Paris and Rome and a few other places. How do you know John and Jean?
Jo John's my brother.
Sam Oh, right.

Check your answers

Jo My name's Jo and yours?
Sam Sam.
Jo So, where do you come from Sam?
Sam I'm from New York. I work in a bookshop there.
Jo Do you like it?
Sam Yes, I really enjoy it, actually. I love books. So, do you know this town well?
Jo Quite well. I come for a holiday from time to time. How about you? Where do you go on holiday?
Sam I like going to Europe for my holidays – I love London and I know Paris and Rome and a few other places. So, how do you know John and Jean?
Jo John's my brother.
Sam Oh, right.

2 Correcting people – *actually*

Example from *The Story*:

Tasha: 'So, whereabouts in England do you live, Oliver?'
Oliver doesn't live in England. He lives in Scotland.
He says: 'I live in Scotland, **actually**.'

He doesn't say the wrong information, 'I don't live in England.' This can sound rude. He says 'I live in Scotland, actually.' He says the correct information + *actually*.

With *actually* the correction is less direct.

★ *Actually* goes at the beginning or the end of the correction,
Example: 'Actually, I live in Scotland' OR 'I live in Scotland, actually.'

→ Read the short dialogues below.
→ Correct the 'mistakes'.

Recording 2

Example:	**A**	Good morning, Jo.	**B**	***My name's Sam, actually.*** (Your name's Sam)
1	**A**	So, what's it like working for Sony?	**B**	________________ (You work for Panasonic)
2	**A**	Excuse me ... here's your bag.	**B**	________________ (The bag isn't yours)
3	**A**	Would you like some wine?	**B**	________________ (You don't drink alcohol)
4	**A**	Please take me home.	**B**	________________ (You can't drive)
5	**A**	So, whereabouts in France are you from?	**B**	________________ (You're from Italy)
6	**A**	Peter's really nice, isn't he?	**B**	________________ (You don't know Peter)
7	**A**	(On the phone) Sue?	**B**	________________ (You're Sue's mother)
8	**A**	Lovely, isn't it?	**B**	________________ (You're not very keen on it)
9	**A**	What sort of work does your husband do?	**B**	________________ (You're not married)

Check your answers

1 (Actually), I work for Panasonic, (actually).
2 (Actually), it's not mine, (actually).
3 (Actually), I don't drink alcohol, (actually).
4 (Actually), I can't drive, (actually).
5 (Actually), I'm from Italy, (actually).

6 (Actually), I don't know him, (actually).
7 (Actually) I'm her mother, (actually).
8 (Actually) I'm not very keen on it, (actually).
9 (Actually) I'm not married, (actually).

→ Listen to Recording 2 and say the responses.

3 *Abroad*

Example from *The Story*:

Tasha's father works abroad.

★ *Abroad* has no preposition and no **article** ('the').

It isn't correct to say:
'He works ~~in the~~ abroad.'
'He goes ~~to~~ abroad for his holiday.'

→ Complete these answers with *abroad* and information about Oliver and Tasha from the recording.

1 Is Tasha's mother in England?
No, ____________

2 Does Tasha live in England?
No, she___________

3 Oliver __________ a lot for his job.

4 Tasha's father __________ quite a lot.

5 What sort of holidays do you like?
I enjoy (travel) ___________

Check your answers

1 No, she's abroad. **2** No, she lives abroad. **3** Oliver travels abroad a lot for his job. **4** Tasha's father works abroad quite a lot. **5** I enjoy travelling abroad.

How do you pronounce it?

He, she, it and *who?* forms of present simple

Recording 3, part 1

Example from *The Story*: My mother organises her work.

→ Read the question below.
→ Listen to the sentence on the recording and choose **a** or **b**.

The verb *organise* has three syllables – or-gan-ise.

'Organises' has **a** three / **b** four } syllables?

Check your answer

b 'organises' has four syllables - or-gan-is-es. / ˈɔ:gənaɪzɪz /
Remember, a syllable is part of a word with a vowel sound.

★ Some verbs add an extra syllable / ɪz / with *he* and *she*, *it* and *who?*

→ Listen to Recording 3, part 2 and repeat these verbs.

Recording 3, part 2

close	fin-ish	re-lax	watch	dance
clos-es	fin-ish-es	re lax-es	watch-es	danc-es

Pronunciation – 3rd person singular, present simple

Situation Kate and Joey are married. Joey has a shop and his wife works in a supermarket. Who does what in their house?

→ Read Joey's sentences on page 108.
→ Complete the verbs and write the number of syllables in the brackets ( ). All the verbs here change.
→ Practise the extra syllable. Read the verbs aloud as you write.

My wife and I

Example: I close (1) my shop at 6.00 but Kate's supermarket ***closes*** (2) at 9.00.

I finish ( ) work early but she ______ ( ) late.

At home I wash ( ) the dishes and she ______ ( ) the clothes.

I fix ( ) the car and she ______ ( ) things in the house.

I relax ( ) in the bath but she ______ ( ) with a book.

I watch ( ) sport on T.V. but Kate ______ ( ) news programmes.

I dance ( ) a bit but my wife ______ ( ) well.

I use ( ) soap but my wife ______ ( ) shower gel.

I change ( ) the baby in the morning and Kate ______ ( ) her at night.

I sneeze ( ) when I'm ill but she ______ ( ) every morning.

I organise( ) the money and she ______ ( ) the holidays.

I kiss ( ) my wife and my wife ______ ( ) me.

Check your answers *(Recording 3, part 3)*

I close (1)…the supermarket closes (2)
I finish (2)…she finishes (3)
I wash (1)…she washes (2)
I fix (1)…she fixes (2)
I relax (2)…she relaxes (3)
I watch (1)…Kate watches (2)
I dance (1)…my wife dances (2)
I use (1)…my wife uses (2)
I change (1)…Kate changes (2)
I sneeze (1)…she sneezes (2)
I organise (3)…she organises (4)
I kiss (1) my wife and my wife kisses (2) me.

→ Listen to the answers above on Recording 3, part 3 and repeat.
→ Pay special attention to the extra syllable for *she*.

Asking *who*? – pronunciation 3rd person singular '*-es*'

Who does these things? Kate or Joey?

→ Complete the questions with one word only.

Who ________( ) the dishes?	Joey.
Who ________ ( ) work at 9.00?	Kate does.
Who ________ ( ) sport on T.V.?	Joey does.
Who ________( ) things?	They both do.

Check your answers

1 Who washes the dishes?
2 Who finishes work at 9.00
3 Who watches sport on T.V?
4 Who fixes things?

Note
Not: ~~Who does wash the dishes?~~
When *who* is the subject, no *do*.

Q When do we add an extra syllable for 'he, she, it' and question 'who'?

A When it's difficult to say the 's' without adding an extra vowel sound. An extra vowel sound = extra syllable (It's the same reason as the plural nouns in Topic 3.)

→ Look at the summary below.

Pronunciation and spelling summary

3rd person singular

★ For *he, she, it* and *who* add an extra syllable to verbs ending in:

- se	**-ce**	**-ge**	**- ze**	**-ss**	**-sh**	**-tch**	**-x**
close use organise	dance	change	sneeze	kiss	wash finish	watch	relax fix
				Here, the spelling changes too. Add 'es'			

→ Look at the verbs below.
→ Which ones change with *he, she, it* and question *who*?

touch	cross	read	think	want	drink
fax	pass	manage	pronounce	wish	

Check your answers

Touch, cross, fax, pass, manage, pronounce, wish.
All these words have an extra syllable in 3rd person singular.

What's the right word?

The family: close relatives

Who's who in this family?

→ Look at the family diagram on page 111 and the vocabulary in the boxes.
→ Complete the sentences on page 112.
→ Use your dictionary if necessary.

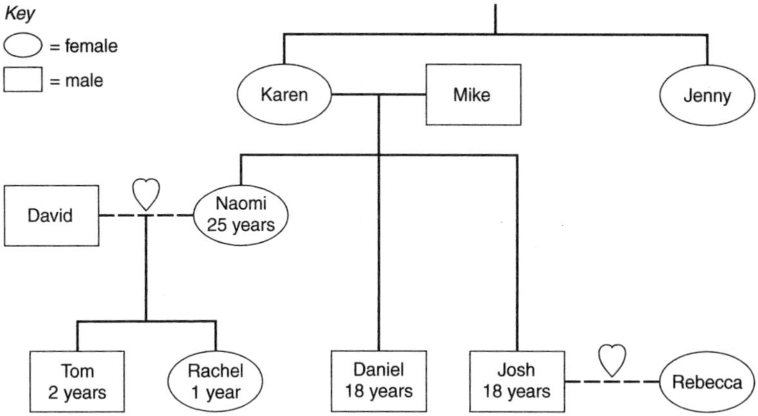

Karen ⟷ Mike
Wife Husband
Karen and Mike are married
Mike is married to Karen

Karen/Mike ⟷ Naomi, Josh, Daniel
Parents Children

Karen/Mike ⟷ Naomi/Daniel
Mother/Father ⟷ Daughter/Son

Naomi ⟷ Daniel/Josh
Sister Brother(s)
Josh ← Twin brothers → Daniel

Naomi lives with David
Partner ⟷ Partner

Josh is going out with Rebecca
Boyfriend ⟷ Girlfriend

Rebecca isn't related to Jenny.
Tom and Josh are related.

Naomi →	Karen	'Hello, Mum'
Tom →	Naomi	'Hello, Mummy' (young children)
Naomi →	Mike	'Hello, Dad'
Tom →	David	'Hello, Daddy' (young children)
David →	Tom/Rachel	'Hello, kids' (informal)

→ Now complete thesc sentences with the vocabulary from the diagram and boxes above.

1 Mike: Could I speak to Karen, please? It's her ______ here.'

2 This is Karen, Josh's mother. Is my ______ there, please?'

3 I'm Naomi, Daniel's sister. Is my ______ here, please?

4 **A** Who's David? **B** Naomi's ______ .

5 **A** Josh, are you ______/______ to Mike? **B** Yes, he's my dad.

6 Mike: Naomi's a lovely ______ .

7 Mike: I'm married to Karen now. Sue's my first ______ .

8 Naomi: Daniel's my ______ .

9 Josh is Daniel's ______/______. They look exactly alike.

10 Josh is in love with his ______. He wants to marry her. He asks her, 'Will you marry me?'

11 When David goes to work, little Tom says, 'Bye, bye ______.'

12 **A** Naomi, is Daniel a ______ of yours? **B** Yes, he's my brother.'

13 'We always give our ______ flowers on Mother's Day.'
*Mother's Day is usually in April in Britain.

14 It's Daniel here, Naomi's brother. Can I leave a message for my ______, please?'

15 **a** Naomi and David have got two ______.
b When Naomi takes them out, she says 'Come on ______ . We're going out.'

16 Daniel: I need to talk to Mum. Naomi: Mum isn't here but ______ is. Shall I get him?'

17 Tom is in a shop. He can't find Naomi. He says, 'Where's my ______?'

18 Naomi and Josh are ______ and ______.

19 **A** Who's Karen ______/______? **B** Mike

20 **A** Who's Rebecca ______/______/______? **B** Her ______'s name's Josh.

Check your answers

1 husband **2** son **3** brother **4** partner **5** related to (preposition! Not: '~~related with~~') **6** daughter **7** wife **8** brother **9** twin brother **10** girlfriend **11** Daddy **12** relative/relation **13** Mum **14** sister **15 a** children **b** kids

*It is rude to use the singular in this way. Instead we use the name e.g. 'Come on David', not '~~Come on kid~~'.

16 Dad **17** Mummy **18** brother and sister **19** married to (preposition! Not: ~~married with~~') **20** going out with/boyfriend

Family relationships

Possessive *'s* contraction of *is* and *has*

A sentence can have more than one possessive **'s**.
→ Look at the examples below.

1 Who**'s** Karen? Mike**'s** wife (Not: ~~The wife of Mike~~)
is **possessive 's**

2 Karen**'s** daughter**'s** name**'s** Naomi. (Not: ~~The name of the daughter of Karen is Naomi~~)
possessive ' s **is**

3 What**'s** David**'s** son's name? (Not: ~~What's the name of the son of David~~)
is **possessive 's**

OR What**'s** the name of David**'s** son?
is **possessive 's**

4 Daniel has a friend, Jack.
Who**'s** Jack? A friend of Daniel**'s**. (Not: ~~A friend of Daniel~~.)
is **possessive 's**

1 **A** Who's Josh? **B** M____'_ / s_____
2 **A** Who'_ Mike? **B** K____'_ / h______
3 Daniel' __/m____'_/n______'_/ Karen.
4 Josh'_/ f_______'s/ n_____'_/ Mike.
5 Mike'_ / d______'_ / n ____' _ Naomi.
6 **A:** What'__/ K___n'_ / d_____'_ / n____? **B:** Naomi.
7 **A:** Who'_ Daniel? A f _____ / o__/ J ____'_.

Check your answers

1 Mike's son. **2** Karen's husband. **3** Daniel's mother's name's Karen. **4** Josh's father's name's Mike. **5** Mike's daughter's name's Naomi. **6** What's Karen's daugher's name? **7** Who's Daniel? A friend of Jack's.

Write about you and your family

→ Choose the right information below to make a paragraph about you and your family.
→ Delete, circle, complete or tick the right answers about you.
→ Use your dictionary if necessary.

For example: I'm { married
~~not married~~

My husband's
wife's name's Mary/John
partner's
girlfriend's
boyfriend's

I've got 1
2 children ✓
3

About you

My name's _________
My family and friends call me _________
I'm { married
not married
I've got a { partner
girlfriend
boyfriend

About your partner

My { husband's
wife's name's _________
partner's
girlfriend's
boyfriend's

OR
I haven't got a partner/girlfriend/boyfriend
OR
I'm too young to have a girlfriend/boyfriend

About your brothers and sisters

I've got	1 brother	His name's _________
	2 brothers	Their names are ________ and _______
	3 brothers	Their names are _______, ______ and ______
	4 etc. brothers	Their names are __________________ ________ and _________
I've got	1 sister	Her name's ________
	2 sisters	Their names are ________ and ________
	3 sisters	Their names are _______, ______ and_______
	4 etc. sisters	Their names are ____________________ _________ and ________

OR
I haven't got any brothers or sisters. I'm an only child

About your parents

Both my parents are alive. They live in _______

{ Both my parents are alive but they aren't together.
My mother lives in _______ and my father lives in _______

My mother's alive but my father's dead. She lives in _______
My father's alive but my mother's dead. He lives in _______
Both my parents are dead

About your children

I haven't got any children
I've got one child, a son. His name's
I've got one child, a daughter. Her name's _______
I've got two, three, four etc. children. Their names are _______ __________ and ______

Grammar and communication 1

Possessive pronouns – *mine*, etc.

Examples from *The Story*:

1 The woman asks the man his name.
He says, 'Oliver.' Then he asks the same question.
He says, 'And **yours**?'

2 Why is Tasha going to England?
She says, 'To see some friends of mine.'

★ 'They're friends of mine' is more common than 'they're my friends.'

→ Use the possessive pronouns in the box to complete the table below.

Subject		Possessive adjective		Possessive pronoun
I	→	my	→	________
he	→	his	→	________
she	→	her	→	________
you	→	your	→	________
we	→	our	→	________
they	→	their	→	________

ours	*mine*	*theirs*	*his*	*yours*	*hers*

Check your answers

Subject	Possessive adjective	Possessive pronoun
I	my	mine
he	his	his
she	her	hers
you	your	yours
we	our	ours
they	their	theirs

Possessive pronouns

→ Complete the sentences below with the correct possessive pronoun.

1 **A** My birthday's in April. When's ______? **B** In November.
2 We're seeing friends of _______ for dinner tomorrow.
3 **A** Does David know Jack? **B** Yes, Jack's a friend of ________
4 That isn't their car. _______ is blue.
5 **A** Is Jo a classmate of _______? **B** Yes, we're in the same English class.

6 The family is going on holiday.
- **a** Which bag is yours? That big one's ________
- **b** And John's? The red one's ________
- **c** Where's Mary's? _______ is this black one.
- **d** How about Kay's and Mike's? ______ are in the car.
- **e** And we can take _______. Come on, let's go.

Check your answers

1 yours **2** ours **3** his **4** theirs **5** yours **6 a** mine **b** his **c** hers **d** theirs **e** ours

Grammar and communication 2

Present progressive – temporary actions

Example from *The Story*:

1 Tasha's parents aren't in England now.
She says, '**My father's working** in the States until June.'
is

The name of the tense is the **Present Progressive**.
What's the meaning and form?

→ Choose the right answers.

Meaning

1 Here the present progressive is for **a** the past.
b the present.
c the future.

2 The action is **a** permanent.
b temporary.

Form

1 The verb has **a** one word.
b two words.

2 The present of 'be' **a** is / **b** isn't } part of this tense

Check your answers

Meaning **1 b** the present **2 b** temporary.
Form **1 b** two words **2 a** The present of 'be' is part of this tense.

★ Here the **present progressive** is for **a temporary action** in the **present**.

Present progressive – form

→ Complete the table on page 118 with the correct part of the verb *be*.
→ Write the contractions in the brackets, for example I am (I'm).

Affirmative ('yes')		**Negative ('no')**	
I _ _ ('m)	working.	I _ _ not ('m)	working.
He She _ _ It ('_)		He She _ _ not It ('_) OR _ _ n't	
You We _ _ _ They ('_ _)		You _ _ _ not We ('_ _) They OR _ _ _ n't	

Questions		Question tags – to make conversation Echo questions – to express interest	
		Positive	**Negative**
_ _ I	working?	_ _ I?	aren't I?
_ _ he she it		_ _ she? it?	_ _ n't he? she? it?
_ _ _ you we they		_ _ _ you? we? they?	_ _ _ n't you? we? they?

Check your answers

Affirmative ('yes')		Negative ('no')	
I am ('m)	working	I am not ('m)	working
he she is it ('s)		he she is not it ('s) OR isn't	
you we are they ('re)		you are not we ('re) they OR aren't	

Questions		Question tags – to make conversation Echo questions – to express interest **Positive**	**Negative**
Am I	working?	am I?	aren't I?
Is he she it		is he? she? it?	isn't he? she? it?
Are you we they		are you? we? they?	aren't you? we? they?

More questions! Present progressive – form

→ Answer *Yes/No* to these questions

1 The main verb is always with 'ing'. Yes/No
2 To make questions, you use auxiliary *do*. Yes/No
3 To ask a question, you change the word order. Yes/No
4 In questions the verb *be* is before the person. Yes/No
5 The negative can have two forms. Yes/No
6 The 'I' form of the negative question tag is irregular. Yes/No

Check your answers

1 Yes **2** No **3** Yes **4** Yes **5** Yes **6** Yes (aren't I?)

Temporary actions in the present – present progressive

What's happening at home?

Situation Mark arrives home. He's talking to his brother, Dave. They've got one sister, Sharon and a brother, Jamie.

→ Complete the conversation. Use the correct parts of the present progressive and appropriate verbs.

Mark Where's Dad?
Dave He'_/______ the car. This water's for him.
Mark And Mum?
Dave She's in the kitchen – ________ a cake for your birthday.
Mark What' __ Jamie ______?
Dave _____ T.V in his room.
Mark __/__?

Mark _____ Sharon _____ her homework?
Dave Of course she __'__. She's upstairs with some friends. They'__/ l_______/ to music.
Mark They a____'t /l_______/__ my new CD, a___/ they?

[Mark goes to Sharon's room]

Mark Sharon, what / __/you/ l_______/ t__?
Sharon Your new CD. It's great! I'__ really _______ it!
Mark A____/y____? Now come on. Give it back to me.
Sharon Sorry! Here you are.

Check your answers

Mark Where's Dad?
Dave He's washing the car. This water's for him.
Mark And Mum?
Dave She's in the kitchen – making a cake for your birthday.
Mark What's Jamie doing?
Dave Watching T.V in his room.
Mark Is he?

Mark Is Sharon doing her homework?
Dave Of course she isn't. She's upstairs with some friends. They're listening to music.
Mark They aren't listening to my new CD, are they?

[Mark runs up to Sharon's room]

Mark Sharon, what are you listening to?
Sharon Your new CD. It's great! I'm really enjoying it!
Mark Are you? Now come on. Give it back to me.
Sharon Sorry! Here you are.

Q ***In the conversation above, what's the difference between the two answers below.***

Mark What's Jamie doing?
a Dave **He's watching** T.V.
b Dave **Watching** T.V.

A Both are correct and common.

a is always appropriate. ***b*** is more informal.

Q ***In the story, why is it:***

'My father's living in the States until June?'
present progressive

Can I also say, 'My father lives in the States?'
present simple?

A This is a very important question. The grammar in both sentences is correct. They mean different things.

With the **present progressive**, ('My father's living') the situation is **temporary**.
With the **present simple**, ('My father lives'), the speaker thinks the situation is **permanent**. So, 'My father lives in the States until June' is wrong. ✗

Q **Situation** ***It's 3.00. Where's Sharon?***

Is it correct to say, 'She's sleeping?'

This answer is not wrong but it's not common. 'She's asleep' is more common.
It's the same with questions and the negative.

'Is she asleep?' is more common than 'Is she sleeping?'.
'She isn't asleep' is more common than 'She isn't sleeping'.

Present simple or present progressive?

→ Circle the correct verb form. Choose present simple for permanent situations. Choose present progressive for temporary situations.

1 Your teacher's ill, so today I teach/I'm teaching your class.
2 Are you in a hotel? No, I stay/I'm staying with friends.
3 My son lives/is living with me until his new flat is ready.
4 Now, come on Joseph, you are/you're being very naughty today. Stop that and sit down. Usually you are/you are being a very good boy.
5 Normally, I work/I'm working hard but this month I don't/ I'm not. – it's very quiet.
6 Does your daughter live/Is your daughter living at home?
Yes, she's only 14.

☑ Check your answers

1 I'm teaching. **2** I'm staying. **3** Is living. **4** You're being…. You are. **5** I work…..I'm not. **6** Does your daughter live?

Present progressive – future arrangements

Example from *The Story*:

Oliver is on a plane on his way to London.
He says, 'I'm **staying** in London for a couple of weeks.'

Meaning

→ Answer these questions. For **1**, **2** and **4** find the right answer. For **3** answer 'Yes' or 'No'.

1 Here, this tense is for an action in the

(a) Past **(b) Present** **(c) Future**

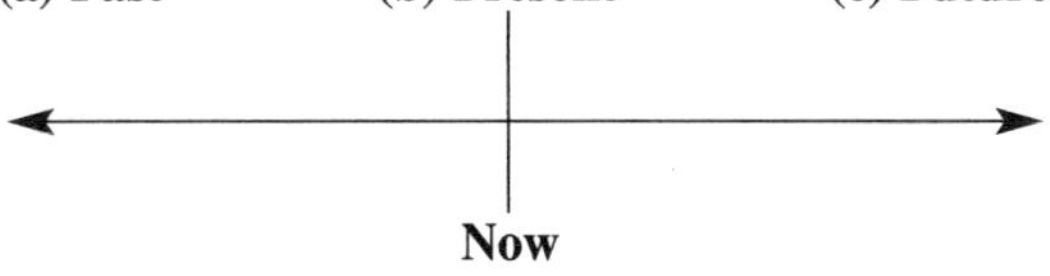

2 The decision to stay in London is

(a) In the past **(b) In the present** **(c) In the future**

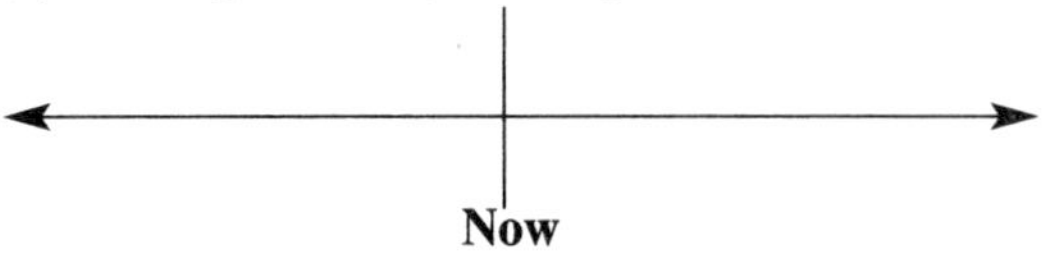

3 **a** The plan is for Oliver to spend two weeks in London. Yes/No
b Action to arrange the time in London is in the past. Yes/No

4 The arrangement is **a** personal **b** part of a timetable?

Check your answers

1 c future **2 a** in the past **3 a** yes – planned **b** yes – arranged **4 a** personal

★ Here the **present progressive** is for **personal future arrangements**.

→ Complete this conversation between two friends.

A What __/you ____ this evening?
B I' __/_____ to the cinema with Don. Would you like to come with us?
A No, thanks, Jim'_ / _____ in a minute. We' _/_______ out for a drink.
B Which pub ____/you/____/ __?
A The one by the river.

Check your answers

A What are you doing this evening?
B I'm going to the cinema with Don. Would you like to come with us?
A No, thanks. Jim's arriving in a minute. We're going out for a drink.
B Which pub are you going to? **A** The one by the river.

Example:
'I'm going to the cinema this evening.'

Q ***Can I also say, 'I go to the cinema this evening'? ✗***

A No. This is a personal arrangement in the future. The present progressive is the only correct tense.
(The present simple is only used for the future to talk about timetables, schedules and itineraries – see Topic 8.)

Present and future actions

→ Read the sentences below. They are all in the present progressive.
→ Which sentences refer to an action in the present?
→ Which sentences refer to a personal future arrangement?
→ Write 'present' or 'future'.

1 I'm doing it right now! ________
2 I'm leaving soon. ________
3 Is he arriving on Friday? ________

4 I'm busy talking on the phone at the moment. ________
5 I'm seeing him in the morning ________
6 The telephone's ringing – Can someone please answer it? ________
7 I'm having dinner with him tomorrow evening. ________
8 They're having a holiday at the end of the contract. ________
9 You're not meeting John after work, are you? ________
10 **A** Mummy, I can't sleep.
B I'm coming in a minute, darling. ________

Check your answers

1 Present **2** Future **3** Future **4** Present **5** Future **6** Present **7** Future **8** Future **9** Future **10** Future

Future arrangements – present progressive

→ Read the mini-dialogue below about arrangements for next weekend.
→ Underline the personal future arrangements.

A So, what are you doing next weekend?
B Well, on Saturday morning I'm visiting a friend. Then, in the evening we're having dinner in the new pizza restaurant. On Sunday my parents are coming for the day.

Check your answers

A So, what are you doing next weekend?
B Well, on Saturday morning I'm visiting a friend. Then, in the evening we're having dinner in the new pizza restaurant. On Sunday my parents are coming for the day.

Find the mistakes with the verbs

→ There are five mistakes in this mini-dialogue. Write the correct dialogue below.

A Do you come to class tomorrow? **B** No, I won't.

A Why you can't come? **B** Because tomorrow comes my mother from Germany. I go to the airport to meet her.

A ______________________ **B** ______________________

A ______________________ **B** ______________________

Check your answers

A Are you coming to class tomorrow? **B** No, I'm not.
A Why can't you come? **B** Because tomorrow my mother is coming from Germany. I'm going to the airport to meet her.

→ What are you doing next weekend? Write or prepare to tell a friend.
→ Write a minimum of three things about your arrangements for next weekend.

Grammar and communication 3

Saying why - *to, so that, because*

Examples from *The Story*:

1 Tasha: 'I'm going to England **to see** some friends.'

2 Tasha: 'My mother organises her work **so that** she can travel with my father.'

3 Why does Tasha go to England every year?
She says, '**because** I need to see other relatives and friends.'

4 Why is Oliver staying in London for 2 weeks?
Because of his job.

Summary – Saying why
A Why is Tasha travelling to England? **B** { To / Because she wants to/likes to/needs to / So (that) she can } visit friends and family.
A Why is Oliver staying in London? **B** Because of his job (because of noun +)

Answers to '*Why?*'

→ Why is Tasha travelling to England?
→ Write *because*, *because of* or *so (that) she can.*

a .... buy new books for her job.
b .... her friends and relatives.
c .... it's her country.
d .... have a holiday.

Check your answers

a So that she can buy new books for her job.
b Because of her friends and relatives.
c Because it's her country.
d So that she can have a holiday.

Common mistake – Saying why

Example from *The Story*:

Tasha says 'I'm going to England **to see** some friends.'
This is **the infinitive of purpose**. In other words, it answers the question *Why?* or *What for?*

Not: 'I'm going to England ~~for to see~~ some friends.'
Not: 'I'm going to England ~~for seeing~~ some friends.'

How do you pronounce it?

Infinitive of purpose – *to* + verb

→ Look at the words with stress in the phrase below.
'… to see some friends.'

The pronunciation of *to* is weak / tə /. The important word in the phrase 'to see' is *see*.

→ Complete sentences **1–8** with an expression from the box below.

Example: We go to France ***to buy nice wine***.

1 I'm phoning ______________________
2 I go to the coffee bar ______________________
3 I need some change ______________________
4 I'm going to the kitchen ______________________

5 You call 999 ____________________
6 I swim ____________________
7 She's in Italy ____________________
8 I'd like to go to London ____________________

to learn Italian	to relax and keep fit	to make a phone call
to have some tea		to tell you about the party
to get an ambulance	~~to buy nice wine~~	
to talk to my friends and have a snack		to visit the museums

Check your answers *(Recording 4)*

1 I'm phoning to tell you about the party.
2 I go to the coffee bar to talk to my friends and have a snack.
3 I need some change to make a phone call.
4 I'm going to the kitchen to have some tea.
5 You call 999 to get an ambulance.
6 I swim to relax and keep fit.
7 She's in Italy to learn Italian.
8 I'd like to go to London to visit the museums.

→ Listen to the sentences above on Recording 4 and repeat them.
→ Pay special attention to weak form *to* / tə /. The stress is on the verb after *to*.

Saying why

→ Read the questionnaire below and tick ✓ the right answers for you.

Why are you learning English?

☐ Because I like it. It's a hobby.
☐ Because I need it for my job.
☐ Because I need it for my studies.
☐ Because I want to visit England.

- ☐ So I can travel independently.
- ☐ So I can understand and talk to my colleagues and/or visitors.
- ☐ So I can get a better job.
- ☐ To pass exams.
- ☐ Because I want to understand the words of songs in English.
- ☐ Because I like to watch films in English.
- ☐ To help my children with their English studies.
- ☐ Because there is an English-speaking person in my family.

What are your main reasons? ______________________

Why are you using this *Teach Yourself* book?

- ☐ To improve and practise my English in general.
- ☐ To learn how to communicate better in English.
- ☐ To understand speakers of English when they talk.
- ☐ To improve my pronunciation.
- ☐ To improve my vocabulary.
- ☐ To improve my grammar.
- ☐ To find out more about British life and customs.
- ☐ Because I can't go to classes.
- ☐ Because I study on my own.

What are your main reasons? ______________________

What would you say?

1 You are next in a queue in a shop. The shop assistant asks 'Who's next? The person behind you says 'Me'.

____

2 The phone rings. Your brother answers it. You're in your room. Your brother calls you and says 'It's for you'.

____

Possible answers

1 'I think it's my turn, actually' OR 'Excuse me, I think I'm next.'
2 (I'm) coming.'

Revision

How do you say it in your language?

→ Here are some examples of the important points in this topic.
→ Translate the sentences below into your language in the spaces.
→ Remember – translate the idea, not the words.

1 Here's my car. Where's yours?

____

2 Maria's a friend of mine.

____

3 I'm studying English because of my job.

____

4 I listen to the tape or CD to improve my pronunciation.

____

5 I'm working tomorrow.

____

6 **A** Where's Pat? **B** She's having a bath.

____

7 I don't work so that I can be with my children.

____

Join the conversation

→ Look at the text of Recording 1 (page 98), *The Story*, again.
→ Listen to Recording 5.
→ Read the **woman's** words in the spaces.

TEST 5

Which one is right?

Choose **a** or **b**.

1 Where's Sue? **a** She's in holidays.
b She's on holiday.

2 **a** Do you go out this evening?
b Are you going out this evening?

3 I go to the cinema a lot **a** because of I like new films.
b because I like new films.

4 I'm working hard **a** so as to can travel **a** abroad.
b so that I can travel **b** in the abroad.

5 Why are you calling David? **a** To invite him to the party.
b For to invite him to the party.

6 We go there **a** all the weekends.
b every weekend.

7 I like playing tennis **a** even if it's raining.
b if even it's raining.

8 **a** I don't wait any more. I leave right now.
b I'm not waiting any more. I'm leaving right now.

9 **a** Susan is the girlfriend of Paul and Paul's a friend of me.
b Susan is Paul's girlfriend and Paul's a friend of mine.

10 **a** She's a friend of Peter.
b She's a friend of Peter's.

For **11** and **12** choose the appropriate answer.

11 You live at number 2, don't you? **a** No.
b Actually, my house is number 3.

12 I'm a friend of your brother's. **a** Oh, right.
b Yes.

Write a dialogue

Situation You are in a new English class in England. You meet another student. She is not the same nationality as you.

You

1 You say your name
You ask her name

Gloria

2

I'm Gloria

3 You ask why she's studying English

4 Because of my job.

She asks you the same question

5 You answer (work/tourism)

You ask about her arrangements
for after the class

6 She answers (library/homework)
She asks you the same question

7 You answer (lunch/cafeteria)

Check your answers

Which one is right?

1 b **2** b **3** b **4 b** a **5** a **6** b **7** a **8** b **9** b **10** b **11** b **12** a

Dialogue: model answers

1	**You**	Hello, My name's …. What's yours?
2	**Gloria**	I'm Gloria.
3	**You**	Why are you studying English?
4	**Gloria**	Because of my job. How about you?
5	**You**	I'm studying English because I want to work in tourism in my country. What are you doing after the class?
6	**Gloria**	I'm going to the library to do my homework. And you?
7	**You**	I'm having lunch in the cafeteria.

6 STAYING IN CONTACT

Grammar and communication
- Future plans – *going to*
- Making arrangements: possibilities, suggestions and offers
- Telephone language
- Asking for things (2)

Vocabulary
- Numbers
- The alphabet

Pronunciation
- Using stress to correct mistakes

Tasha and Oliver continue their conversation... They exchange personal details and plan future contact.

Understanding the important information

→ Read the sentences below and on page 134
→ Listen to Recording 1 and answer *Yes* or *No*.

1 Oliver would like to see Tasha again. Yes/No
2 Tasha would like to see Oliver again. Yes/No

3 He gives her his contact details. Yes/No
4 She gives him her contact details. Yes/No
5 They arrange a meeting. Yes/No
6 They arrange a telephone call. Yes/No
7 They're arriving in London soon. Yes/No

Recording 1 (and 16) – The Story

Oliver As I'm working in London for two weeks, we could … we could meet for a drink one evening, if you like.
Tasha Yes, that would be nice.
Oliver I don't know where I'm staying but you can phone me at the office, and we can arrange something. Shall I give you my number?
Tasha O.K. Where's my diary?
Tasha opens her bag and gets her diary.
Tasha What's your surname?
Oliver Rees.
Tasha Is that R double E, C, E?
Oliver No, its R, double E, S actually, and the telephone number of the London office is 020 7402 3277.
Tasha 020 7402…?
Oliver 3277. You can get me on extension 159, I think it is. Yes, 159. If you have access to e-mail, my e-mail address is orees@fastpost.com.
Tasha I can give you the telephone number of my friend's house, too.
Oliver Why not? Then I can call you. Just a minute.
Oliver opens his diary.
Tasha My other name's Harrison by the way. Tasha Harrison.
Oliver Harrison, 'H', Tasha Harrison. And your friend's number is…?
Tasha 020 8549 6682.
Oliver 020 8949…
Tasha No, it's 020 8549 6682… Yes, that's it.
Oliver When would you like me to call, during the day or in the evening?

Tasha I don't mind. I'm going to visit relatives and do other things but I'm going to spend time at home with my friends, too. So, any time's alright with me, really. I'm on holiday!

Oliver Right then, I'll telephone you some time next week, Tasha, if that's O.K.

Tasha Yes, I'll look forward to it.

Oliver Oh, look, the 'Fasten your seat belts' sign is on. We're landing in a minute.

Check your answers

1 Yes **2** Yes **3** Yes **4** Yes **5** No **6** Yes **7** Yes

Understanding more

→ Cover the text of Recording 1, *The Story*.
→ Read the questions below.
→ For **1** and **5** listen and tick ALL the correct answers.
→ For **2**, **3** and **4** complete the information where possible.

1 Oliver talks about
a dinner
b a drink
c the cinema
} next week.

2 Oliver's details
a his family name ________
b the name of his hotel ________
c his home telephone number ________
d his office telephone number ________
e his e-mail address ________

3 Tasha's details
a her family name ________
b her friend's name ________
c her friend's address ________
d her friend's telephone number ________
e her e-mail address ________

4 Tasha's plans for her holiday
a ____________________
b ____________________
c ____________________

5 Who's phoning who and when?

a Oliver's phoning Tasha
b Tasha's phoning Oliver
c next weekend
d next week
e in the day
f in the evening

Check your answers

1 b. **2 a** Rees **b** X. **c** X. **d** 020 7402 3277. **e** orees@fastpost.com. **3 a** Harrison. **b** X. **c** X. **d** 020 8549 6682. **e** X. **4 a** visit relatives. **b** do other things. **c** spend time with her friends. **5 a d e f**.

What do they say?

→ Read the sentences below.
→ Listen to Recording 1 again and try to complete the words.
→ Then read the text of the recording on page 134 to help you if necessary.

1 a Oliver would like to see Tasha again.
He suggests a drink. He says, 'We c _ _ _ d meet for a drink…'.

b Tasha responds. 'Yes, t_ _ t / w _ _ _ d / be / n _ _ e.'

2 a Oliver talks about possible contact.
He says, 'I don't know where I'm staying but you / c _ _ / phone me at the office and we / _ _ _ / arrange something.'

b Tasha also talks about possible contact.
She says, 'I / _ _ _ / give you the telephone number of my friend's house.'

3 Oliver offers to give Tasha his telephone number.
He says, 'S _ _ _ _ / _ / give you my number?'

4 a Oliver offers to phone Tasha next week.
He says, 'I'_ _ / telephone you some time next week.'

b Tasha feels positive about it.
She says, 'I'_ _ / l _ _ k / f _ _ w _ _ d / t _ / i _ .'

5 a Oliver asks Tasha for a time.
He says, 'When w _ _ _ _ / you / l _ _ _ / m _ / t _ / call?'

6 Tasha talks about her plans for her holiday.
She says, 'I' _ / g _ _ _ _ / t _ / v _ _ _ t / relatives and do other things but I'm / g _ _ _ _ / t _ / s _ _ _ _ / time at home with my friends, too.'

Check your answers

1 a 'We could meet for a drink …'
b 'Yes, that would be nice.'
2 a 'You can phone me … and we can arrange something.'
b 'I can give you…'
3 a 'Shall I give you…?'
4 a 'I'll telephone you…'
b 'I'll look forward to it.'
5 a 'When would you like me to call?'
6 'I'm going to visit relatives and do other things but I'm going to spend time at home with my friends, too.'

What's the right word?

Numbers 1–10

→Write the numbers next to the words. Use your dictionary if necessary.

- eight   - zero   - one

- nine   - ten

- six

- three

- five

- four

- two   - six

Check your answers

0 – zero; 1 – one; 2 – two; 3 – three; 4 – four; 5 – five; 6 – six; 7 – seven; 8 – eight; 9 – nine; 10 – ten

→ Practise saying the numbers backwards as fast as possible: ten, nine, etc.
→ Practise counting in twos.
→ What are the *even* numbers? 2, 4, etc.
→ What are the *odd* numbers? 1, 3, etc.

How do they say it?

Telephone numbers

→ Read the sentences below.
→ Listen to the telephone numbers on Recording 2 and choose **a** or **b**

1 For '0' they say **a** zero
b O (the name of the letter).
2 For 8549 they say **a** eight – five – four – nine
b 85 – (eighty-five), 49 (forty-nine).
3 When two numbers are the same, for example '77', they say **a** 'two sevens' or **b** 'double seven'.

Check your answers

1 **b** (**a** is also correct but it is more formal.) **2 a 3 b**

Recording 2

Oliver …and the telephone number of the office is 020 7402 3277.
Oliver And your friend's number is…?
Tasha 020 8549 6682.

Find the words and phrases

→ Read the sentences below.
→ Read text of Recording 1 again (page 134) and complete the words.

1 Oliver would like to meet Tasha for a drink. Does he say exactly when?
No. He says, 'We could meet o _ _ / e _ _ _ _ _ g.'

2 a Oliver checks it is alright with Tasha. He says,
'We could meet for a drink…… , i _ / y _ _ / l _ _ _ .'

b Later he checks that a phone call is alright.
He says, ' i _ / t _ _ _ ' s / _ . _ .'

3 He doesn't know the telephone number of his hotel. He says,
'You can phone me /_ _ / t _ _ / o _ _ _ _ _.'

4 Is the meeting fixed? No.
Oliver says, 'You can phone me… and we can a _ _ _ _ _ _ /
s _ _ _ _ _ _ _ g.'

5 People often write names and telephone numbers in the special pages in their d _ _ _ _ .

6 S _ _ _ _ _ _ means the same as family name.

7 7402 3277 isn't Oliver's direct number. His telephone is
e _ _ _ _ _ _ _ n 159.

8 Tasha hasn't got a computer in London but perhaps her friends have got e-mail. Oliver says, 'If you h _ _ _ / a _ _ _ _ s / t _ /
e-mail.'

9 Oliver gives Tasha his phone number and she gives him her number t _ _ .

10 Oliver needs time to find his diary. He says 'J_ _ _ / a minute.'

11 Does he need Tasha's surname? Yes. Has he got it? No. Tasha gives him this information. She says 'My other name's Harrison,
b_ / t _ _ / w _ _.'

12 a Does Tasha choose 'day' or 'evening' for the phone call?
No. She says, 'I / d _ _ ' _ / m _ _ d.'

b Oliver can phone in the day and he can phone in the evening. He can phone / a _ _ / t _ _ _.

13 Tasha accepts Oliver's suggestion. Oliver starts his promise to call her next week with the phrase, 'R _ _ _ _ / t _ _ n.'

14 Which day is Oliver calling Tasha? We don't know exactly. He says 'S _ _ _ / t _ _ _ / next week.'

15 This is a 'fasten your seatbelts' / s _ _ _. Is it _ _? Yes. Why? Because they're arriving soon.

16 Planes take off and l _ _ _.

17 Verb *get*.

a Why does Tasha open her bag? – to *get* her diary.

b Oliver says, 'You can *get* me on extension 159.'

Which one means *contact*, which one means *take*?

Check your answers

1 We could meet one evening. **2 a** We could meet for a drink, if you like. **b** If that's O.K. **3** at the office (preposition!) **4** You can phone me and we can arrange something. **5** diary **6** surname **7** extension **8** If you have access to e-mail. (electronic mail) **9** too **10** Just a minute. **11** My other name's Harrison, by the way. **12 a** I don't mind. **b** any time **13** Right then. **14** Some time next week. **15 a** sign **b** on (preposition!) **16** land **17 a** take **b** contact

Using these words and phrases

1 Some time and *any time*

For example, 'I'm going home **some time** next week.'

Some time means:

a I'm going next week.
b The time of the trip is fixed.
c I don't know the time OR I don't remember the time.

Any time means: **a** the time isn't fixed.
b The person can choose the time.

For example, 'You can call me *any time* tomorrow.'
The person can call at 9, or 10, or 11, etc. – when they like.

Another example: 'We can meet *at any time* between 11 and 1.'
The person can choose a time between 11 and 1.

→Complete these sentences with *some time* or *any time*:

1 When's John coming back from Australia?
_____________tomorrow, I think.

2 When can I use the computer?
_____________ you like.

3 When can we visit him in hospital?
_____________ between 10 a.m. and 9 p.m.

4 When's your appointment at the dentist's?
__________ next Wednesday.

Check your answers

1 Some time tomorrow. **2** Any time you like. **3** Any time between 10 a.m. and 9 p.m. **4** Some time next Wednesday.

2 By the way

We know that indirect language is very common in English. *By the way* is another example.

In the story, Oliver opens his diary to write Tasha's telephone number. He needs her surname. Before he asks, she gives him the extra information. She says, 'My other name's Harrison, *by the way*.'

★ Without *by the way* the sentence or question is:
– correct
– communicative
– direct.

★ With *by the way* the sentence or question is:
– correct
– communicative
– indirect.

When do I use this expression?

★ Use *by the way* to
a give extra information

b introduce a new topic in an indirect way
(*so* on page 103 is more direct)

c introduce a difficult topic.

★ *By the way* can go at the beginning or the end of the sentence.

By the way

→ What would you say in these situations?

1 Your colleague's talking to you about her husband. You want to know her husband's job. Ask her.

____

2 You're talking to a friend. You can't remember her boyfriend's name.

____

3 Your colleague's baby is very ill. He is in hospital.
You're talking to your colleague. Ask about the baby.

____

4 You buy a new computer.
You're at work, talking to your colleagues. Tell them.

____

5 You're at a friend's house. Your friend is having a party tomorrow. You would like your new girlfriend to come to the party. Ask your friend.

____

6 Your friend Mary is thinking about a trip to England.
You want to know her decision.

____

7 Your friend promises to give you the telephone number of a new friend. It's a week later. Ask for the number.

____

8 You invite a new friend to dinner. You want to cook fish. You're talking to the friend on the phone. Check that he likes fish.

____

9 A colleague is having a meeting with a new client. You join the meeting and introduce yourself.

____

Check your answers

1 By the way, what does your husband do*? **2** By the way, what's your boyfriend's name*? **3** By the way, how's your baby*? **4** By the way, I've got a new computer* **5** By the way, is it O.K. if my new girlfriend comes to the party*? **6** By the way, are you going to England*? **7** By the way, have you got X's phone number*? **8** By the way, do you like fish*? **9** Hello, *my name's X, by the way.

* *By the way* can go here, too.

How do you pronounce it?

Using stress to correct mistakes

★ In English we often use stress to correct mistakes.
How do you correct, for example, a wrong telephone number in your language? Some languages use extra words. For example, 'No, it's not 3 it's 2'.

→Listen to this example from *The Story* on Recording 3, part 1.

Recording 3, part 1

Oliver And your friend's number is…?
Tasha 020 8549 6682.
Oliver 020 8949…
Tasha No, 020 8549.

★ To correct a person, we stress the right number(s).

→Read the four mini-dialogues below and on page 144.
→Underline the different number in **B** – the number(s) where there is a mistake.

Recording 3, part 2

1 A Is that 8954 6210?
B Sorry, this is 8954 3210.

2 A I'm calling 01223 55 31 13.
B Sorry, you've got the wrong number. This is 01223 55 31 31.

3 A Good morning. Kodak.
B I'm trying to get 8749 4168.
A Sorry, this is 4178.

4 A Hello! Vicky!
B Sorry, there's no-one called Vicky here.
A Isn't that 01932 214218?
B No, I'm afraid it's not. This is 01532 214218.

Check your answers

1 3210. **2** 55 31 31. **3** 4178. **4** 01532.

→ Now listen to the four mini-dialogues above on Recording 3, part 2 and correct the mistakes.

Correcting other 'mistakes'

Where are the 'mistakes' in the mini-dialogues below? Some of the 'mistakes' are only a different opinion.

→ Underline the 'corrections', the syllable with stress in **B**.

Recording 3, part 3

1 A I'd like to meet your girlfriend.
B Julie? She's my sister.

2 A The meeting's on Thursday.
B I think it's on Wednesday.

3 A He's a good singer.
B He's a fantastic singer.

4 A We need some sandwiches.
B We need lots of sandwiches.

5 A The dictionary's not on the desk.
B No, it's under the desk, on the floor.

6 A I can telephone you tomorrow.
B No, it's my turn, I'll call you.

Check your answers

1 sister **2** Wednesday **3** fantastic **4** lots 5 under, floor, 6 my, I'll, you

→ Now, listen to the dialogues on Recording 3, part 3 and correct the mistakes, using stress.

Grammar and communication 1

Future plans – *going to*

Example from *The Story*:

Tasha talks about her holiday plans.

She says, '**I'm going to** visit relatives and do other things but **I'm going to** spend time at home with my friends, too.'

The name of this **tense** is the '*going to*' future.

Meaning

Here, *going to* is for future plans.

Form

The form is the verb *go* in present progressive + *to* + verb.

→ Make mini-dialogues. Match sentences **1–9** with the correct sentence or question (**a–i**) from the box on page 146.

1 A ______________________
B Because he's not at home.
2 A ______________________
B After the news.
3 A ______________________
B Oh, is he? Who to?
4 A ______________________
B Is he? I hope he passes.
5 A ______________________
B Are you? That's nice.
6 A ______________________
B Oh, just a sandwich, I think.

7 **A** ______________________

B Yes, I think they are.

8 **A** ______________________

B I can, if you like.

9 **A** ______________________?

B Aren't you? Why not?

a I'm going to visit my parents next week.
b Are your friends going to buy that house?
c He's going to take his driving test soon.
d We aren't going to invite them.
e What are you going to have for lunch?
f Why aren't you going to call him?
g Who's going to make some tea?
h When are you going to put the T.V. off?
i He's going to get married.

☑ **Check your answers**

1 f **2** h **3** i **4** c **5** a **6** e **7** b **8** g **9** d

Grammar and communication 2

Making arrangements: possibilities, suggestions and offers

Examples from *The Story*:

'**We could** meet for a drink one evening.'
'**You can** phone me at the office.'
'**I'll call** you some time next week.'
'**Shall I** give you my number?'
'**When would you like me to** call you?'

★ Here, *can*, *could*, *I'll*, *shall I? would you like me to?* are all similar in meaning.

Situation Your friend is ill, in hospital. You want to visit him/her. You are talking to his/her partner.

Summary – Possibilities, suggestions, offers	
I can I could I'll }	go to the hospital tomorrow.
Shall I Would you like me to }	go to the hospital tomorrow?

★ All these expressions are correct and appropriate.
★ *Could* is a little less direct than the others.
★ *Shall I?* and *Would you like me to?* are questions. Here, *I can*, *I could* and *I'll* aren't questions but they need a response.
★ To say *yes* you can use an echo question. (Echo questions are in Topic 2.)
★ *Can you? Could you?* and *Would you?* are echo questions for the expressions above.
★ The offer and the echo question can have different verbs.

Examples: 1 A I'll do that for you.
B Can you?
2 A I could ask him.
B Would you?

Q ***Can I say 'It's possible for me to (go to the hospital tomorrow)' for offers?***

A The grammar is correct.

Students of English often say *It's possible, Is it possible? It isn't possible.* It is more common to say *I can, I could, I'll, shall I?* or *Would you like me to?* for offers.

Possibilities, suggestions and offers

Situation Debbie is my neighbour. She's got four young children. I arrive at her house.

→ Read the conversation below and answer these two questions.

1 Debbie is **a** fine
b not very well

2 I offer to do four things for her. Write them below with her answers:
– a tick for *yes* ✓
– a cross for *no* ✗

a Take __________ Answer ☐ **c** ______________ Answer ☐
b ______________ Answer ☐ **d** ______________ Answer ☐

Recording 4

Me	Hi! Debbie. Isn't it cold today? How are you?
Debbie	Not very well at all actually, and it's nearly time for school.
Me	I can take the children to school for you if you like.
Debbie	Really? Are you sure?
Me	Yes, of course.
Debbie	That's very kind of you. I feel really terrible!
Me	Right, now you just go and sit down and I'll make you a cup of tea. Shall I call the doctor?
Debbie	Could you? Thanks.
Me	Where can I find the number?
Debbie	In the little book by the phone. Could you ask for an appointment as soon as possible, please?
Me	No problem. How about dinner this evening? Would you like me to cook for you all? The children could eat at my house.
Debbie	Thanks for the offer, but it's alright. My husband doesn't mind cooking, actually.

Check your answers

1b. 2a Take the children to school – yes. **b** Make a cup of tea – yes. **c** Phone a doctor – yes. **d** Cook dinner – no.

★ 'Really? Are you sure?' It is common to check an offer of help before you say yes.

★ 'Not very well at all, actually' is more common than 'I'm ill'.

→ Read the sentences below. Find the exact words in the dialogue on p.148.

1 I offer to take the children to school. Debbie says Yes.
I say ______________________ She says __________

2 I offer to make a cup of tea.
I say ______________________

3 I offer to call the doctor. Debbie says Yes.
I say ______________________ She says __________

4 I need help to find the number.
I ask ______________________

5 I offer to cook dinner.
I say ______________________

6 I suggest the children eat at my house. Debbie says No.
I say ______________________ She says __________

Check your answers

1 I can take the children to school for you if you like. Debbie says yes. She says, ' That's very kind of you.' **2** I'll make you a cup of tea. **3** Shall I call the doctor? Debbie says yes. She says, 'Could you?' **4** Where can I find the number? **5** Would you like me to cook? **6** The children could eat at my house. Debbie says no. She says 'Thanks for the offer, but it's alright.'

→ Now listen to the dialogue on Recording 4 and repeat it.

Common mistake – offers and suggestions

'Would you like me to make some tea?'
(Not: '~~Would you like **that I** make some tea?~~')

would like		*to* + verb
Would you like When would you like I'd like	us Richard the children	to help you? to do the job? to come with us.

Possibilities, suggestions and offers

Situation You are on the phone to your friend. Your friend is bored.

→ Read the conversation and complete with the correct phrase.

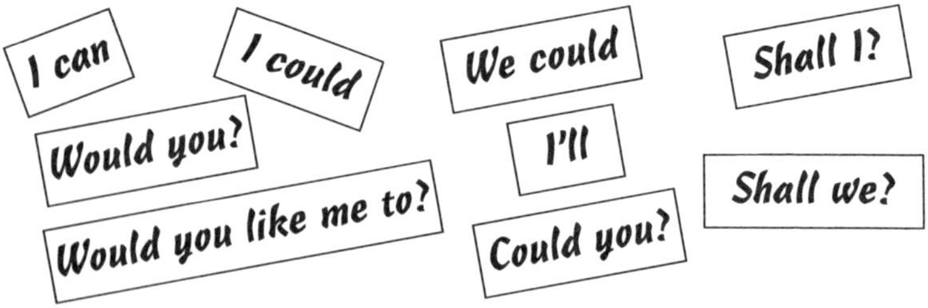

Your friend I'm bored.
You ____________(1) go to the cinema (?)
Your friend That's a good idea. _________(2) go to the ABC(?) They've got nine screens there.
You Why not? I've got the car tonight. _________(3) pick you up on the way (?)
Your friend ___________?(4) Great! Thanks!
Your friend Do you know what time the films start there(?)
You I've got no idea. __________(5) call and ask(?)
Your friend Don't worry, I think it's usually about 8 o'clock.
You Fine. _______(6) get to your house around seven(?) Is that O.K.?
Your friend Yes, an hour is plenty of time to get there, decide which film to see and buy the tickets.
You See you later, then. Bye.
Your friend Bye!

Check your answers

1 We can / We could } go to the cinema.
Shall we go to the cinema?

2 We can / We could } go to the ABC.
Shall we go to the ABC?

3 I can
I could } pick you up on the way.
I'll

Shall I
Would you like me to } pick you up on the way?

4 Can
Could } you?
Would

5 I can
could } call and ask.
I'll

Shall I
Would you like me to } call and ask?

6 I can
I could } get to your house around seven.
I'll

Shall I
Would you like me to } get to your house around seven?

→Now look at these responses from the dialogue above. Do they mean *yes* or *no*?

→Write a tick ✓ or cross ✗ in the boxes.

Suggestions/offers	**Responses**
1 We could go to the cinema.	That's a good idea. ☐
2 Shall we go to the ABC?	Why not? ☐
3 Shall I pick you up on the way?	Can you? or Could you? or Would you? ☐
4 I'll call and ask (the times).	Don't worry. ☐

Check your answers

1 ✓ 2 ✓ 3 ✓ 4 ✗

Here's a summary of all the responses from the three conversations about offers and suggestions in this topic. (Recording 1 and 5 and the dialogue above.)

Summary – Saying *Yes* and *No* to offers and suggestions	
Yes That's very kind of you (Yes), That's a good idea (Yes), Why not? (Yes), that would be nice O.K. Could you? Can you? Would you?	**No** Thanks (for the offer), but it's alright Don't worry

You can see from these expressions that

★ It is very common to say *yes* without the word 'yes'.
★ It is very common to say *no* without the word 'no'.
★ These are more examples of indirect language.

What's the right word

i **British culture – surnames/family names**

Q ***How do I answer the question, 'What's your name?'***

A In an informal situation give your first name.
In a more formal situation give your first name and then your family name(s).
In official situations give your family name.

- Nowadays, at work most people are informal – they use first names.
- When women get married they usually change their name to their husband's surname, for example, Brenda Dickens marries Jack Green. Her new name is Brenda Green or Mrs Green.

- Nowadays, some women don't change their surname.
- What are the most common family names in Britain? Here are some from the telephone book: Baker, Mills, Walker, Moore, Brown, Ward, Campbell, Newman, Reid, Wilson, O'Brien, Harris, Evans, Dixon, Fisher, Hall, Dickinson, King, Mann, Woods, Lee, Green, Young, Taylor, Thomas, Matthews, Palmer, West, White.
- The most common name for a man is David Jones and for a woman Margaret Smith.
- Some surnames are male first names + 's'.
  For example,
  First name: Edward; family name: Edwards.

→ Look at the two lists below. They are the same except for the 's' at the end of the surname.

First names	**Surnames**
William	Williams
Daniel	Daniels
Peter	Peters
Richard	Richards
Steven	Stevens
Hugh	Hughes
Matthew	Matthews
Edward	Edwards

First names and surnames

Which name is it, the first name or surname?

→ Recording 5 on page 154 has eight mini-dialogues – one for each pair of names above.

→ Listen and tick the 'first name' or the 'surname' in the boxes above.

Check your answers *(Recording 5)*

1 Hello, my name's **Williams**.
2 A What's your name? **B Daniel**.
3 Hi! I'm **Peter**.
4 A And your name is…? **B Richards**.
5 A Could I have your name, please sir? **B** Yes, it's **Stevens**.
6 Is that **Hugh**?
7 Her father's name's **Matthews**.
8 No, **Edward**'s his other name.

Names in your country

→ Read the questions below.
→ Either write your answers or prepare to tell a friend.

How many names do people usually have in your country?

____

Which names do people use more at work, first names or family names?

____

What happens to a woman's name when she gets married?

____

What are the most common family names in your country?

____

In your language have you got special words or names for people who are special to you? Give some examples.

____

Do you have special titles for older people?

____

British culture – special telephone services

→ Cover the text of Recording 6.
→ Read the information below.
→ Listen to the recording and complete the numbers for Britain.

	And in your country?
International phone calls	
The international code for Britain is ____	____________
Special services	
■ Emergency – fire } ________	____________
police } This number	____________
ambulance } is free	____________
■ **Operator** National ________	____________
International ________	____________
■ **Directory enquiries**	
National ________	____________
International ________	____________

Check your answers *(Recording 6)*

To phone a number in Britain from abroad, the international code is 44.
For emergency services – fire, police or ambulance – dial 999. This is a free number.
Operator services are on 100, one, zero, zero.
For the international operator, dial 155.
To ask for a telephone number call 192 for numbers in Britain or 153 for international directory enquiries.

→ What are these numbers in your country? Complete the list on the right above.

Grammar and communication 3

Using the telephone

What do these **telephone sounds** mean?

→ Read the sentences below.
→ Listen to Recording 7 and match **1–6** with **a–e**.

Recording 7

1 —	**4** —
2 —	**5** —
3 —	**6** —

a It's engaged. Try again later.
b Oh dear! It's out of order.
c That means you've got a line. You can dial now.
d **A** What's happening? **B** The computer is dialling the number.
e Wrong number? Dial it again.
f It's ringing. Someone'll answer it in a minute.

Check your answers

1 d **2** c **3** f **4** a **5** e **6** b

Hello! – Telephone language

★ We say 'This is', (Not: '~~I am~~…')
'Is that?' (Not: '~~Are you~~…?')

'Speaking' (Not: 'Yes, ~~I am X~~')
'John speaking'
'It's John speaking'
'It's John here' (Not: '~~I am John~~')
'John here'

→ Listen to the two mini-dialogues on Recording 8.

Recording 8

[Ring ring]
Rachel 6537. Hello?
Richard Can I speak to Rachel, please?
Rachel Speaking.

[Ring ring]
Rachel Hello?
Matt This is Matt. Is that Rachel?
Rachel Yes, it's me.

→ Complete these dialogues with the phrases above.

1

Tom Hi, ______ Tom. ______ Andrea?

Vicky Hello, Tom. No, ______ Vicky. Hang on a minute and I'll call her. Andrea, ______ Tom on the phone for you.

2

Peter Hello. Is David there, please?

David ______________________

Check your answers

1 **Tom** Hi, This is Tom. Is that Andrea?
Vicky Hello, Tom. No, this is Vicky … Andrea, it's Tom on the phone for you.
2 Speaking *or* This is David *or* This is David speaking.

Asking for numbers on the telephone

Situation You need the codes for some of the big towns in the British Isles. You phone Directory Enquiries on 192 and ask for the codes.

→ Cover the text of Recording 9.
→ Look at the map below.
→ Read the names of the towns.
→ Listen to the recording and write the code number under the name of the town.

Tip: Most codes begin with 01. The list is in alphabetical order.

Recording 9

Example: Operator Directory Enquiries. Which name, please?
Caller Hello, yes. Could I have the code for Canterbury, please?
Operator Yes, the code for Canterbury is 01227.
Caller Thank you. Goodbye.

1 Operator Directory enquiries, Lynn speaking. Which name, please?
Caller Yes, Could you tell me the code for Bath, please?
Operator Yes, the code for Bath is 01225.
Caller Thanks. Bye.

2 Operator Directory enquiries. Which name, please?
Caller Hello. I'd like the code for Birmingham, please.
Operator Birmingham – that's 0121.
Caller Many thanks. Goodbye.

3 Operator Directory enquiries, Nick speaking. Can I help you?
Caller Yes, can you give me the code for Brighton, please?
Operator Brighton – yes that's 01273.
Caller Thanks very much. Bye.

4 Operator Directory enquiries. Which name, please?
Caller Hello. Could I have the code for Dover, please?
Operator Yes, Dover's 01304.

5 Operator Directory enquiries, Diane speaking. Which name, please?
Caller Hello, yes. What's the code for Edinburgh, please?
Operator One second please. Yes, that's 0131.

6 Operator Directory Enquiries. Which name, please?
Caller Hello. Could you tell me the code for London, please?
Operator Yes the new code for inner London is 020 7. And 020 8 for outer London.

7 Operator Directory Enquiries. Which name please?
Caller Hello. Can you give me the code for Plymouth, please?
Operator Sorry, which town, caller?
Caller Plymouth, please.
Operator The code for Plymouth is 01752.

Check your answers

1 Bath – 01225 **2** Birmingham – 0121 **3** Brighton – 01273 **4** Dover – 01304 **5** Edinburgh – 0131 **6** Inner London – 020 7, Outer London – 020 8 **7** Plymouth 01752

Grammar and communication 4

Asking for things

→ Read the text of Recording 9 on page 159.
→ Find five expressions to ask for things.
→ Write them below.

a C _ _ _ _ / I / h _ _ _ ...?

b C _ _ _ _ / y _ _ / t _ _ _ / me...?

c I ' _ / l _ _ _ ...

d C _ _ / y _ _ / g _ _ _ / m _...?

e W _ _ _ ' _ / t _ _ / code for...?

Check your answers

a Could I have...? **b** Could you tell me...? **c** I'd like... **d** Can you give me...? **e** What's the code for...?

Asking for telephone numbers

→ Look again at the map on page 158.
→ Cover the text of Recording 10 below.
→ You need the codes for the other four places on the map, (1) Cardiff, (2) Oxford and (3) Norwich and (4) Dublin.
→ Listen and use the questions above to ask for the codes.
→ Write the codes on the map.

Check your answers *(Recording 10)*

1	**Operator**	Directory enquiries. Which name, please?
	You	______________________________ .
	Operator	Yes, the code for Cardiff is 029 20.
2	**Operator**	Directory enquiries. Mandy speaking. Which name, please?
	You	______________________________ .
	Operator	The code for Oxford is 01865.
3	**Operator**	Directory enquiries. Which name would you like?
	You	______________________________ .
	Operator	The code for Norwich is 01603.

4	**Operator**	Directory enquiries. Which name would you like?
	You	______________________________.
	Operator	The code for Dublin is 003531.

How do you pronounce it?

Do you know your a, b, c (alphabet) in English?

Q ***How many letters are there in the alphabet?***

A 26.

Q ***How many sounds are there in English?***

A 44

Q ***How many vowels are there in the alphabet?***

A Five, 'a', 'e', 'i', 'o', 'u'. But there are 20 vowel sounds in English.

Q ***How many consonants are there in the alphabet?***

A 21. But there are 24 consonant sounds in English.

★ English spelling doesn't always help with the pronunciation. (This is why I always suggest you listen to the recordings several times before you read the words. Listening to English before you read it always helps with good pronunciation.)

★ In English one pronunciation can have different spellings and different meanings.

For example *no* and *know*
see and *sea*
right and *write*
meet and *meat*

★ Because English sounds can have different spellings, it is very common to ask for spellings of words, especially names and addresses.

→ Look at the columns of letters below.
The letters in each column have the same sound.

→ Listen to Recording 11, part 1 and repeat the names of the letters. You will hear each letter twice.

Recording 11, part 1

a	b	f	i	o	q	r
h	c	l	y		u	
j	d	m			w	
k	e	n				
	g	s				
	p	x				
	t	z				
	v					

Can you say the names of the letters?

→ Listen to the first letter from each column on Recording 11, part 2.
→ Say the others with the same vowel sound.

Spelling

Situation: I teach a class of people who want to be English teachers. Here is my register (list of students). Some names are missing. The spelling of some names is wrong.

→ Listen to Recording 12 and write or correct the surnames.

CLASS REGISTER

1 Lesley__________
2 Denise Varnish
3 Matt Hanant
4 Anne __________
5 Simon __________
6 John Pierson
7 Joan __________
8 Liz Thomson-Smith

Recording 12

Me	So, could you tell me your surnames, please? Lesley, What's your surname?
Lesley	Crowley.
Me	How do you spell that, Lesley?
Lesley	C – R – O – W – L – E –Y.
Me	And yours, Denise?
Denise	My family name's Farnish.
Me	Is that with an 'F' or a 'V'?
Denise	With an 'F'. F – A – R – N – I – S – H.
Me	And how about you, Matt? What's your other name?
Matt	Hannant. That's H – A double N – A – N – T.
Me	Anne, your surname is…?
Anne	Johnson, spelt J – O – H – N – S – O – N.
Me	Simon, yours next, please.
Simon	Lawrence.
Me	How do you spell it?
Simon	L – A – W – R – E – N – C – E.
Me	And John? I've got Pierson here. Is that right?
John	Yes. P – E – A – R – S – O – N.
Me	Oh, I've got P – I – E.
John	No, it's P – E – A at the beginning.
Me	And Joan – How about you? What's your other name?

Joan Rawlings. R – A – W – L – I – N – G – S.
Me And the last one is Liz, please.
Liz My surname's Thompson-Smith.
Me Is that Thompson with a 'P' or without?
Liz With a 'P' and 'Smith' at the end.
Me Thanks very much everybody. Now let's start the lesson.

Check your answers

1 Lesley Crowley **2** Denise Farnish **3** Matt Hannant **4** Anne Johnson **5** Simon Lawrence **6** John Pearson **7** Joan Rawlings **8** Liz Thompson-Smith

→ What's the question?

The answer is S – M – I – T – H.
The question is ________________________?

(Answer: 'How do you spell it?' (Not: 'How do you write it?') ☹

How do you spell it?

It is easy to confuse some letters, for example 's' and 'f' or 'p' and 'b', especially on the telephone. To make the difference, we say, for example, 'F for 'Foxtrot' or 'S for Sierra'. Some people use other common words or names for this, for example, A for 'apple'.

On page 165 is the International Phonetic Alphabet (NATO Alphabet).

→ Look at this example:

Telephonist What name is it, please?
Caller Eva Rach.
Telephonist Is that R – A – **T** for Tango?
Caller No, it's R – A– **C** for Charlie – H.

→ Listen to Recording 13 and repeat the letters and words.

Recording 13

A – Alpha	N – November
B – Bravo	O – Oscar
C – Charlie	P – Papa
D – Delta	Q – Quebec
E – Echo	R – Romeo
F – Foxtrot	S – Sierra
G – Golf	T – Tango
H – Hotel	U – Uniform
I – India	V – Victor
J – Juliet	W – Whisky
K – Kilo	X – X-Ray
L – Lima	Y – Yankee
M – Mike	Z – Zulu

→ Help to spell aloud this Japanese surname correctly

S A K O T A

It's 'S' for ____
'A' _________
____
____
____
____

Check your answers

'S' for Sierra
'A' for Alpha
'K' for Kilo
'O' for Oscar
'T' for Tango
'A' for Alpha

Which letter is it?

Example from the class register exercise on page 163:

A My name's 'Farnish'
B Is that with an 'F' or a 'V'?
A With an 'F'.

→ Look at the pairs of names below.
→ Listen to Recording 14 and choose the correct spelling **a** or **b**.

1	**a** Hallis	**b** Harris
2	**a** Fraser	**b** Frazer
3	**a** Stephens	**b** Stevens
4	**a** Simms	**b** Sims
5	**a** Stupps	**b** Stubbs
6	**a** Initial 'F'	**b** Initial 'S'

Recording 14

1
A My name's Hallis.
B Double 'R' is that?
A No, double 'L', H – A – double L – I – S.

2
A The name's Frazer.
B Do you spell that with an 'S' or a 'Z'?
A With a 'Z'.

3
A My name's Stevens.
B Is that with 'PH' or a 'V'?
A With a 'V'.

4
A My name's Simms.
B Is that one 'M' or two?
A S - I - double M - S.

5
A Her name's Helen Stubbs.
B Is that 'P' for Papa or 'B' for Bravo?
A Double 'B' for Bravo.

6
A What's your initial?
B 'S'.
A Is that 'F' for Foxtrot or 'S' for Sierra?
B 'S' for Sierra.

Check your answers

1 a **2** b **3** b **4** a **5** b **6** b

Spelling vowels

Many learners of English have problems with the names of English vowels (a,e,i,o,u). Here's some practice.

→ Listen to Recording 15 and complete the spelling of these surnames.

1 P _ P _ R
2 S N _ _ T H _
3 S M _ _ T _ N
4 T _ Y L _ R
5 S H _ R _ D _ N
6 R _ _ D _ R
7 S _ M _ _ L S

Check your answers *(Recording 15)*

1 Piper, that's P–I–P–E–R.
2 My name's Snaithe, spelt S–N–A–I–T–H–E.
3 Yes, it's Smeaton, S–M–E–A–T–O–N.
4 And my surname is Taylor, T–A–Y–L–O–R.
5 The family name's Sheridon, S–H–E–R–I–D–O–N.
6 And the second name is Reeder, that's spelt R–E–E–D–E–R.
7 Samuels, S–A–M–U–E–L–S.

Spelling your name aloud and giving your contact details

→ Practise spelling your names and address aloud – clarify difficult letters.
→ Practise saying the numbers aloud.

First name______________________________
Middle name(s) ______________________________
Surname(s) ______________________________
Telephone number (home) _______(work)_______(mobile) _______
E-mail address______________________________
Address ______________________________
Passport number ______________________________

What would you say?

1 You telephone a friend in England from your country. You get a wrong number.

____

2 You are on the telephone. The line is very bad. You can't hear the other person.

____

Possible answers

1 I'm very sorry. It's the wrong number.
Advanced alternative: Sorry to disturb you. I think I've got the wrong number.
2 I'm sorry, this line's terrible. I can't hear you.
Advanced alternative: I'm sorry, this line's terrible. Could you speak up a bit, please?

Revision

How do you say it in your language?

Here are some examples of the important points in this topic.

→ Translate the sentences below into your language.
→ Remember – translate the idea, not the words.

1 **a** We could go out for a pizza tonight. **b** That's a good idea!

____

2 **a** I'll book the restaurant for tomorrow. **b** I'll look forward to it.

____

3 **a** Shall I make some coffee? **b** Yes, please.

____

4 **a** Can I help you? **b** It's very kind of you, thank you, but it's alright.

____

5 By the way, how's your mother today – is she better?

____

6 I'm going to buy a car tomorrow.

____

Join the conversation

→ Look at the text of Recording 1 (page 134), *The Story*, again.
→ Listen to Recording 16.
→ Read **Oliver's** words in the spaces.

TEST 6

Which one is right?

→ Choose **a** or **b**.

1 Three and five is
  a nine
  b eight.

2 'surname', 'family name' and 'other name' mean
  a the same
  b something different.

3 You ask someone to wait. You say,
  a 'A moment'
  b 'Just a minute, please.'

4 Beer or wine?
- **a** I don't mind.
- **b** It is not matter.

5 I can't speak to Peter. His number is
- **a** occupied.
- **b** engaged.

6 I can't use the machine. It's
- **a** out of operation.
- **b** out of order.

7 On the telephone
- **a** Here speaks Rodica. **a** Is that Peter?
- **b** This is Rodica. **b** Are you Peter?

8 **a** Please, it is possible I speak with Jenny?
- **b** Could I speak to Jenny, please?

9 Your telephone number is in my
- **a** diary.
- **b** agenda.

10 The shop is open 24 hours a day. You can go shopping
- **a** all the times.
- **b** at any time.

11 **a** Would you like that I go with you?
- **b** Would you like me to go with you?

12 Shall I ask him?
- **a** Yes, you shall. **b** Yes, please.

13 Shall we go out for a drink after work?
- **a** Sorry, I go out with my wife to a family dinner.
- **b** Sorry, I'm going out with my wife to a family dinner.

14 **a** Why he is going to sell the house?
- **b** Why is he going to sell the house?

Which one is better?

15 Would you like me to translate that for you? I speak Japanese.
- **a** Yes, I would.
- **b** Thanks.

16 Shall I do that?

a No.

b I'm alright, thanks.

Which ones are right?

17 I'll do that for you, shall I?

a Can you? Thanks.

b Could you? Thanks.

c Would you? Thanks.

Write a dialogue

Situation You are on the phone to your friend.

1 You	**Your friend**
	What can we do this evening?
Suggest a Chinese meal and a video at his house.	
	2 Yes
3 You offer to get the food and video on the way.	
	4 Yes. He asks you to get Chinese chicken with rice.

5 You say yes.
You offer to get some beer.

6 No. He's got some.

7 You ask what type of film he'd like to see.

8 He has no preference.

Check your answers

1 b **2** a **3** b **4** a **5** b **6** b **7** b a **8** b **9** a **10** b **11** b **12** b **13** b **14** b **15** b **16** b **17** a, b, c

Dialogue: model answers

1 You	We could have a Chinese meal and watch a video at your house.
2 Your friend	Yeah, why not?
3 You	Shall I get the food and the video on the way?
4 Your friend	That would be good. Could you get me a Chinese chicken with rice, please?
5 You	No problem. I could get some beer, too.
6 Your friend	No, don't worry about that. I've got some.
7 You	What sort of film would you like to see?
8 Your friend	I don't mind.

7 TRAVELLING AND HANDLING MONEY

Grammar and communication
- Inviting people to do things
- Suggesting doing something together – *let's*
- Asking people to do things
- Asking for help – indirect questions

Vocabulary
- Numbers (2)
- Money
- Travel

Pronunciation
- Pronouncing groups of words – linking

The plane is arriving in London at Heathrow Airport

Understanding the important information

Situation The pilot of the plane talks to all the passengers. He makes an announcement.

→ Cover the text of Recording 1, *The Story* on page 174.
→ Read the sentence above it.
→ Listen to the recording and choose ALL the correct answers.

The captain talks about

a seat belts
b passports
c the time
d the arrival time
e the temperature
f the weather

Recording 1 – The Story

Pilot Good morning, ladies and gentlemen. This is your captain speaking again. In a few moments, we will begin our descent into London's Heathrow Airport. Please return to your seats and fasten your seatbelts. If you would like to adjust your watches, the time in London is now 6.50 in the morning and the temperature on the ground is -2 degrees centigrade, that's 29 degrees Fahrenheit. Our estimated time of arrival is 7.15. That's a quarter past seven on the ground in London. The forecast for today is cold … but bright … .

Check your answers

a c d e f

Understanding more

→ Cover the text of Recording 1, *The Story*.
→ Read the questions below.
→ Listen and choose **a** or **b**.

1 The time in London is now **a** six fifteen (6.15) **b** six fifty (6.50).
2 The temperature is **a** 2 degrees centigrade **b** -2 degrees centigrade.
3 They're landing at **a** seven fifteen (7.15) **b** seven fifty (7.50).

Check your answers

1 b **2** b **3** a

*In Britain we measure temperature in both centigrade (Celsius) and Fahrenheit. 0C = 32ºF.

How do they say it?

Pronouncing groups of words – Linking words

★ When we speak, we often join a word to the next word.
★ This happens when one sound is a consonant and the other a vowel.
★ Two examples from the story above are, 'ladies‿and', 'this‿is'.
★ Sometimes the last **letter** isn't a consonant. It's the last sound that's important, for example, 'time‿in London' – the last **sound** in 'time' is /m/.

→ Read the phrases below. They are from *The Story* on page 174.
→ Listen to these phrases on Recording 2 and repeat them.
→ Pay special attention to linking the words marked.

Recording 2

Ladies‿and gentlemen
This‿is your Captain speaking again
In‿a few moments
The time‿in London‿is now 6.50
That's‿a quarter past seven‿on the ground‿in London

What's the right word?

Numbers to 100

→ Complete this table with the numbers on page 176.

1 one	11________		
2 two	12________	20________	
3 three	13 ***thirteen***	30 ________	
4 four	14 ________	40________	
5 five	15 ________	50 ________	
6 six	16 ________	60 ________	
7 seven	17 ________	70 ***seventy***	
8 eight	18 ________	80 ________	
9 nine	19 ________	90 ________	100 ***a hundred***

eleven twelve twenty ~~thirteen~~ fifteen thirty fourteen ~~seventy~~ forty fifty sixteen sixty seventeen eighteen nineteen ninety eighty

☑ Check your answers

1 one	11 eleven		
2 two →	12 twelve →	20 twenty	
3 three	13 thirteen	30 thirty	
4 four	14 fourteen	40 forty	
5 five	15 fifteen	50 fifty	
6 six	16 sixteen	60 sixty	
7 seven	17 seventeen	70 seventy	
8 eight	18 eighteen	80 eighty	
9 nine	19 nineteen	90 ninety	100 a hundred

→ Write these numbers in figures.

ninety-nine ___	twelve ___	forty-three ___	thirty-one ___
eleven ___	seventy-six ___	eighty-five ___	twenty-two ___
sixty-four ___	fifty-seven ___	seventeen___	a hundred ___

☑ Check your answers

Ninety-nine – 99; Twelve – 12; Forty-three – 43; Thirty-one – 31; Eleven – 11; Seventy-six – 76; Eighty-five – 85; Twenty-two – 22; Sixty-four – 64; Fifty-seven – 57; Seventeen – 17; A hundred – 100

→Write these numbers in words.

Example: 72 – ***Seventy-two***

18________	59________	13 ________
93 ________	15 ________	21 ________
86 ________	16 ________	45 ________
19 ________	37 ________	12 ________
14 ________	68 ________	100 ________

Check your answers

18 eighteen	59 fifty-nine	13 thirteen
93 ninety-three	15 fifteen	21 twenty-one
86 eighty-six	16 sixteen	45 forty-five
19 nineteen	37 thirty-seven	12 twelve
14 fourteen	68 sixty-eight	100 a hundred

→Now try some mental maths. Say these sums aloud when you do them.

1 Eleven and five and seventeen and forty-two is ________
You say, 'Eleven and five is sixteen, and seventeen is... and forty-two is...

2 Nine and six and twenty-three and eighteen is ________

3 Four and twelve and two and fourteen is ________

Check your answers

1 Eleven and five is sixteen, and seventeen is thirty three and forty-two is seventy-five. **2** Nine and six is fifteen, and twenty-three is thirty-eight and eighteen is fifty-six. **3** Four and twelve is sixteen, and two is eighteen and fourteen is thirty-two.

→Say these numbers aloud as quickly as possible.

a Say the **even** numbers up to twenty – two, four, six, etc...

b Say the **odd** numbers up to twenty – one, three, five, etc...

c Count in 5s up to 50. Five, ten, etc...

d Count in 3s up to 36. Three, six, etc...

e Can you say the 'eight times table' in English?
One eight is eight
Two eights are sixteen
Three eights are …

Check your answers

a Two, four, six, eight, ten, twelve, fourteen, sixteen, eighteen, twenty
b One, three, five, seven, nine, eleven, thirteen, fifteen, seventeen, nineteen
c Five, ten, fifteen, twenty, twenty-five, thirty, thirty-five, forty, forty-five fifty
d Three, six, nine, twelve, fifteen, eighteen, twenty-one, twenty-four, twenty-seven, thirty, thirty-three, thirty-six
e One eight is eight
Two eights are sixteen
Three eights are twenty-four
Four eights are thirty-two
Five eights are forty
Six eights are forty-eight
Seven eights are fifty-six
Eight eights are sixty-four
Nine eights are seventy-two
Ten eights are eighty

Maths talk

→ Write the sums below in figures.
Use the numbers and signs in the box to help you.

a Twenty plus ten equals thirty 20_____10_____30
b Twelve minus one is eleven __________________________
c Four multiplied by six equals twenty-four__________________
d Twenty-seven divided by three is nine____________________

4	12	30	11	3	10	27	6	1	24	9	20
				+	−	×	÷	=			

Check your answers

a $20 + 10 = 30$. **b** $12 - 1 = 11$. **c** $4 \times 6 = 24$. **d** $27 \div 3 = 9$.

Q ***How do you say this? 3 X 6 = 18.***

A There are 3 ways
a three sixes are
b three times six is
c three multiplied by six equals
(more formal/technical)
} eighteen

Find the words and phrases

→Read the sentences below.
→Read the text of Recording 1 (page 174), *The Story*, and find the correct words and phrases.

1 The pilot wants to talk to all the people on the plane.
He says 'Good morning, l _ _ _ _ s / and g _ _ _ l e _ _ n.'
2 Does he say 'I am your captain?' No, he uses telephone language. He says, 'T _ _ _ / _ _ / your captain.'
3 We don't call the pilot 'Pilot Smith', we say 'C _ _ _ _ _ _ Smith'.
4 The pilot invites the passengers to change the time on their watches. He says 'I_ / y _ _ / w _ _ _ _ / l _ k _ / t _ / adjust your watches, the time in London is…'
5 Does the pilot know the exact time they are arriving in London? No, he says, 'Our e _ _ _ _ _ _ _ d / time / o _ / a _ r _ _ _ l / is 7.15.'
6 What television programme is immediately after the news? Usually it's the weather f _ _ _ _ _ _ _ where they talk about the weather for the rest of today, tomorrow, etc.

Check your answers

1 ladies and gentlemen. *These words are often on public toilet signs. **2** This is. **3** captain. **4** If you would like to adjust your watches. **5** estimated time of arrival. **6** forecast.

Grammar and communication 1

Inviting people to do things

Example from *The Story*:

The pilot invites the passengers to change the times on their watches.
He says, '**If you would like to** adjust your watches…'

★ We use *if you would like to* for two situations:
1 to invite people
2 to ask and tell people to do things in a polite, indirect way.

For example:
1 'We're having a small dinner party on Saturday. If you would like to join us…' Meaning: I'm inviting you to the dinner party.

2 'If you would like to take a seat for a moment...' Meaning: Please sit down and wait.

★ When you are asking someone to do something, it is common not to finish the sentence.

For example:

Situation At the reception of a small hotel.

Receptionist: 'If you would just like to follow me, please...' (and s/he doesn't say 'I can show you to your room' – the meaning is clear from the situation. She doesn't need to finish the sentence.)

★ This expression is particularly common in formal and new situations.

Asking someone to do something

Where can you hear these 'invitations'?

→ Read the 'invitations' below and choose the place. You can use each place more than once.

office

dentist's

shop

school

dinner party

1 If you would like to come back for your watch some time later this afternoon... around 4 ...
2 If you would like to sit there, Kevin, next to my husband ...

3 I've got your son here. I'm afraid he's not very well so if you would like to come and pick him up …
4 I'm sorry but Mr Smith isn't here this afternoon. If you would like to give me your name and number …
5 If you would like to come with me to the cash desk …
6 If you would like to go through to the waiting room …
7 If you would like to go in, the manager can see you now …
8 If you would like to just open your mouth and say 'aah'…oh yes …
9 If you would all like to come to the table …
10 If everybody would like to be quiet now, please …

Check your answers

1 shop **2** dinner party **3** school **4** office **5** shop **6** dentist's **7** office **8** dentist's **9** dinner party **10** school

Q ***What are the possible responses to these 'invitations'? Is it OK to say 'Yes'?***

A 'Yes' alone isn't appropriate. ☹

→ Look at these responses.

1 You can say, 'Thank you'
'Yes, that's fine'
'Yes, of course'
'Yes, I'll' + verb

2 You say nothing and 'do' the action.
3 If you are following someone, you can say, 'After <u>you</u>.'

→ Match these sentences from the exercise above with an appropriate response from the box on page 182.

1 In a shop:
A If you would like to come back for your watch some time later this afternoon… around 4 …
B ____________________________

2 In a school:
A I've got your son here. I'm afraid he's not very well so if you would like to come and pick him up …
B ____________________________

3 In an office:

A I'm sorry but Mr Smith isn't here this afternoon. If you would like to give me your name and telephone number …

B ____________________

4 In a shop:

A If you would like to come with me to the cash desk …

B ____________________

5 In an office:

A If you would like to go in, the manager can see you now.

B ____________________

a Thank you
b Yes, I'll be there as soon as I can
c Yes, of course, have you got pen and paper, it's 7859…
d Yes, that's fine
e After you

Check your answers

1 d **2** b **3** c **4** e **5** a

Our story continues. Oliver and Tasha get off the plane

→ Look at pictures **1–6** on page 183.
In Recording 3 on page 184, the conversation between Oliver and Tasha is in six parts, **a–f**. The parts are in the wrong order.

→ Listen and write the correct letter **a–f** in the first box under the pictures.

1

2

3

4

5

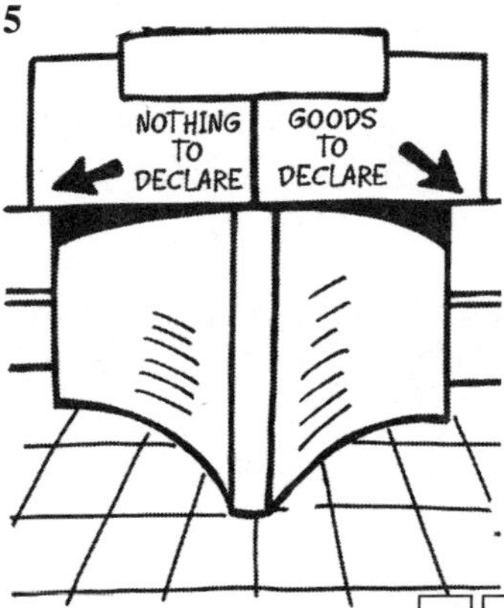

6

Recording 3 – The Story

a

Oliver Well, it's been really nice talking to you, Tasha.
Tasha Yes, and thanks for the help with the luggage.
Oliver I'll be in touch next week, then.
Tasha Yes, bye.
Oliver Bye.

b

Oliver Wow, this suitcase is a bit heavy – is that it now?
Tasha The suitcase, the small bag and my handbag – yes, that's everything.

c

Oliver Now, it's this way. You haven't got anything to declare, have you?
Tasha No, nothing.
Oliver We can go through the green channel, then. Over there.

d

Immigration officer Thank you madam. Sir, your passport please. Thank you.

e

Oliver Do you need a trolley?
Tasha That would be a good idea – I've got quite a lot of luggage.
Oliver They're just over here. Now, let's find the rest of the luggage.

f

Tasha Would you mind waiting for just a minute, Oliver?
Oliver Of course not. The suitcases aren't here yet, anyway.
Tasha Could you look after my trolley, oh, and can you take my coat, please?
Oliver Sure, go ahead.
Tasha asks for help at the information desk.
Airport employee Can I help you?

Tasha	Yes, could you tell me where the ladies' is, please?
Airport employee	Of course, madam. Just over there. Can you see the sign?

Check your answers

1 d **2** e **3** f **4** b **5** c **6** a

→ Write the correct words on the signs in the pictures on page 183.

INFORMATION DESK

CUSTOMS

ARRIVALS

PASSPORT CONTROL

TROLLEYS

BAGGAGE RECLAIM 5

Check your answers

1 Passport Control **2** Trolleys **3** Information desk **4** Baggage Reclaim 5 **5** Customs **6** Arrivals.

→ Read the sentences and mini-dialogues below. Where are the people?

→ Write the letters **A** to **F** in the second box, under the correct picture (**1–6**) on page 183.

A 'Could you open your bag for me, please?'
'Yes, of course.'

B 'Hello, Rachel, it's lovely to see you again. How are you?'

C 'Excuse me, I'm from this flight but my suitcase isn't here.'

D 'Have you got a visa?'
'Yes, it's on the next page.'

E 'I think we need two, don't you? One isn't enough for all this luggage.'

F 'How can I help you, sir?'
'Where can I change some money, please?'

Check your answers

1 D 2 E 3 F 4 C 5 A 6 B

Understanding more

→ Read the questions below.
→ Read the text of Recording 3 on page 184 and choose **a** or **b**.

1 a Tasha has got 1 piece } of luggage.
b 2 pieces

2 a They go to the red } channel at customs.
b green

3 Tasha needs to **a** change some money.
b go to the toilet.

Check your answers

1 b **2** b **3** b

What do they say?

→ Read the sentences below.
→ Read the text of Recording 3 on page 184 and complete the sentences.

1 They get the trolley. Oliver suggests they find their suitcases.
He says, 'Now, l _ _ ' _ / find the rest of the luggage.'

2 a Tasha asks Oliver to wait for her. She says,
'W _ _ _ _ / you / m _ _ _ / w _ _ _ _ _ g/ for just a minute?'
b Oliver responds, 'Of / c _ _ _ _ e / n _ t .'
c Tasha asks Oliver to look after her trolley and take her coat.
She says, 'C _ _ _ _ / y _ _ / look after my trolley?
Oh, and / c _ _ / y _ _ / take my coat, p _ _ _ _ _ ?'
d Oliver responds, /'S _ _ _ -/ g _ / a _ _ _ d.'

3 a The person at the information desk offers Tasha help.
She says, 'C_ _ / I / h _ _ _ / y _ _ ?'
b Tasha asks help to find the ladies' toilets.
She asks, 'C _ _ _ _ / y _ _ / t _ _ _ / m _ / where the ladies'/ _ _ /, please?'

Check your answers

1 Now let's find the rest of the luggage. **2 a** Would you mind waiting for just a minute? **b** Of course not. **c** Could you look after my trolley and can you take my coat, please? **d** Sure. Go ahead. **3 a** Can I help you? **b** Could you tell me where the ladies' is please?

★ The ladies' is the short expression for '*the ladies' toilets*'.
★ The men's or gents' are short expressions for 'the (gentle)men's toilets'.
★ We say 'the ladies'/men's is over there'. (Not: '~~are~~')
★ The words *ladies* and *gents* are for public toilets only.

Find the words and phrases

→ Read the questions below.
→ Read the text of Recording 3 again and complete the words and phrases.

1 Oliver has only got one suitcase but Tasha's got q _ _ _ _ / a / l _ _ / of / l _ _ g _ _ e.

2 Are the suitcases on the way? Yes.
Are the suitcases there? No, not y _ _.

3 Tasha asks Oliver to wait. To wait isn't a problem because the suitcases aren't there. Oliver says, 'The suitcases aren't here yet, a _ _ w _ _.

4 How can you ask, 'Is that all (your luggage?)' in two other ways?
'Is that / _ _ /? ' or 'Is that e _ _ _ _ t _ _ _ g?'

5 When you take someone somewhere, you can say, 'It's t _ _ _ / w _ _.'

6 a Oliver checks Tasha hasn't got anything to declare.
He says, 'You / h _ _ _ _' _ / got / a _ _ th _ _ _ / to declare, / h _ _ _ / y _ _ ?'
b Has Tasha got anything to declare? No, n _ _ _ _ _ g.

7 Oliver is happy about meeting Tasha on the plane. He says, 'I_ ' _ / b_ _ n / r _ _ _ _ y / n _ _ e / t _ _ k _ _ g / t _ / you / Tasha.'

8 Tasha thanks Oliver f _ _ the help with her suitcase.

9 He says he'll contact her next week. He says, 'I'_ _ / b _ / i _ / t _ _ _ _ / next week.

10 Verb *get*: In part **e** 'I'll go and *get* one' (trolley).
Here, *get* means **a** buy **b** bring one here?

Check your answers

1 Tasha's got quite a lot of luggage. **2** No, not yet. **3** The suitcases aren't there, anyway. **4** 'Is that it?' 'Is that everything?' *'Is that it?' is informal, 'Is that everything?' is always appropriate. **5** It's this way. **6** You haven't got anything to declare, have you? **7** It's been really nice talking *to* you Tasha (Preposition!) **8** Tasha thanks Oliver *for* his help (Preposition!) **9** I'll be *in* touch next week (Preposition!) **10** b.

Q ***What are the differences between suitcase, luggage and baggage?***

A Answer:

Meaning

1 This is a suitcase.

2 This is luggage.

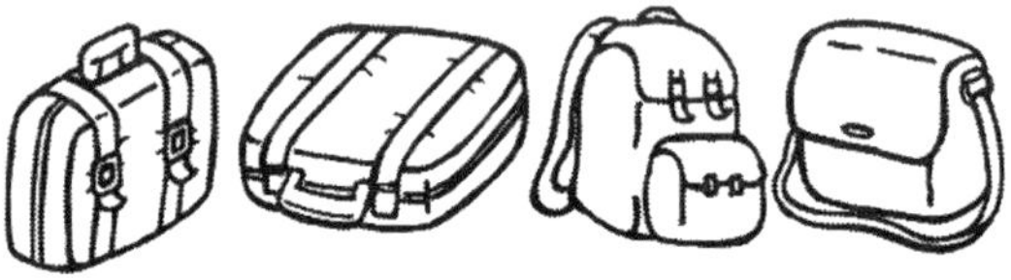

3 This is baggage.

Form

Suitcase is countable – one *suitcase* (two syllables), two *suitcases* (three syllables).

Luggage and *baggage* are uncountable/mass words.

Example: Our suitcases and bags are in the car OR
Our luggage is in the car.

★ The unit word for *luggage* is *piece*. For example, an airport employee: 'How many pieces of luggage have you got?'
★ We sometimes say *case* for *suitcase*.

→ Complete the sentences below with *(suit)case(s)*, *luggage*, *piece(s)* of *luggage* or *baggage*.

1 People take guitars, boxes, and all sorts of __________ on planes.
2 Passengers can take one small piece of hand __________ into the plane with them.
3 On flights from Europe to America you can take two __________ of __________ .
4 Let's go kids! Are your __________ in the car?

Check your answers

1 baggage **2** hand-luggage **3** pieces of luggage **4** (suit)cases (Luggage is wrong here because the verb is plural – *are*)

Grammar and communication 2

Suggesting doing something together – *let's*

Example from *The Story*:

They get the trolley. Oliver suggests they find their suitcases.
He says, 'Now **let's** find the rest of the luggage.'

Meaning

Who is making a suggestion? Oliver.
Does the suggestion include Oliver? Yes.

★ Use *let's* when the suggestion includes *you*.

Form

Let's + verb

★ The negative is *let's not* + verb.
★ The short answer is, *Yes, let's.*
★ The question tag is *Let's (go), shall we?*

Let's – summary of responses		
Positive responses are	O.K./Alright Yes, why not? That's a good idea Yes, why don't we?	☺
Possible negative responses are	Do you really want to? I'm not too sure Perhaps not Actually, I'm not too keen	☹

Situation You live with Chris, a friend of yours.

→ Write suggestions and responses for these situations.

1 It's very hot. You and Chris are sitting in the garden, talking. You're thirsty.
You ______________________________
Chris ______________________________ ☺

2 **Situation** You both have a friend, Hilary. Hilary is ill. Suggest you both go and visit her this afternoon.
You ______________________________, _______?
Chris ___________________________ ☹

3 Chris puts the T.V. on. There's a football match on. You don't like football and there's a good film on Channel 5.
You ____________the football. Why don't we watch the film on Channel 5 instead?
Chris_____________ ☺

4 You are talking about a holiday. Suggest Mexico.
You ______________________Mexico.
Chris_________________ ☺

Chris suggests inviting Sam (another friend) too.
Chris _____________________
You ____________________ ☹

5 You are going to a party tonight. You're very tired. You don't want to go.
You _______________to the party. _________ stay here instead.
Chris Shall we have a Chinese meal?
You Yes ____'__!

Check your answers

1 Let's have a drink. **2** Let's go and visit Hilary this afternoon, shall we? **3** Let's not watch the football. Why don't we watch the film on Channel 5 instead? **4** Let's go to Mexico. Let's invite Sam, too. **5** Let's not go to the party. Let's stay here instead. Yes, let's!

Responses

☺ Any response from the ☺ list in the box on page 190.

☹ Any response from the ☹ list in the box on page 190.

Q *What's the difference between 'We could'*
'We can...' } *(Topic 6)*
and 'Let's' ...?

A **Here are two examples:**

Situation You're with a friend, talking about this evening.

a 'We could go to the cinema.'
b 'Let's go to the cinema.'

With **a** *We could...* the cinema is a possibility.

With **b** *Let's...* you would like to go to the cinema and you would like the other person to go, too.

In summary, *we could* is less direct.

Grammar and communication 3

Asking people to do things

Examples from *The Story*:

1 Tasha asks Oliver to wait for her. She says, '**Would you mind** waiting for just a minute?'
Oliver responds, 'Of course not.'

2 Tasha asks Oliver to look after her trolley and take her coat.
She says, '**Could you** look after my trolley, oh, and can you take my coat, please?'
Oliver responds, 'Sure. Go ahead.'

Grammar summary – Asking someone to do something		
Request	**Responses – it's O.K.**	**Responses – it isn't O.K.**
Can you + verb…? Could you + verb…?	Sure Of course Of course I can/could Yes, that's no problem	I'm afraid I can't I'm sorry but I can't I'm sorry but + reason
Would you mind + verb/ing?	Of course not Not at all	

★ A response isn't always necessary. The person can 'do' the action without a response.

★ It is very common to say *please* when you ask someone to do something.

★ Answers *Yes, I can*, *Yes, I could*, *No, I can't*, *No, I wouldn't*, etc. alone are not usually appropriate. ☹

★ *Would you mind?* means 'Is it a problem for you to…?'
If it is not a problem, the response is negative, *No, of course not.*

★ When you say *no*, it is common to give a reason.
Example 'Could you cook the dinner tomorrow, please?'
'I'm sorry, I can't. I'm going out to dinner with Julie.'

★ *Could* is less direct than *can.*

★ *Would you mind...?* can be more formal than *can you?/could you?*

Asking someone NOT TO do something	
Would you mind not + *verb*/'ing'?	<u>Positive response</u> Oh! I'm sorry
	<u>Negative response</u> Is it really a problem?

Asking people to do things – *Can you..? Could you...? Would you mind...?*

→Read the situations below.

→Complete the requests.

→Choose an appropriate response from the box on page 194, where necessary.

1 Someone speaks to you in English but you don't understand. Ask them to say it again.
You ***Ca***________________________________, please?

2 You are eating with friends. You would like some water. The bottle is at the other end of the table.
You ***Co***____________________________________

Your friend ____________________________

3 Your child asks for help with his/her English homework.
Mum/Dad, ca _______________________?
You ______________________

4 You are a tourist and you've got a camera. You want a photo with your friends. You ask another tourist.
W________________________________?
The tourist ______________________

5 The telephone rings. You are just going in the shower. Ask the person to call you back in 10 minutes.
Ca____________________________________ ?
The caller ______________________

6 A friend is staying in your house. She smokes in the kitchen. You really don't like it. Ask her not to.
You ***W***____
Your friend ________________________________

7 Someone tells you a new word in English. You want to write it but you don't know the spelling.
You ***Co***____?
The other person __________________________

Responses

Of course. What is it?

I'm sorry but I'm going out right now and it's urgent

Oh, sorry!

Not at all – what do I do?

Yes, it's T – H – A...

Yes, here you are

Check your answers

1 Can you say that again, please? *This is more common than 'Can you repeat that, please?' **2** Could you pass the water, please? Yes. Here you are. **3** Mum/Dad, can you help me with my homework? Of course. What is it? **4** Would you mind taking a photo of us, please? Not at all. What do I do? **5** Can you call me back in 10 minutes, please? I'm sorry but I'm going out right now and it's urgent. **6** Would you mind not smoking in the kitchen? Oh, sorry! **7** Could you spell that for me, please? Yes, it's T – H – A...

Asking people to do things – official announcements

Situation On a plane or at an airport.

→ Cover the text of Recording 4.
→ Read the flight attendants' requests and invitations below (**a–h**)
→ Listen to the announcements on Recording 4, (**1–8**).
→ Just try to understand the message – it is not necessary to understand all the words.
→ Match the requests and the announcements, for example **1–f**.
→ Write the number in the box.

a 'Could you please go back to your seat, sir? We're landing soon.' ☐
b 'Would you mind not smoking, please, sir? This is a non-smoking flight.' ☐
c 'I'm sorry, could you please sit down again, madam? The plane is still moving.' ☐
d 'Could you put those bags in the overhead compartments, please?' ☐
e 'Could you please hurry, sir? The aircraft is ready to leave.' ☐

f 'Could you please stay in your seat, sir, and fasten your seatbelt? It's a little bumpy ahead.' ☐

g 'If you wouldn't mind filling this in, madam…You'll need it at passport control.' ☐

h 'If you would like to report to the special desk sir, when you get off the plane…' ☐

Recording 4

1 Passengers are requested to remain in their seats with their seat belts fastened – we are entering an area of turbulence.
2 Passenger Smith going to Rome is requested to go immediately to Gate 12 where the flight is now closing.
3 All transfer passengers are requested to report to the transfer desk.
4 All passengers are requested to return to their seats. We are beginning our descent.
5 Passengers are requested to put all hand luggage in the storage space above your heads.
6 All passengers are required to complete a landing card for the immigration authorities.
7 Passengers are requested to remain in their seats until the plane comes to a complete halt.
8 Passengers are respectfully reminded that smoking is not allowed on this flight.

Check your answers

a 4 b 8 c 7 d 5 e 2 f 1 g 6 h 3

★ In hotels, restaurants, airports, shops, etc., the staff say *sir* to a man and *madam* to a woman. Clients and customers don't use *sir* or *madam* with staff.

★ If we use the family name, we say *Mr.* or *Mrs.* + family name.

Grammar and communication 4

Asking for help – indirect questions

The person at the information desk offers Tasha help.
She says, 'Can I help you?'

Tasha asks for help to find the toilets.
She says, '**Could you tell me** where the ladies' is please?'

Direct question 'Where's the ladies', please?'
Indirect question 'Could you tell me where the ladies' **is**, please?'

★ Both are grammatically correct.
★ *Could you...* is very common because it is indirect.
★ Use *Could you tell me...*
Can you show me...
Would you mind explaining... } to ask for help.
★ In other words, expressions for 'asking for help' and 'asking someone to do something' are the same.

! Common mistake – indirect questions – word order

'Can you tell me how much **this is**, please?' ✓
(subject + verb ✓)

(Not: 'Can you tell me how much ~~**is this**~~, please?) ✗
(Verb + subject ✗)

★ Word order is important with indirect questions.

Q ***Where is the question form in indirect questions?***

A At the beginning.
Can you...
Could you...
Would you mind... } is the question. (verb + subject)

The question is at the beginning.
The second part of the sentence is not a question. For this reason there is no question form here.

Grammar summary – Indirect Questions – verb *be*			
Indirect question phrase	**question words**	**subject**	**verb**
Can you tell me Could you tell me Would you mind telling me	where how much when who	it	is?

→ Below are six direct questions asking for help.
→ Ask the questions in a polite (indirect) way.
→ Start with *Excuse me,...*

1 'Where's the coffee bar?'
Excuse me, ca________________________________

2 'Where are the toilets?'
Excuse me, co________________________________

3 'How much is this?'
Excuse me, co________________________________

4 'How much are these?'
Excuse me, w________________________________

5 'How much is this magazine?'
Excuse me, ca________________________________

6 'How much are these crisps?'
Excuse me, co________________________________

☑ Check your answers

1 Excuse me, can you tell me where the coffee bar is, please?
2 Excuse me, could you tell me where the toilets are, please?
3 Excuse me, could you tell me how much this is, please?
4 Excuse me, would you mind telling me how much these are, please?
5 Excuse me, can you tell me how much this magazine is, please?
6 Excuse me, could you tell me how much these crisps are, please?

British culture – money – sterling

- The currency (unit of money) in Britain is the pound (£). (Today £1 is US about $1.60.)
- The sign '£' goes in front of the number, for example £15. (Not: ~~15£~~)
- There are 100 pence (we often say 'p') in £1.
- The coins are:
  1p 2p 5p 10p 20p 50p £1 £2

- The notes are:
  £5 £10 £20 £50

Q ***How do we say, for example, £3.20?***

A We can say, 'Three pounds, twenty pence' (more formal).

OR 'Three pounds, twenty' } less formal
OR 'Three pounds, twenty p' }

About your country: money

→ Read the questions below.
→ Either write your answers or prepare to tell a friend.

1 What is the currency in your country?

____

2 What are the coins?

____

3 What are the notes?

____

4 How do you write it?

____

5 How do you say it?

____

Our story continues. Oliver is in a shop in the airport.

Understanding the important information

→ Cover the text of Recording 5.
→ Read the questions below.
→ Listen to Recording 5 and answer the questions.

1 Oliver buys 1, 2, 3, 4, things?
2 Oliver's got the right money. Yes/No

Recording 5

Oliver	Excuse me, do you sell *Computing Weekly*?
Seller	Yes, sir, they're here.
Oliver	And a packet of mints – have you got Polos?
The seller gets a packet of Polos.	
Oliver	£2.86 please, sir.
Oliver	Sorry, I haven't got any change. Is £20.00 alright?
Seller	Yes, no problem. Seventeen pounds, 14p change.
Oliver	Thanks.

Check your answers

1 Oliver buys two things. **2** No, Oliver hasn't got the right money.

Understanding more

→ Cover the text of Recording 5 again.
→ Read the sentences below.
→ Listen and choose the correct answer.

1 Oliver buys **a** a newspaper.
b a magazine.

2 He buys **a** a Mars bar
b a packet of polos
c a packet of crisps
d a bar of chocolate
} too.

3 The total price is **a** £1.86.
b £2.68.
c £2.86.

4 Oliver gives the man **a** £5.
b £10.
c £20.

5 The change is **a** £17.40.
b £7.14.
c £7.40.
d £17.14.

6 The change is **a** right.
b wrong.

Check your answers

1 b **2** b **3** c **4** c **5** d **6** a

What's the right word?

Snacks

→ Label the pictures. Choose one expression from **Box 1** and one word from **Box 2** on page 202.
→ Use your dictionary if necessary.

Example:
a packet of polos

1

2

3

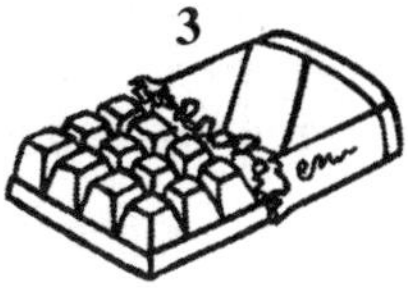

4

6

7

8

5

Box 1

a bar of	a carton of
a can of	a packet of
a bottle of	

Box 2

water	sweets
fruit juice	crisps
chocolate	biscuits
chewing gum	Coke

Check your answers *(Recording 6)*

1 a packet of crisps
2 a can of Coke
3 a bar of chocolate
4 a packet of chewing gum
5 a packet of biscuits
6 a bottle of water
7 a carton of fruit juice
8 a packet of sweets

How do you pronounce it?

Saying groups of words together – linking

→ Look at the link lines and stress on the expressions above.
The word *of* is weak in all the sentences, so the vowel is *schwa* / ə /.

→ Listen to Recording 6 and repeat the list.
Pay special attention to
a stress **b** linking words **c** weak *of*.

British culture – snacks

- Snacks are very common in Britain.
- Sweet things are very popular, especially sweets and chocolate, for example, Polos (mint sweets) and Mars bars.
- It is common to have biscuits and cakes, especially with tea and coffee.
- Nowadays, savoury snacks, for example, crisps and nuts, are also popular.
- All the snacks in the exercise above are very common.
- People eat snacks at any time of the day.
- At work, a snack with tea and coffee is very usual.
- In the summer, ice cream is a popular snack.

About you: snacks

→ Write answers to the questions below or prepare to tell a friend.

1 What do people eat and drink between meals in your country?

____

2 Write two lists:
a snacks you like. ____________ ____________
b snacks you don't like. ____________ ____________

Understanding numbers

Is it 13 or 30?

Look at the stress pattern.

13 thir**teen**	30 **thir**ty
14 four**teen**	40 **for**ty
15 fif**teen**	50 **fif**ty
16 six**teen**	60 **six**ty etc.

Can you hear the difference?

→ Listen to Recording 7 and tick ✓ the correct picture.

1 a 

b 

2 a 

b 

3 a 

b 

4 a 

b 

5 a 

b 

6 a 3:15 **b** 3:50

7 a 

b 

8 a ●→● 18 miles
b ●————→● 80 miles

Recording 7

1	**A**	Excuse me, how much is this, please?
	B	50p.
2	**A**	How much does this cost, please?
	B	£13.
	A	Sorry, is that £13 or £30?
	B	£13, sir.
3	**A**	Do you know how much this is, please?
	B	£4.90.
4	**A**	Excuse me, could you tell me how much this costs, please?
	B	Of course. That's £17.99.
	A	Is that one, seven or seven '0'?
	B	One seven, seventeen.
5	**A**	Where do you live?
	B	At number 60.
6	**A**	At what time?
	B	At 3.15.
7	**A**	Where is it?
	B	On page 40.
8	**A**	How far is it to the town?
	B	18 miles.

Check your answers

1 b **2** a **3** b **4** a **5** b **6** a **7** b **8** a

What do they say?

Asking the price

→ Read questions 1–4 of Recording 7 above.
→ Copy below the four questions to ask the price.
→ Choose *direct* or *indirect* for each one.

1 ______________________________? Direct/Indirect
2 ______________________________? Direct/Indirect
3 ______________________________? Direct/Indirect
4 ______________________________? Direct/Indirect

Check your answers

1 Excuse me, how much is this, please? (Direct) **2** How much does this cost, please? (Direct) **3** Do you know how much this is, please? (Indirect) **4** Excuse me, could you tell me how much this costs, please? (Indirect)

→ Listen to Recording 7 again and repeat the questions and answers.

Common mistake – indirect questions

★ The word order in indirect questions is always the same.
The question is at the beginning and the rest is normal word order – subject first, then verb.

'Excuse me, could you tell me how much **this costs**, please?'

(Not: 'Excuse me, could you tell me how much ~~**does this cost**~~, please?')

★ Use *if* with yes/no indirect questions.
For example: Direct question. 'Does this shop open on Sundays?'
Indirect question. 'Do you know if this shop opens on Sundays?'

Asking for help – indirect questions

→ Which one is correct? Complete the questions with **a**, **b** or **c**.

1 Excuse me, do you know how much ________, please?
a are these **b** these are

2 Could you tell me ________________, please?
a where the coffee bar is **b** where is the coffee bar

3 Do you know when ________________ ?
a starts the film **b** the film starts

4 Excuse me, can you tell me ________________?
a where this train goes **b** where does this train go

5 Do you know what ______________?
a does he do? **b** he does

6 Excuse me, can you tell me ____________ to the town centre, please?
a how far is it **b** how far it is

7 Could you tell me ____________ there?
a how do I get **b** how to get

8 Do you know when ____________?
a he is arriving **b** is he arriving

9 Can you tell me what _____________ in English?
a is this **b** this is

10 Can you tell me ______________ to London?
a does this train go **b** if this train goes

11 Could you tell me ___________ the right bus for the airport, please?
a if this is **b** is this

12 Do you know _______________ ?
a what means this word
b what this word means
c what does mean this word

This one's difficult for very many learners of English – have you got it right?

Check your answers

1 b **2** a **3** b **4** a **5** b **6** b **7** b **8** a **9** b **10** b **11** a **12** b

What would you say?

1 You buy something in a shop.
The person gives you the wrong change.

____

2 You are at baggage reclaim at the airport. Your suitcase doesn't come.

____

Possible answers

1 How much is it again? OR I'm sorry but I don't think this change is right.
I don't think X is right is more common than 'x is wrong'.
I don't think X is right is less direct.
Advanced alternative: I'm sorry but I think there's a mistake here.
2 Excuse me, I don't know where my suitcase is. Could you help me please?

Revision

How do you say it in your language?

→ Here are some examples of the important points in this topic.
→ Translate the sentences into your language in the spaces.
→ Remember – translate the idea, not the words.

1 You arrive at a restaurant. The person working there says 'If you would like to follow me… (I'll show you to your table)

____

2 **A** 'What shall we do today?' **B** 'Let's go to my brother's.' **A** 'Fine, why not?'

____

3 **A** 'Shall we walk there?' **B** 'I'm not too keen on that idea. Let's go by car.'

____

4 **A**'Can I help you?' **B** 'Yes, Could you tell me where the coffee bar is, please?'

____

5 **A** 'I'm sorry I can't go tomorrow. Would you mind changing the meeting to Wednesday?' **B** 'Of course not – that's no problem.'

____

6 At the end of a conversation you say, 'It's been nice talking to you.'

____

7 'Do you need a trolley? I'll go and get one.'

____

Join the conversation

→ Look at the text of Recording 8 on page 208. It's the complete conversation from Recording 3, when Oliver and Tasha get off the plane. Notice the linking.
→ Listen to Recording 8 and read Tasha's words in the spaces.
→ Pay special attention to the linking between the words.

Recording 8

Immigration officer	Thank you madam. Sir, your passport please. Thank you.
Oliver	Do you need a trolley?
Tasha	That would be a good idea – I've got quite a lot of luggage.
Oliver	They're just over here. Now, let's find the rest of the luggage.
Tasha	Would you mind waiting for just a minute, Oliver?
Oliver	Of course not. The suitcases aren't here yet anyway.
Tasha	Could you look after my trolley, oh, and can you take my coat, please?
Oliver	Sure, go ahead.
Tasha asks for help at the information desk.	
Airport employee	Can I help you?
Tasha	Yes, could you tell me where the (ladies'/gent's) is, please?
Airport employee	Of course, (madam/sir). Just over there. Can you see the sign?
Oliver	Wow, this suitcase is a bit heavy – is that it now?
Tasha	The suitcase, the small bag and my handbag – yes that's everything.
Oliver	Now, it's this way. You haven't got anything to declare, have you?
Tasha	No, nothing.
Oliver	We can go through the green channel, then. Over there.
Oliver	Well, it's been really nice talking to you, Tasha.
Tasha	Yes and thanks for the help with the luggage.
Oliver	I'll be in touch next week, then.
Tasha	Yes, bye.
Oliver	Bye.

TEST 7

Which one is right?

→ Choose **a** or **b**.

1 Thirty-five and twenty-nine are
  a forty-six.
  b sixty-four.

2 If you would like to go in now, madam…
  a Yes, I would.
  b Thank you.

3 **a** Would you mind to wait, please?
  b Would you mind waiting, please?

4 **a** I'm hungry. Let's have something to eat!
  b I'm hungry. Let's to have something to eat!

5 Could you help me, please?
  a Yes. What do you want?
  b Of course. What would you like me to do?

6 Excuse me, can you tell me where station is, please?
  a Yes, I can.
  b Yes, it's just over there.

7 **a** I'll get a trolley for the luggages.
  b I'll get a trolley for the luggage.

8 The information desk?
  It's **a** in this way.
  b this way.

9 **a** 'Bye, I'll see you tomorrow.'
  b 'Bye, I see you tomorrow.'

10 Would you mind coming back later? (You can go back later.)
  a Yes.
  b Sure, it's no problem.

11 **a** Can you tell me where are the taxis, please?
  b Can you tell me where the taxis are, please?

12 £24.75. This is
  a pounds twenty four, seventy-five.
  b twenty-four pounds, seventy-five.

Write a dialogue

Situation Eva is an au-pair with the Lewis family. (She works in the family, helping with the children and the house.) It's the morning and Barbara, Lewis and Eva are talking about the day.

Barbara

1 Barbara asks Eva to take the children to school. She's working this morning.

Eva

2 Eva says 'yes'

____ Would you like me to go to supermarket on the way back?

3 Barbara says yes and asks her to buy bread, milk and cartons of fruit juice.

4 Eva responds.

Does Barbara need more things from the shop?

5 Barbara says no and asks Eva to take the children to the park after school.

She also asks her to work on Saturday evening.

6 Eva can take the children to the park but she can't work on Saturday evening. She's going to a party.

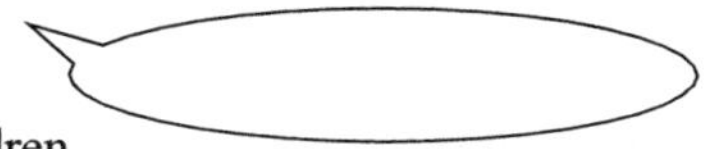

7 <u>It's the afternoon</u>
Eva is in the park with the children. One of the children sees an ice cream van and suggests they all have an ice cream.

Check your answers

1 b **2** b **3** b **4** a **5** b **6** b **7** b **8** b **9** a **10** b **11** b **12** b

Dialogue: model answers

1 Barbara	Could you take the children to school, please? I'm working this morning.
2 Eva	Of course. Would you like me to go to the supermarket on the way back?
3 Barbara	Could you? Can you get some bread, some milk and some cartons of fruit juice?
4 Eva	Fine. Do you need anything else?
5 Barbara	No, thanks. Could you take the children to the park after school and would you mind working on Saturday evening?
6 Eva	I can take the children to the park but I'm sorry, I can't work on Saturday evening – I'm going to a party. [In the afternoon]
7 Child	Let's all have an ice cream!

8 USING PUBLIC TRANSPORT

Grammar and communication
- Prepositions at the end of questions
- Asking for instructions, giving instructions
- Asking for and understanding travel information
  – the time, timetables, itineraries

Vocabulary
- Public transport
- The time

Pronunciation
- Stress – place names

Oliver is at the information desk at the airport. He needs to get to the centre of London.

Understanding the important information

→Cover the text of Recording 1, *The Story*.
→Read the question below.
→Listen to the recording and answer the question.

How is Oliver going to the centre? – By train, by bus or by taxi?

Recording 1 – The Story

Airport employee	Can I help you?
Oliver	Yes, could you tell me how to get to the centre of town, please?
Airport employee	You can go by bus, by train or by underground, sir. Which part of London are you going to?
Oliver	I need to get to Victoria Station.
Airport employee	Then you can take the A1 Airbus. It goes all the way to Victoria.
Oliver	The A1, right. And where do I get the bus from?
Airport employee	Just over there, sir. You see the sign that says, 'Airbus?' You follow that sign.
Oliver	Oh, I see! Do you know when the next bus leaves?
Airport employee	In ten minutes', sir – at 8.05.
Oliver	And how long does it take to get there?
Airport employee	I'm not sure – the best thing to do is ask the driver.
Oliver	Many thanks for your help.

Check your answer

By bus

Understanding more

→Cover the text of Recording 1.
→Read the questions on page 214.
→Listen and choose the right answers.

1 Choose ALL the right answers.
The man says Oliver can go by bus, or by
- **a** coach
- **b** taxi
- **c** underground
- **d** train

(2 – 6 Choose the right answer.)

2 Where exactly in London is Oliver going?
- **a** Waterloo Station
- **b** Paddington Station
- **c** Victoria Station
- **d** Euston Station

3 What's the name of the bus?
- **a** London bus
- **b** Airbus
- **c** Central bus
- **d** Express bus

4
- **a** It's a long walk to the bus.
- **b** The bus is very near.
- **c** The bus goes from the train station.
- **d** The bus is downstairs.

5 The next bus leaves
- **a** in an hour
- **b** in half an hour
- **c** in two minutes' time
- **d** in ten minutes' time

6 When does the bus arrive in London?
- **a** we don't know
- **b** in one hour
- **c** in half an hour
- **d** in ten minutes

Check your answers

1 c and d **2** c **3** b **4** b **5** d **6** a

What do they say?

→ Read the sentences below.
→ Listen to Recording 1 again and try to complete the words.
→ Then read the text on page 213 to help you if necessary.

1 a Oliver doesn't know how to get to the centre of town. He asks for help. He says, 'C _ _ _ _ / you / t _ _ _ / me / h _ _ / t _ / g _ _ / t _ / the centre of town, please?'

b There are three possibilities.
The man says, 'You / c _ _ / g _ / b _ bus, / b _ / train or b _ / underground.'

2 a The man asks where exactly in London Oliver is going. He says, 'Which part of London / a _ _ / y _ _ / g _ _ _ g / t _ ?'

b Oliver answers, 'I / n _ _ _ / t _ / g _ _ / t _ Victoria Station.'

3 a The man suggests the Airbus.
He says, 'Y _ _ / c _ _ / t _ _ _ / the A1 Airbus.'

4 a Oliver doesn't know where the buses are. He asks, 'Where / d _ / I / g _ _ / t _ _ / b _ _ / f _ _ _?'

b The man gives Oliver instructions.
'Y _ _ / f _ ll _ _ / the sign that says 'Airbus'.'

5 Is it necessary to change?
No, the A1 bus goes a _ _ / t _ _ / w _ _ / to Victoria Station.

6 Oliver wants to know the time the journey takes. He asks, 'H _ _ / l _ _ _ / d _ _ _ / it / t _ _ _ / t _ / g _ _ / there?'

Check your answers

1 a Could you tell me how *to* get to the centre of town, please? (preposition!) **b** You can go *by* bus, *by* train or *by* underground (preposition!). **2 a** Which part of London are you going *to*? (preposition!). **b** I need to get to Victoria Station. **3** You can take the A1 Airbus. **4 a** Where do I get the bus *from*? (preposition!) **b** You follow the sign that says 'Airbus'. **5** No, the A1 bus goes all the way to Victoria Station. **6** How long does it take to get there?

How do you pronounce it?

London's main stations – stress

The logo is a registered trademark in the name of the Secretary of State for the Environment, Transport and the Regions.

Example from the story:

The man asks Oliver: 'Which part of London are you going to?'
Oliver answers: 'I need to get to Victoria.'

→ Cover the text of Recording 2 below.
→ Look at the Underground map on page 217 with the names of the main train stations.
→ Listen to Recording 2.
→ Repeat the names and underline the stress for each one.

Check your answers *(Recording 2)*

1 Victoria
2 Paddington
3 Marylebone
4 King's Cross
5 St Pancras
6 Euston
7 Liverpool Street
8 Waterloo

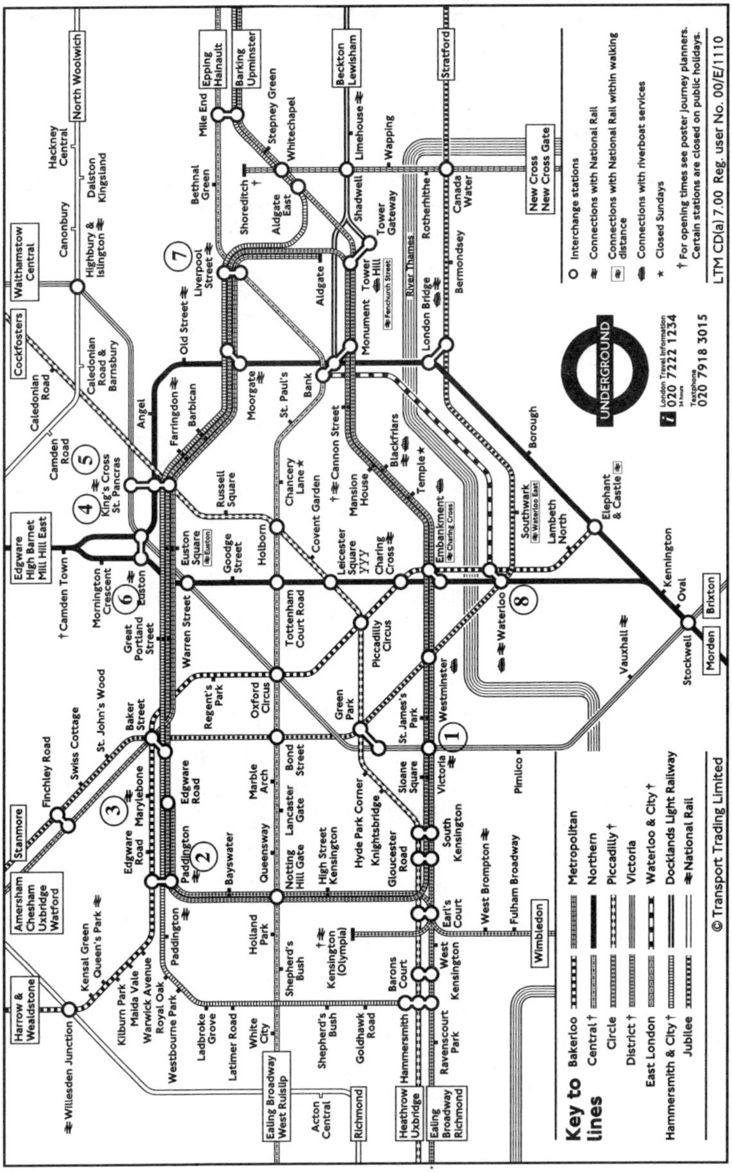
Key to lines
Bakerloo
Central †
Circle
District †
East London
Hammersmith & City †
Jubilee
Metropolitan
Northern
Piccadilly †
Victoria
Waterloo & City †
Docklands Light Railway
National Rail
© Transport Trading Limited
Interchange stations
Connections with National Rail
Connections with National Rail within walking distance
Connections with riverboat services
Closed Sundays
† For opening times see poster journey planners. Certain stations are closed on public holidays.
LTM CD(a) 7.00 Reg. user No. 00/E/1110
UNDERGROUND
London Travel Information 24 hours 020 7222 1234
Textphone 020 7918 3015
Harrow & Wealdstone
Amersham Chesham Uxbridge Watford
Stanmore
Cockfosters
Walthamstow Central
North Woolwich
Epping Hainault
Barking Upminster
Beckton Lewisham
Stratford
New Cross New Cross Gate
Edgware High Barnet Mill Hill East
Ealing Broadway West Ruislip
Richmond
Heathrow Uxbridge
Ealing Broadway Richmond
Wimbledon
Morden
Brixton
Willesden Junction
Kensal Green
Queen's Park
Kilburn Park
Maida Vale
Warwick Avenue
Royal Oak
Westbourne Park
Paddington
Ladbroke Grove
Latimer Road
White City
Acton Central
Shepherd's Bush
Goldhawk Road
Hammersmith
Ravenscourt Park
Barons Court
West Kensington
Holland Park
Kensington (Olympia)
Earl's Court
West Brompton
Fulham Broadway
Edgware Road
Bayswater
Notting Hill Gate
Queensway
High Street Kensington
Gloucester Road
South Kensington
Lancaster Gate
Marble Arch
Hyde Park Corner
Knightsbridge
Sloane Square
Victoria
Pimlico
Bond Street
Finchley Road
Swiss Cottage
St. John's Wood
Marylebone
Baker Street
Regent's Park
Oxford Circus
Green Park
St. James's Park
Westminster
Great Portland Street
Warren Street
Tottenham Court Road
Piccadilly Circus
Waterloo
Vauxhall
Stockwell
Oval
Kennington
Camden Town
Mornington Crescent
Euston
Euston Square
Goodge Street
Holborn
Leicester Square
Charing Cross
Embankment
Lambeth North
Southwark
Elephant & Castle
Borough
King's Cross St. Pancras
Camden Road
Caledonian Road
Caledonian Road & Barnsbury
Russell Square
Chancery Lane
Covent Garden
Mansion House
Blackfriars
Temple
Angel
Farringdon
Barbican
St. Paul's
Cannon Street
Highbury & Islington
Canonbury
Old Street
Moorgate
Bank
Monument
London Bridge
Liverpool Street
Aldgate
Tower Hill
Fenchurch Street
River Thames
Bermondsey
Hackney Central
Dalston Kingsland
Bethnal Green
Shoreditch
Aldgate East
Tower Gateway
Mile End
Stepney Green
Whitechapel
Shadwell
Limehouse
Wapping
Rotherhithe
Canada Water

Understanding the important information

→ Read the sentences below.
→ Read the text about the London Underground and answer True or False.

1 London has twelve Underground lines. True/False
2 There are ninety-five Underground stations. True/False
3 Each line has a number. True/False
4 There is only one fare. True/False
5 It costs the same all day. True/False
6 You can use a travelcard on the buses and trains. True/False
7 It doesn't cost much to use public transport in Britain. True/False

British culture – the London Underground or 'The Tube'

UNDERGROUND

London Travel Information
020 7222 1234
24 hours

Textphone
020 7918 3015

- There are just over 450 kms of Tube tunnel under London's streets, with 12 Underground lines and more than 250 stations. Over 100,000 people a day use Victoria station.
- Each line has a name and a colour. For example, the District Line is green and the Circle Line is yellow. London is divided into six fare zones. Central London is Zone 1. The fare you pay depends on the number of zones you travel in. It is cheaper to travel after 9.30 in the morning when you can buy a one-day travelcard. You can use this ticket on the buses and trains too. Family tickets are also available.
- Public transport is quite expensive in Britain.

Check your answers

The correct answers are in brackets. **1** True. **2** False (more than 250). **3** False (each line has a name). **4** False (the fare depends on the number of zones). **5** False (it's cheaper after 9.30). **6** True. **7** False (it's quite expensive).

Famous places in London – stress

You are on a tourist bus in central London.

→ Look at the bus route below with the famous places.
→ Listen to the announcement on Recording 3.
→ Underline the syllable with stress for each place.

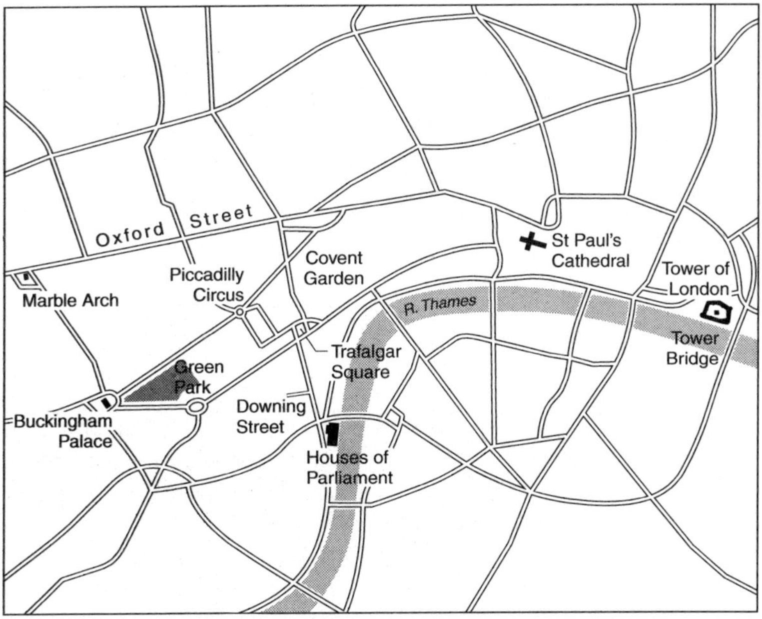

1 Marble Arch	**2** Oxford Street	**3** Green Park
4 Buckingham Palace	**5** Piccadilly Circus	**6** Trafalgar Square
7 Downing Street	**8** Houses of Parliament	**9** Covent Garden
10 St Paul's Cathedral	**11** London Bridge	**12** The Tower of London

He's getting off the bus and she's getting on the bus

Check your answers *(Recording 3)*

Good morning, ladies and gentlemen. Welcome to the Tour of London bus. If you would like to look at your maps for a moment, I can tell you a little bit about our route. This bus stops at the following famous places:

1 Marble Arch
2 Oxford Street
3 Green Park
4 Buckingham Palace
5 Piccadilly Circus
6 Trafalgar Square
7 Downing Street
8 The Houses of Parliament
9 Covent Garden
10 St Paul's Cathedral
11 Tower Bridge
12 The Tower of London

Passengers are reminded that you can get on or off the bus at any one of these stops. We hope you enjoy your tour with us this morning.

★ The stress is at the beginning on two names, Oxford Street and Downing Street.

★ For most place names the stress is on the second word, like *Park*, *Palace*, *Square*, *Road*, *Bridge*, for example, London Bridge, Kensington Palace.

★ *Street* is different – the stress is on the first word.

→ Listen to Recording 3 again and repeat the names of these famous places.

How do you pronounce it?

Stress on place names – addresses

★ English has lots of words for *Road* or *Street*.

→ Listen to Recording 4 and repeat these street names.
→ Underline the syllable with stress.

Park Road	*High Street*	*Eton Avenue*
Buckingham Gardens	*Tudor Drive*	*Moor Close*
West Hill	*Elm Crescent*	*Rose Walk*
River Lane	*Church Grove*	*Esher Place*
Orchard Way	*Maple Court*	*Nova Mews*

Check your answers *(Recording 4)*

Abbreviations are in brackets ( ).

Park Road (Rd)	High Street (St)	Eton Avenue (Ave)
Buckingham Gardens (Gdns)	Tudor Drive (Dr)	Moor Close (Cl)
West Hill	Elm Crescent (Cres)	Rose Walk (Wlk)
River Lane (La)	Church Grove (Gr)	Esher Place (Pl)
Orchard Way	Maple Court (Ct)	Nova Mews

★ When we say or write an address, the number is first, before the name of the street, for example, 2 Park Road, 57 Eton Avenue.

Grammar and communication 1

Prepositions at the end of questions

Examples from *The Story:*

1 The man asks Oliver exactly where in London he's going
He says, 'Which part of London are you going **to**?' (preposition!)

Affirmative 'I'm going to Victoria.'

Question 'Which part of London are you going to?'

2 Oliver doesn't know where the buses are.
He asks 'Where do I get the bus **from**?' (preposition!)

Possible answer 'You get the bus from the bus stop outside the terminal.'

★ The grammar is correct with the preposition at the end.
★ Nowadays it is common to put the preposition at the end of the question.

→ Complete these mini-dialogues with the correct question from the box below.

1 A ____________________? **B** My brother – I call him every week.
2 A ____________________? **B** This picture. Isn't it attractive?
3 A ____________________? **B** My girlfriend. It's her birthday today.
4 A ____________________? **B** My boyfriend. I miss him.
5 A ____________________? **B** My keys. Do you know where they are?
6 A There's an urgent e-mail for you. **B** ________________?
7 A I like reading. **B** ________________________________?
8 A She's married. **B** ________________________________?
9 A I'm going to that new restaurant this evening. **B** ________________?
10 Taxi-driver **A** ____________________? **B** The station please.
11 A We could go and see that new film this weekend.
B ______________?
12 A I'd like to book a Eurostar ticket to Paris, please. **B** ______________?

> **a** Do you know who it's from? **b** Oh, is she? Who to?
> **c** They're nice flowers. Who are they for? **d** Who are you talking to?
> **e** Of course, sir. When for? **f** Are you really? Who are you going with?
> **g** What are you looking at? **h** What's it about?
> **i** Do you? What sort of books are you interested in?
> **j** What are you looking for? **k** Who are you writing to?
> **l** Where to, madam?

☑ Check your answers

1 d **2** g **3** c **4** k **5** j **6** a **7** i **8** b **9** f **10** l **11** h **12** e

What's the right word?

Public transport

→ Write the names of these vehicles. Choose words from **Box 1** below.
→ Where do they go from? Choose the place from **Box 2** and write it next to the picture.
→ Use your dictionary if necessary.

1

2

3

4

5

Box 1

taxi	train
underground (train)	
coach	bus

Box 2

station	coach station
bus-stop	taxi-rank
	platform

Check your answers

1 Train/station/platform **2** underground (train)/station/platform **3** bus/bus stop **4** coach/coach station **5** taxi/taxi-rank

Getting around on public transport

→ Read the mini-dialogues and look at the words in the box on page 225.

→ Listen to Recording 5 and complete the dialogues with the correct word(s) from the box.

1

2

3

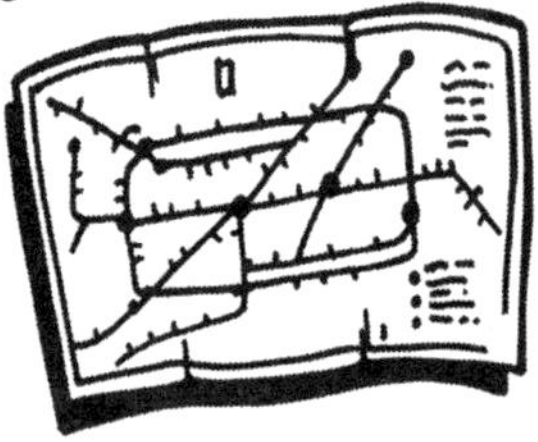

4

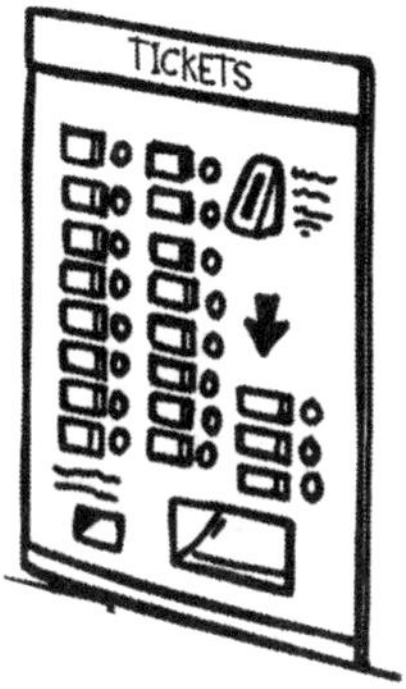

5

Recording 5

1 **A** I don't know the Underground.
Could you give me a _______ please?
B Of course. Here you are.

2 **A** Excuse me, do you know the time of the next train, please?
B I'm not sure. There's a ___________ over there, on the wall.

3 **A** Excuse me, how much is a _____________ to London?
B Is that a _______?
A No, a ________ please. I'm coming back this evening.

4 **A** I want to buy a ticket but the _________/_________ is closed.
B You can get one at the ________ / __________ over there.

5 **A** Which ________ does the train go from, please?
B Number five, right at the end, over there.

6 **A** What's the ________ to the town centre please?
B 70p.

7 **A** Which _______is Victoria in?
B One, I think. It's in the centre, isn't it?

8 **A** Which _______is Heathrow on?
B The blue one, but I don't know the name of it.

9 **A** Are you going to Edinburgh?
B I'd like to but it takes 10 hours.
A That's a long _________

10 **A** Is this a ________train? **B** No, I'm afraid it stops at all stations.

11 **A** Is this a _________ train? **B** No, sorry, change at the next stop.

12 **A** I'm not sure which platform to go to.
B Let's listen to the __________.

13 **A** We're going on an _________ to Cambridge tomorrow.
B Oh, are you? What time does your coach leave?

14 **A** In a taxi. 'The fare is £4.50. How much ______shall I give him?'
B 'If you give him £5.00 that's fine.'

direct	platform	journey	ticket machine	timetable		fare
line	ticket	excursion	fast	announcements	tip	zone
single return	map	ticket office				

Check your answers

1 map **2** timetable **3** ticket, single, return **4** ticket office, ticket machine **5** platform **6** fare **7** zone **8** line **9** journey **10** fast **11** direct **12** announcements **13** excursion **14** tip

Label the pictures

→ Now label the pictures on page 224.

Check your answers

1 fare **2** timetable **3** map **4** ticket machine **5** ticket office

Common mistake

'This is a long travel.' ✗

'This is a long journey.' ✓

Q ***What's the difference between 'travel' and 'journey'?***

A *Journey* is usually a countable noun.
Journey is the time and/or distance from A to B.

For example: 'It's a long journey from England to North America.'

Travel can be **a** a verb **b** an uncountable noun

Travel is general movement.
For example: a 'I travel a lot for my job.'
b 'Foreign travel is good for a person's education.'

Travel or journey?

→ Complete with *journey* or *travel.*

1 It's a long _________ to get here.
2 He's a ________ agent.
3 Foreign ______ helps people understand other cultures.
4 How long does the _________ take?

Check your answers

1 journey **2** travel **3** travel **4** journey

What's the right word?

Trips

→ Choose the correct phrase from the box to complete the sentences below.
→ Use your dictionary if necessary.

change your ticket get on book a ticket go on the excursion find out about times and prices get off cancel the trip

You would like to go on an excursion.

1 First you ______________
2 Then you ______________
3 If something happens and you can't go, you can either **a** ____________ or **b** ___________
4 On the day of the trip you **a** __________ the coach. When you get there you **b** __________the coach and have a good time!

Check your answers

1 First you find out about times and prices. **2** Then you book a ticket. **3** You can either change your ticket or cancel the trip. **4 a** You get on the coach **b** You get off the coach.

Grammar and communication 2

Asking for instructions, giving instructions

Examples from *The Story*:

Asking for instructions

1 The man at the information desk says, 'Can I help you?' Oliver says, 'Yes, could you tell me how to get to the centre of town, please?'

2 The man says 'You can take the A1 Airbus.'
Oliver asks, 'Where do I get the bus from?'

Giving instructions

The man answers, 'You **follow** the sign that says 'Airbus'.'

→ Answer these questions about instructions.
Examples: 'Where do I **get** the bus from?' 'You **follow** the sign…'

Meaning

In the two examples above, *get* and *follow* are
a in the past
b in the present
c in the future.

Form

The tense is
a present simple
b present progressive
c future simple.

Check your answers

Meaning c
Form a

★ We can use the present simple to ask for and give instructions.

Asking for instructions

→ Read the seven questions below.
→ How many are correct?

Direct questions
How do I get to the town centre?
How can I get to the town centre?
How could I get to the town centre?

Indirect questions
Can you tell me how to get to the town centre?
Could you tell me how I get to the town centre?
Do you know how I can get to the town centre?
Do you know how I could get to the town centre?

Check your answers

All the questions are correct.

Q ***What are the differences?***

A All the questions are appropriate in most situations.
The indirect questions are very common.
Could is the most indirect.\

<table>
<tr><td colspan="7">Summary – Instructions</td></tr>
<tr><td colspan="7">1 Asking for instructions</td></tr>
<tr><td colspan="7">Direct questions</td></tr>
<tr><td>How</td><td>do
can
could</td><td colspan="5">I get to the town centre?</td></tr>
<tr><td colspan="7">Indirect questions</td></tr>
<tr><td>Can</td><td rowspan="2">you</td><td>tell
show</td><td>me</td><td rowspan="2">how</td><td rowspan="2">I
I can
I could
to</td><td rowspan="2">get to the town centre?</td></tr>
<tr><td>Could</td><td>explain</td><td>to me</td></tr>
<tr><td colspan="3">Do you know how I</td><td>can
could</td><td colspan="3">get to the town centre?</td></tr>
<tr><td colspan="7">2 Giving instructions – present simple</td></tr>
<tr><td colspan="7">You go… You follow… You take…</td></tr>
<tr><td colspan="7">3 For more than one possibility</td></tr>
<tr><td colspan="7">You can + verb (without ‘to’) + ‘or’ + verb (without ‘to’)
For example: ‘You can walk or go by bus.’</td></tr>
</table>

Asking for instructions

→ Put the words in the right order to complete the question.

1 Excuse me, __________ the station from here, please?
to/how/I/do/get

2 Excuse me, ____________ a ticket for tomorrow?
can/where/I/book

3 Excuse me, ____________________________ excursions to Oxford?
out/I/how/find/about/could

4 Can you show me __________ a ticket from this machine, please?
to/how/buy

5 Could you tell me __________ the coach station, please?
to/get/I/how

6 Do you know ____________ this door, please?
how/open/can/I

7 Do you know ______________________ my return ticket, please?
change/I/could/how

Check your answers

1 how do I get to **2** where can I book **3** how could I find out about **4** how to buy **5** how I get to **6** how I can open **7** how I could change

Giving instructions

Example from *The Story*:

Oliver asks: 'Where do I go to get the bus?'
The man says: 'You follow the sign that says 'Airbus'.'

★ To give **instructions**, use the **present simple**.

Situation You want to make a trip from London to Paris on the Eurostar train. You ask a friend for instructions.

→ Complete your friend's instructions with the correct verb phrases from the box below.
→ It's not necessary to understand all the words. Just try to get the general idea.

She's going down the escalator.

He's going up the escalator.

He's going through the door.

When you get to Waterloo, ____________(1) the signs to 'Eurostar'. ↘__________(2) the escalator and ________(3) your ticket from the ticket office. Then ______________(4) ticket check and security control. After that __________(5) in the departure lounge. When you hear the announcement to board the train ↗__________(6) the right escalator or travelator for your part of the Eurostar platform and ____________(7) the train, ________(8) your luggage in the special luggage racks and __________(9) your seat. If you need refreshments during the journey – tea, coffee, something to eat, _______(10) the buffet car.

you go to	you put	you go up	you wait	you go down
you look for	you get on	you go through	you follow	
you collect				

☑ Check your answers

1 you follow **2** you go down **3** you collect **4** you go through **5** you wait **6** you go up **7** you get on **8** you put **9** you look for **10** you go to

Asking for help

→ Correct these questions if necessary. Some of the verbs are wrong.

1 Where I sign? ______________________

2 Can you tell me what do I write in this card?____________________

3 Where pay I, please? ______________________

4 Can you tell me where I go now, please? ____________________

5 How do I get a taxi? _____________________

6 How I open this door? ______________________

7 Do I write this in English or my language?_____________________

8 I give a tip or not? _____________________

☑ Check your answers

1 Where do I sign? **2** Can you tell me what to write/what I write in this card? **3** Where do I pay, please? **4** correct – Can you tell me where I go now, please? **5** correct – How do I get a taxi? **6** How do I open this door? **7** correct – Do I write this in English or my language? **8** Do I give a tip or not?

→ Now match the questions (**1–8**) above with the possible answers (**a–h**) below.

a If you could just wait over there, please sir.

b At the bottom, just here.

c At the cash desk over there please.

d Yes, people usually give about 10%.

e 'Happy Birthday' is fine.

f I can call one for you, madam.

g They open automatically when the train stops.

h Either, it doesn't matter.

☑ Check your answers

1 b **2** e **3** c **4** a **5** f **6** g **7** h **8** d

British culture – an invitation to dinner
I don't know what to say – I don't know what to do

Situation Your English colleague invites you to his house for dinner.
You don't know about British customs and habits.
You ask a friend to help you.

→ Look at the questions below and then the answers.
→ Write the correct question with the answer.

a What do I say if she offers me more food and I don't want it?
b What do I do if they speak very fast and I don't understand?
c Do I shake hands when I arrive?
d Do I take a present? And if so, what sort of present do I take?
e I don't know his wife's name? What do I call her? Do I call her 'madam'?
f What do I say if I want to use the bathroom?
g What do I say when I want to leave?
h The invitation is for seven o'clock. What time do I arrive?
i What do I wear?
j Do I do anything the next day?
k What do I do and say when I leave?
l What time do I leave?

Example:

1 **You** *What do I wear?*
Your friend Informal clothes are fine.

2 **You** ______________________________?
Your friend A box of chocolates or flowers is the most common type of present. Lots of visitors like to give a little present from their country. That's fine too.

3 **You** ______________________________?
Your friend Punctuality's quite important here so it's best to get there within about 10 minutes of the time, but not before the time.

4 **You** ______________________________?
Your friend Yes, the usual thing is to shake hands and say 'Pleased to meet you' or 'How do you do?' when you meet his wife. *How do you do* is more formal than *Pleased to meet you.*

5 **You** __________________________?
Your friend No, we only use that word in shops and places like that. If you call her 'Mrs. Parker' to start with, she'll tell you her first name, I'm sure.

6 **You** ____________________________?
Your friend You just ask them to speak more slowly.

7 **You** ______________________

Your friend You say, 'No thanks. I'm fine.'

8 **You** ______________________?
Your friend You just say, 'Is it alright if I use the toilet?'

9 **You** __________________________?
Your friend You can say, 'It's getting late. I'd better go now.'

10 **You** ____________________________?
Your friend Between ten and eleven o'clock is normal.

11 **You** ____________________________?
Your friend You shake hands again and say, 'Thank you for inviting me – it was a lovely evening.'

12 **You** ____________________________?
Your friend You can say 'thank you' again to your colleague at work if you like but it's not necessary to write a letter. Some people write a short note or card. This is a formal thank you.

✓ Check your answers

1 i **2** d **3** h **4** c **5** e **6** b **7** a **8** f **9** g **10** l **11** k **12** j

→ Answer these questions about the meaning and form of the verbs in questions **a–l** on page 233.

Meaning

In the exercise, the dinner is
a in the past
b in the present
c in the future.

Form

The tense in the questions is
a present simple
b present progressive
c future simple

Check your answers

Meaning c. Form a

★ We use the **present simple** to ask for and give instructions/help with systems. In the exercise above you are asking for help with the cultural systems, in other words, the habits and customs.

Q ***What's the difference between, for example, 'What shall I wear?'*** (Topic 7) ***and 'What do I wear?'?***

A *What shall I* (+ verb)…? asks for a suggestion.
What do I (+ verb)….? asks for help with a system. In other words, 'What is the right thing to do/say/wear, etc., in this situation?'

About your country: Invitations

→ Read the questions below.
→ Either write your answers or prepare to tell a friend.

Situation A colleague invites me to dinner.
Answer my questions about customs and habits in your country.

1 In England it's common to invite someone to the house. Which is more common in your country, an invitation to the house or to a restaurant?

____

2 What do I wear?

____

3 Do I take a present? If so, what sort of present do I take?

---

4 The invitation is for seven. Is that a usual time here for a dinner invitation? What time do I arrive?

---

5 What do I do when I arrive? Do I shake hands with him, with his wife?

---

6 I don't know his wife's name. What do I call her?

---

7 What time do I leave?

---

8 Do I do or say anything the next day?

Our story continues... Oliver is walking towards the A1 Airbus. A man talks to him

Understanding the important information

→ Cover the text of Recording 6 on page 237.
→ Read the question below.
→ Listen and choose the correct answer.

What's the time? **a** 8.00
b 7.55
c 7.52
d 5.28

Recording 6 – The Story

Man	Excuse me, can you tell me the time, please?
Oliver	Yes, it's five to eight.
Man	Many thanks.

Check your answer

b

What do they say?

The time

→ Cover the text of Recording 6 again.
→ Read the questions below.
→ Listen and complete the words.

1 The man asks Oliver the time. He says,
'Excuse me, c _ _ / y _ _ / t _ _ _ / m _ / t _ _ / t _ _ _ /, please?'
2 Oliver answers,
'Yes, i _ ' _ / f _ _ _ / t _ / e _ _ _ t.'
3 The man thanks Oliver. He says 'M _ _ _ / t _ _ _ _ _ .'

Check your answers

1 Excuse me, can you tell me the time, please? **2** Yes, it's five to eight. **3** Many thanks.

Grammar and communication 3

Asking for and understanding travel information

Saying the time

→ Read **1–6** on page 238 and draw the hands on these watches.

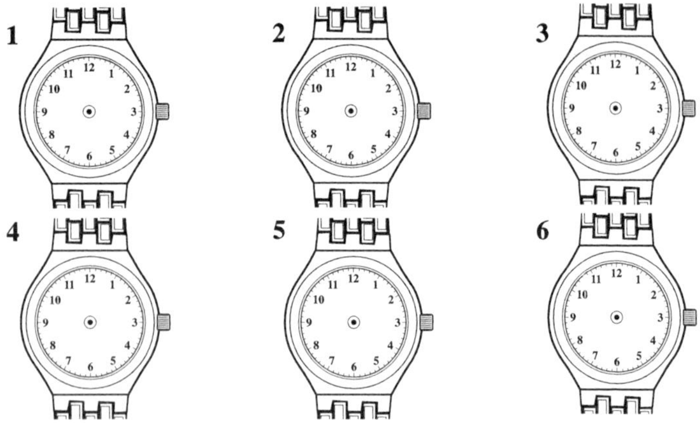

1 Eleven o'clock
2 Half past three
3 A quarter past four
4 A quarter to six
5 Ten to nine
6 Twenty-five past ten

Check your answers

1 11:00 **2** 3:30 **3** 4:15 **4** 5:45 **5** 8:50 **6** 10:25

Timetables

★ There are two ways to say the time. The exercise above is the usual way in spoken English.

★ When we want to be very specific, for example, for a timetable:
- we use the twenty-four hour clock
- we say the exact number of minutes past the hour, even if it's more than 30. For example, '8.43' is 'eight forty-three' and '11.56' is 'eleven fifty-six'.
- We say 'O' like the name of the letter for timetables.

Timetables

Can you give me times of the trains to …, please?

→ Cover the text of Recording 7.
→ Listen and write down the times you hear.

Times of the trains to go	**To come back**
1 ______________	1 ______________
2 ______________	2 ______________
3 ______________	3 ______________
4 ______________	4 ______________

Check your answers

To go	**To come back**
1 6.22 (six twenty-two)	**1** 13.05 (thirteen '0' five)
2 7.49 (seven forty-nine)	**2** 14.50 (fourteen-fifty)
3 8.13(eight thirteen)	**3** 15.32 (fifteen thirty-two)
4 9.56 (nine fifty-six)	**4** 16.09 (sixteen '0' nine)

Recording 7

The first train in the morning leaves at 6.22, then there's another at 7.49, one at 8.13, and another at 9.56. To come back you can leave at 13.05, or 14.50, or there are later trains at 15.32 and 16.09.

Frequency – how often do the trains go?

→ Read the expressions in the boxes below.
→ Read the timetables on page 240.
→ Match each timetable (**a,b,c**) with one phrase from **Box 1** (**1,2,3**) and one phrase from **Box 2** (**A,B,C**).
→ Write the number and letter in the boxes after the timetables.

Box 1

1 four times an hour

2 twice an hour

3 every hour

Box 2

A on the hour

B at five past, twenty past, twenty-five to and ten to the hour

C at a quarter past and a quarter to the hour

The timetables

a	6.00, 7.00, 8.00, 9.00, 10.00, 11.00, 12.00	☐	☐
b	6.15, 6.45, 7.15, 7.45, 8.15, 8.45, 9.15, 9.45	☐	☐
c	6.05, 6.20, 6.35, 6.50, 7.05, 7.20, 7.35, 7.50	☐	☐

Check your answers

a 3 A Every hour on the hour. **b 2 C** Twice an hour, at a quarter past and quarter to each hour. **c 1 B** Four times an hour, at five past, twenty past, twenty-five to and ten to the hour.

How long from now?

Example from *The Story*: Oliver asks, 'When does the bus leave?'
The employee answers 'In ten minutes'(time) at 8.05.'

In ten minutes' time

→ Make four mini-dialogues. Match the questions (**1–4**) with the correct response (**a–d**).

1 When's the next train?

2 When's my Mummy coming?

3 When do they get to Australia?

4 When are you going back to your country?

a In a week('s time). They're in Hong Kong at the moment.

b In two minutes('time). Come on, let's run!

c In 6 months('time), at the end of my course.

d In a few minutes('time). She's on her way.

Check your answers

1 b **2** d **3** a **4** c

How long?

Example from *The Story*:

Oliver wants to know the time the journey takes. He asks, 'How long does **it take** to get there?'

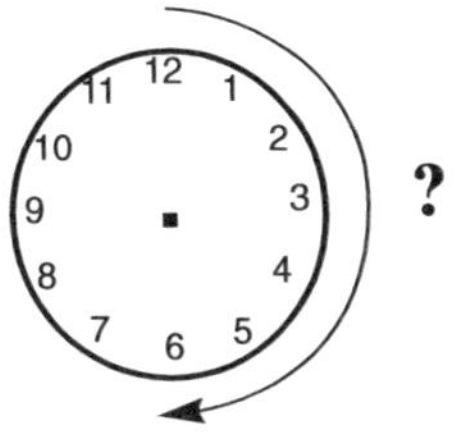

★ To talk about length of time for an activity we use the verb *take*.

★ *It takes* (impersonal subject *it* + verb *take*) + verb with *to*.

→ Complete these mini-dialogues (**1–4**) with (**a–d**).

1 How long does it take to get there?

2 Does it take a long time to do that?

3 It doesn't take long to walk there.

4 It takes my daughter a long time to get ready in the mornings.

a No, only a few minutes. It's easy.

b I know. Mine's the same.

c About 10 minutes. It's not far.

d No, it's very near.

Check your answers

1 c **2** a **3** d **4** b

★ To talk about a specific person with the expression *it takes*, we say *it takes* + person + verb with *to*.

For example:

It takes	my daughter	a long time	to get ready.
Or with the pronouns *me, you, him, her, us, them*			
It takes	her	a long time	to get ready.

How long does it take you?

→ Tell me some things about you.

How long does it take you to have breakfast? ____________

How long does it take you to get ready in the morning?____________

Does it take you a long time to get to work/school? Is it far?____________

How long does it take your best friend to get to your house from his/her house? ____________

How long does it take you to get to the nearest supermarket from your house? ____________

Possible answers

You can write short phrases – for example, 'Ten minutes.'
Or 'It takes me/him/her about (10) minutes.'

Does it take you long?

→ Write questions for these answers.

1 ________________________?
I don't eat much in the mornings, really – about 10 minutes, I suppose.

2 ________________________?
No time at all – I work from home

3 ________________________?
I can walk there in about 5 minutes – I go shopping there most days.

4 ________________________?
School starts at 8.45 and they leave at 8.15 so it's about a half-hour walk.

☑ Check your answers

1 How long does it take you to have breakfast? **2** How long does it take you to get to work? **3** How long does it take you to get to the nearest supermarket? **4** How long does it take the children to walk to school?

Asking and giving the time

→ Look at the clocks below.
→ Cover the text of Recording 8.
→ Listen to the six mini-dialogues asking and giving the time.
→ Write numbers **1–6** below the correct clock(s).

	a	**b**	**c**
	12.58	13.00	13.04
Example:	1 ________	________	________

Recording 8

1	**A**	Dad, what's the time?
	B	It's a few minutes to one.
2	**A**	Excuse me, could you tell me the time, please?
	B	Of course. Er, actually, it's exactly one o'clock.
3	**A**	John, have you got the time?
	B	Yeah, it's just before one.
4	**A**	Could you tell me what the time is, please?
	B	Yes, it's just after one.
5	**A**	Excuse me, can you tell me what time it is, please?
	B	Sorry, I haven't got a watch but I think it's around one.
6	**A**	Do you know what the time is, Sharon?
	B	Let me see, it's almost one.

Check your answers

a 1, 3, 5, 6. **b** 2, 5. **c** 4, 5.

Asking the time

On Recording 8 there are five different expressions for asking the time.

→Cover the text of Recording 8.
→Listen again and, this time, complete the questions below.

1 Dad, /_____'_/____ time?

2 Excuse me,/ c_____/_____/____/____/___/time, please?

3 John, / _______ /____ /_____/______ time?

4 Could/_____/____/____/what/_____/_____/____, please?

5 Excuse me, /____/____/_____/____/____/ time/ ____/___, please?

6 ____/ you/____/_____/the time/______, Sharon?

Check your answers

1 Dad, what's the time? **2** Excuse me, could you tell me the time, please? **3** John, have you got the time? **4** Could you tell me what the time is, please? **5** Excuse me, can you tell me what time it is, please? **6** Do you know what the time is?

There are lots of ways of asking this simple question in English. Look at the summary below.

<table>
<tr><th colspan="4">Summary – Asking the time</th></tr>
<tr><td>What's
Have you got
Do you know</td><td></td><td>the time (please)?</td><td></td></tr>
<tr><td rowspan="3">Could you
Can you</td><td>tell me</td><td>the time (please)?</td><td></td></tr>
<tr><td rowspan="2">tell me what</td><td>the time</td><td>is (please)?</td></tr>
<tr><td>time</td><td>it is (please)?</td></tr>
<tr><td rowspan="2">Do you know</td><td rowspan="2">what</td><td>the time</td><td>is (please)?</td></tr>
<tr><td>time</td><td>it is (please)?</td></tr>
</table>

★ All the questions are correct and appropriate and common in most situations.

★ The questions in the first group are the most direct.

★ 'Could you tell me
'Do you know } *what time it is?*' can be formal.

Timetables and Itineraries

Situation You are in London. You want to go to Cambridge for the day. You want to leave London between 9.00 and 10.00 a.m. You phone National Rail Enquiries for some information.

→ Cover the text of Recording 9 on page 245.

→ Look at the timetable below.

→ Listen and complete the timetable.

London King's Cross d	08:24	08:45				10:00	10:25
Cambridge a	09:28	09:42				11:09	11:16

d – Departure time **a** – Arrival time

Recording 9

Information officer	National Rail Enquiries – Can I help you?
You	Yes, I'd like some information about the times of trains from London to Cambridge please.
Information officer	Which day are you thinking of travelling?
You	It's for tomorrow.
Information officer	And what time of day would you like to travel?
You	We'd like to leave London between nine and ten in the morning.
***Information officer**	Right. There's one that **leaves** at exactly nine o'clock.
You	What time **does** that get to Cambridge?
Information Officer	The nine o'clock **gets** in at twelve minutes past ten. Then there's the nine twenty-four, which **arrives** at ten sixteen, and also a nine fifty-four, which **gets** to Cambridge at ten forty-six.
You	Let me just repeat that to make sure I've got it right. There are three trains. The nine o'clock **arrives** at twelve minutes past ten, the nine twenty-four gets there at sixteen minutes past ten and the nine fifty-four **arrives** in Cambridge at ten forty-six.*
Information Officer	That's correct.
You	Thank you very much.
Both	Goodbye.

Check your answers

London King's Cross d	08:24	08:45	**09:00**	**09:24**	**09:54**	10:00	10:25
Cambridge a	09:28	09:42	**10:12**	**10:16**	**10:46**	11:09	11:16

→ Verb *get*

In the exercise above *get* means **a** take **b** arrive

Check your answer

b

→ Answer these questions about meaning and form of the **verbs** in **bold** (* to *) in the text of Recording 9 on page 245.

Meaning

In the exercise above the journey to Cambridge is **a** in the past
b in the present
c in the future.

Form

The tense of the verbs is **a** Present Simple
b Present Progressive
c Future Simple

Check your answers

Meaning c. Form a

Q ***Tomorrow is in the future? Why are these verbs in the present simple?***

A Because we are talking about a **timetable**.

★ When we talk about organised future activities and they are part of a timetable or like a timetable, we use the **present simple**.

→ Let's look at another example.

Situation Monica is going on a business trip to Scotland next week. Her secretary, Angie, is telling her the itinerary.

Angie **You leave** on the 10.30 flight on Monday and **you arrive** in Edinburgh at 11.10. **You have** a lunch meeting with Mr Jones at 12.30 and then at 3.30 **you take** the train to Glasgow.

All these verbs are in the **present simple** because they are Monica's itinerary or schedule.

→ Now look at the next part of the conversation.

Monica Where **am I staying** in Glasgow?
Angie I've got you a room at the King's Hotel. **You're staying** there for two nights.

Q ***Why are these verbs in the present progressive?***

A These are personal future arrangements (see Topic 5).

Summary
To talk about fixed future events we use: **a** Present progressive if it's a personal arrangement. **b** Present simple if it's a timetable or like a timetable.

★ Sometimes both the present simple and present progressive are correct. The focus is a little different.

For example: '**I go** home next week' – more factual, more focus on the itinerary.
'**I'm going** next week' – more personal.

Q ***In this situation, can I also say, for example, 'I will go home next week'? (future simple)***

A No, not in this situation. ☹

★ 'I will go home' is grammatically correct.
★ It has a different meaning.

→ Answer these questions about 'I'm going home next week' and 'I go home next week.'

1 In both sentences, the decision is
a in the past?
b in the present?
c in the future ?

2 Actions to organise the trip home are
a in the past?
b in the present?
c in the future?

☑ Check your answers

1 a in the past. **2 a** in the past. For example, you've got your ticket.

'I'll go home next week' is only correct at the moment of making the decision. For example,

Itineraries – present simple

Situation Simon is at a travel agent's, collecting his tickets for a short trip to Italy. The assistant talks about his itinerary.

→ Write the verbs in the correct tense.

Travel agent Here are the tickets for your trip to Italy. You (fly)______(1) to Naples with Alitalia on the 12th of next month. The flight (leave) ______ (2) Heathrow at 10.15. When you get to Naples a coach (pick you up) _______(3) from the airport and they (drive)________ (4) you direct to your hotel. The next morning the coach (take)________(5) you on an excursion to the ruins of Pompeii. In the afternoon you (get) ______ (6) the Eurostar train to Rome.

Simon What (happen) ________ (7) when we arrive in Rome? How (get) __________(8) to the hotel?

Travel agent A bilingual guide (meet) _______ (9) the train and (take) ________(10) you on a city tour. They (show)________(11) you all the important sights such as the Coliseum and the Vatican and then the coach (leave)_________(12) you at your hotel. On the Sunday you (be)__________(13) free in Rome and you (come) _________(14) back to London on the evening flight.

Simon What time (get)_________ (15) back?

Travel Agent I think it's twenty-past nine. Just let me check – yes, nine twenty-five.

Simon That all sounds wonderful. I'm looking forward to it.

Check your answers

1 fly **2** leaves **3** picks you up **4** drive **5** takes **6** get **7** happens **8** do we get? **9** meets **10** takes **11** show **12** leaves **13** are **14** come **15** do we get?

All these verbs are in the present simple because it is an itinerary.

Q ***In the mini-dialogue below, are the verbs in 'B' in the present simple?***

A Can you tell me how I get to Waterloo, please?
B Go to Oxford Street and take the Bakerloo Line.

A No. These verbs are in the **imperative** (verb without *to*).

★ People who work in transport often use the imperative to give instructions.
★ Here the imperative is impersonal and short.
(For more information and practice on the imperative, see Topic 9.)

Summary of travel questions

There are a lot of different questions in this topic. How many can you use now?

→ Read the questions below.
→ Write the correct questions for the answers on page 250.

Example: You ***How can I get to Windsor?*** **(j)**
'Take the train at Platform 5 and change at Egham.'

a Could you tell me how to get to London from here, please?
b How often do the trains run to Waterloo?
c When's the next coach to Glasgow, please?
d How long does it take to get to Cambridge from London?
e Is this the right train for Birmingham?
f Which platform is it for Brighton, please?
g I want to go to Cardiff. Where do I change?
h Do you know if this train stops in Reading?
i How much is a single to Hull, please?
j How can I get to Windsor?

1 **You** *Excuse me, how can I get to Windsor?*
Take the train at Platform 5 and change at Egham.

2 **You** ________________________________?
No, this is a non-stop to Paddington.

3 **You** ________________________________?
Number 7, sir.

4 **You** ________________________________?
£22.

5 **You** ____________________________?
Every half an hour – at ten to and twenty past the hour.

6 **You** ____________________________?
No, this is the Liverpool train.

7 **You** ____________________________?
It's not necessary, this bus goes all the way there.

8 **You** ____________________________?
In ten minutes at half past.

9 **You** __________________________?
Yes, take the next train from Platform 10.

10 **You** _________________________?
On a fast train? – just under an hour.

Check your answers

1 j **2** h **3** f **4** i **5** b **6** e **7** g **8** c **9** a **10** d

Asking for information – transport

→ Listen to Recording 10 and ask the questions from the exercise above in the spaces.

Recording 10

1	**You**	Excuse me, how can I get to Windsor?
		Take the train at Platform 5 and change at Egham.
2	**You**	Do you know if this train stops at Reading?
		No, this is a non-stop to Paddington.
3	**You**	Which platform is it for Brighton, please?
		Number 7, sir.

4 **You** How much is a single to Hull, please?
£22.
5 **You** How often do the trains run to Waterloo?
Every half an hour – at ten to and twenty past the hour.
6 **You** Is this the right train for Birmingham?
No, this is the Liverpool train.
7 **You** I want to go to Cardiff. Where do I change?
It's not necessary, this bus goes all the way there.
8 **You** When's the next coach to Glasgow, please?
In ten minutes, at half past.
9 **You** Could you tell me how to get to London from here, please?
Yes, take the next train from Platform 10.
10 **You** How long does it take to get to Cambridge from London?
On a fast train? – just under an hour.

About your country: public transport

→ Write answers to these questions or prepare to tell a friend.

1 How do you go to work and/or the shops?

____

2 How do people travel long distances without a car?

____

3 What are the names of the big train and bus companies in your country?

____

4 Is public transport cheap or expensive?

____

5 Is there an underground in your town or capital?

____

6 On the buses does the fare depend on distance?

____

7 **a** When do you pay if you want to travel by bus?
b Can you buy a return ticket?
c If you need to take two buses, can you use one ticket?

____

____

What would you say?

1 You are a tourist in London. You are at a station. Someone asks you, 'Excuse me can you tell me how to get to Wimbledon, please?'

____

2 It's late at night. You want to get a train ticket from the machine – the ticket office is closed. You've only got a £20 note. The machine takes only coins and £5 and £10 notes.

____

Possible answers

1 I'm sorry but I'm not from here. **2** Excuse me, have got change for a £20 note, please? I need to buy a ticket from the machine.

Revision

How do you say it in your language?

→ Here are some examples of the important points in this topic.
→ Translate the sentences below into your language in the spaces.
→ Remember – translate the idea, not the words.

1 a Excuse me, can you tell me how to get to the centre of town, please?

____

b Yes, you can go by bus, by train or by taxi.

____

2 Which part of the town are you going to?

____

3 a Where do I pay? **b** Over there, please, at the cash desk.

____

4 Where do I go to get a ticket?

____

5 Who are you talking to?

____

6 Which excursions would you like to go on?

____

7 You get a ticket before you get on the bus.

____

8 **a** Excuse me, have you got the time, please?

____

b Yes, it's just after ten.

____

9 **a** How often do the buses go to the station?

____

10 How long does it take to get to the centre?

____

11 Take the train at platform 6 and change at the next stop.

____

Join the conversation

→ Look at Recording 1 (page 213) again.
→ Listen to Recording 11.
→ Read **Oliver's** words in the spaces.

TEST 8

Which one is right?

→ Choose **a** or **b**.

1 I go to work **a** with / **b** by **car**.

2 The bus **a** leaves / **b** is leaving every hour.

3 **a** Do you know what is the time?
b Do you know what the time is?

4 **a** How long does it take to get to the park?
b How long takes it for go to the park?

5 **A** **a** How often go the trains to London?
b How often do the trains go to London?
B **a** Three times in an hour.
b Three times an hour.

6 **a** How much is it for go and come back?
b How much is a return ticket?

7 **a** What do I do now?
b What I do now?

8 **a** Take that train and change at Broad Street.
b You will take that train and then you are changing at Broad Street.

9 **a** West Road, 24.
b 24, West Road.

10 My English friend has got a new baby.
a What am I writing in this card?
b What do I write in this card?

Write a dialogue

Situation You are at the ticket office at Waterloo Station.
You want two tickets to Hampton Court, a famous palace near London.

1 **Travel clerk**

Next, please. Can I help you?

You

2

3 Single or return?

4 You want returns

5 That's £9.80, please

6 Time of next train?

7 In 10 minutes, at twenty to eleven

8 Return times – how often?

9 From Hampton Court to Waterloo, there are two trains an hour, at ten past and twenty to the hour.

10 Travelling time?

11 About half an hour

12 *Thank you*

13 You are near the platform. You want to know which platform to go to.

14 You are on the train. You want to check this is the right train.

Check your answers

1 b 2 a **3** b **4** a **5 A** b **B** b **6** b **7** a **8** a **9** b **10** b

Dialogue: model answers

2	**You**	Two tickets to Hampton Court, please.
3	**Clerk**	Single or return?
4	**You**	Return, please.
5	**Clerk**	That's nine pounds eighty please.
6	**You**	When's the next train? OR At what time does the next train leave?
7	**Clerk**	In 10 minutes, at twenty to eleven.
8	**You**	And to come back, how often do the trains run?

9 **Clerk** There are two trains an hour, at ten past and twenty to the hour.

10 **You** How long does the journey take?

11 **Clerk** About half an hour.

12 **You** Thank you.

13 **You** Excuse me. Which platform is it for Hampton Court, please?

14 **You** Excuse me. Is this the right train for Hampton Court, please?

OR

Excuse me. Does this train go to Hampton Court, please?

9 MEETING FRIENDS

Grammar and communication
- Impersonal *it*
- Asking for opinions – *how was?*
- Adjectives + *-ed* or *-ing*
- Saying *Thank you*
- Obligation and necessity – *have to*
- The imperative
- Offering, rejecting, insisting, accepting
- Introducing something negative politely

Vocabulary
- Public signs
- Large numbers

Pronunciation
- Intonation
  – expressing strong feelings

Tasha leaves customs. Who's there to meet her? What happens next?

Understanding the important information

→ Cover the text of Recording 1, *The Story*.
→ Read the sentences below. Only one is correct.
→ Listen to the recording and choose the correct answer.

a Tasha gets the bus with Oliver.
b Tasha's friend, Helen, is at the airport to meet her.
c Helen is at the airport with her husband and children.
d Tasha goes to Helen's house by taxi.

Recording 1 – The Story

Helen Tasha, Hi, how are you? It's lovely to see you again!
Tasha Hello, Helen! It's great to see you too. How are things?
Helen I'm fine. We're all fine. How was your flight?
Tasha It was alright – 13 hours is a bit long and tiring, but I'm here now. Thanks for picking me up, by the way.
Helen That's O.K. We're glad you could come. The car's in the car park, this way. David and the children are at home, waiting for you.

Now check your answer

b

Understanding more

→ Cover the text of Recording 1 again.
→ Read the sentences below.
→ Listen and answer *True/False/We don't know*.

1	Tasha's flight was terrible.	True/False/We don't know
2	David is at home with the children.	True/False/We don't know
3	Tasha knows David and the children.	True/False/We don't know
4	Helen meets Oliver.	True/False/We don't know
5	Tasha tells Helen about Oliver.	True/False/We don't know
6	Helen can't drive.	True/False/We don't know

Check your answers

1 False **2** True **3** We don't know **4** False **5** False **6** False

What do they say?

→ Cover the text of Recording 1 again.
→ Read the sentences below.
→ Listen and try to complete the words.
→ Then read the text of the recording if necessary.

1 Helen says, 'Hello' but Tasha says 'H _ !'

2 a Helen is happy to see Tasha.
She says, ' I _ ' _ / l _ _ _ _ y / t _ / s _ _ you again.'

b Tasha is happy to see Helen.
She says, ' _ t' s / g _ _ _ t / _ _ / _ _ _ / you / t _ _.'

3 Helen asks, 'How are you?' but Tasha asks 'H _ _ / a _ _ / t _ _ _ _ s?'

4 a Helen asks Tasha about her journey.
She says, 'H _ _ / w _ _ / y _ _ r / flight?'

b Tasha responds, ' I _ / w _ _ / a _ _ _ _ _ t.'

c Tasha talks about the flight.
She says ' 13 hours is a b_ _ / l _ _ _ / and /t_ _ _ _ _ but I'm here now.'

5 a Tasha is happy Helen is at the airport to meet her. During the conversation Tasha decides to thank her friend.
She says: 'Thanks / f _ _ / p _ _ _ _ _ g / m _ / u _ , b_ / t _ _ / w _ _ .'

b When Tasha says, 'Thanks', Helen responds,
' T _ _ _'_ O.K. W_'_ _ / g _ _ _ / you / c _ _ _ d / c _ _ e.'

Check your answers

1 Hi. (informal) **2 a** It's lovely to see you again. **b** It's great to see you too. **3** How are things ('things' is informal) **4 a** How was your flight? **b** It was alright. **c** 13 hours is a bit long and tiring but I'm here now. **5 a** Thanks for picking me up **b** That's O.K. We're glad you could come.

! Common mistake – impersonal *it*

Example from *The Story*:
Helen is happy to see Tasha again.
She says, '**It's** lovely to see you again.'
Tasha says, '**It's** great to see you too.'

(Not: ~~Is lovely~~ to see you again.
OR ~~Is great~~ to see you too.)

Q ***Why do we say 'it' here?***

A All verbs need a subject in English (except imperatives).

'*It*' is the impersonal subject.

Q ***What's the negative? Can I say, 'It's nice <u>to not work</u> at the weekend?'*** ☹

A No – *not* is before *to*. '*It's nice* **not to** *work at the weekend.*'

Grammar summary – impersonal *it*

Impersonal subject	Verb *be*	Adjective	Verb + *to/not to*
It	is 's	lovely frustrating	to see you again not to understand

→ Complete the sentences on page 261 with
- one adjective from **Box 1** and
- one verb from **Box 2**.

→ Use your dictionary if necessary.

Box 1

difficult wonderful
expensive frustrating
useful hard correct ~~cheap~~
interesting tiring boring
kind important

Box 2

go know say work eat
understand arrive ~~travel~~
get invite see visit

Example:

It doesn't cost much – in fact it's quite ***cheap*** to ***travel*** by coach.

1 It's too____________ to ________ by plane. Let's go by train.

2 A Is it __________to _______'Where are you live?' or 'Where do you live?'

B 'Where do you live.'

3 At first it's ____________ to ___________a foreign language because people speak fast.

4 For some people it's very __________ to _______ museums – they really enjoy it.
For others it's the opposite. They find it really ___________

5 I've got an invitation to stay with my friend abroad. It's very _______ of him to ____________ me.

6 When you travel abroad, it's always __________ to ___________ a few words of the language.

7 It's __________not to ________ late for an exam.

8 It's __________ to _________ long hours.

9 It's ___________ to see old friends after a long time.

10 Every time I try to telephone him there's no reply It's really __________ not to ________ an answer.

11 If you are on a diet, it's ___________ not to ________sweet things!

Check your answers

1 expensive to go. **2** correct to ask. **3** difficult/hard to understand. **4** interesting to visit/boring. **5** kind of him to invite. **6** useful to know. **7** important not to arrive. **8** tiring to work. **9** wonderful to see. **10** frustrating not to get. **11** difficult/hard not to eat.

It's + adjective + verb with *to/not to*

→ Write these words in the correct order.

1 ______________________________

to/again/nice/talk/it's/you/to

2 ______________________________

better/not/it's/go/to

3 ______________________________

with/contact/easy/to/it's/people/e-mail

4 ______________________________

for/wait/it's/someone/time/for/long/boring/to/a

5 ______________________________

country/to/exciting/it's/visit/a/foreign

6 ______________________________

normal/language/understand/not/it's/in/foreign/to/everything/a

Check your answers

1 It's nice to talk to you again. **2** It's better not to go. **3** It's easy to contact people with e-mail. **4** It's boring to wait for someone for a long time **5** It's exciting to visit a foreign country. **6** It's normal not to understand everything in a foreign language.

Grammar and communication 1

Asking for opinions – *how was...?*

Example from *The Story*:
Helen asks Tasha about her journey.
She says: '**How was** your flight?'
Tasha answers: 'It was alright'.

→ Answer these questions about *How was...?*

Meaning

1 Is the flight **a** in the present?
b in the future?
c in the past?

2 In 'How was your flight?' Helen is asking,
 a for a long description of the flight or
 b if the flight was O.K. or not for Tasha.

Form

Was is the past of **a** verb *be*
b verb *do*?

Check your answers

Meaning: 1 c 2 b
Form: a

Grammar summary – Past of *be*	
Affirmative	
I He/she/it } was	You We They } were
Negative	
I He/she/it } wasn't	You We They } weren't
Affirmative	
Was { I he/she/it?	Were { you? we? they

→ Complete these mini-dialogues with *was* or *were* + *not* where necessary.

1 A How ______ your holiday?
 B The hotel ____ bad but the food ______ terrible.

2 A ______ your parents alright last night?
 B My mother _________ fine but my father _______ very well at all, actually.

3 **A** ________ that film boring!
B Yes, it ________ very good at all, ______ it?

4 **A** [On Monday morning] How ______ your weekend?
B Really relaxing and quiet thanks. And yours?
A It _____ nice, very nice.

5 **A** Why ________ you at school yesterday, David?
B I ________ ill, Miss.

6 **A** How many people _______ at the party?
B About 20, I suppose.

7 Nobody _______ at home – the answer-machine _______ on.

Check your answers

1 A was **B** wasn't, was **2 A** were **B** was, wasn't **3 A** wasn't **B** wasn't, was it? **4 A** was **A** was **5 A** weren't **B** was *Children call their teachers *Miss* or *Sir*. **6 A** were **7** was, was

How do you pronounce it?

Was

The vowel 'a' in *was* has two pronunciations.

– weak / ə / when *was* is with an adjective or noun
– strong / ɒ / when *was* is the important word.

For example: '*Was* your flight O.K.?' – weak / ə /.
'Yes, it *was*, thanks.' – strong / ɒ /.

The pronunciation of the 'a' in strong *was* / ɒ / and *wasn't* is the same.

→ Look at the text of Recording 2, with the stress.
→ What is the pronounciation of *was* in each one?
→ Choose 'strong' or 'weak'.

Recording 2

1	How was your **day**?	strong/weak
2	Your **party** – how **was** it?	strong/weak
3	It was fan**tas**tic, thanks.	strong/weak
4	Was your hotel **com**fortable?	strong/weak
5	Yes it **was**, thanks.	strong/weak

Check your answers

1 weak **2** strong **3** weak **4** weak **5** strong

→Now listen to Recording 2 and repeat the sentences.

Intonation – big falls to express strong feelings

In Topic 4 we practise intonation to sound positive. In this topic we practise intonation to express strong feelings.

Examples from *The Story*:
Helen is happy to see Tasha.
She says, 'It's lovely to see you again.'

Tasha responds, 'It's great to see you, too.'

Remember, with flat intonation you express that actually you are not very happy to see the person.

To express strong feelings, the voice moves a lot on the syllable with stress.

→Read the sentences below.
→On Recording 3 you will hear each sentence twice.
→Which expresses stronger feelings, **a** or **b**?

Recording 3

1	It's **won**derful to see you again.	**a** or **b**
2	It's **great** to hear from you.	**a** or **b**
3	I think it's a good i**dea**.	**a** or **b**
4	It's so **kind** of you to invite me.	**a** or **b**
5	I don't know **what** to do.	**a** or **b**
6	But I **can't**!	**a** or **b**
7	I'm so **sor**ry!	**a** or **b**
8	Happy **Birth**day!	**a** or **b**

Check your answers

1 a **2** a **3** b **4** a **5** b **6** b **7** a **8** b

→ Listen to Recording 3 again and repeat the sentences. Pay special attention to the big falls in the sentences with strong feelings.

Grammar and communication 2

Feelings – adjectives + *-ed* or *-ing*

Example from *The Story*:

Tasha talks about the flight. She says, 'It was a bit long and **tiring**…'

In other words, Tasha is **tired** because the flight was **tiring**.

Common mistake

Tasha: 'The flight was a bit long and tiring….'

NOT: ~~'The flight was a bit long and tired'~~…..

BUT: 'Tasha was tired after her flight' is correct

Meanings and forms – adjectives + *-ed* and *-ing*

How is Tasha? She feels **tired**.

Why does Tasha feel tired?
What's the source of her tiredness?

The flight. The flight was **tiring**.

Summary		
Adjectives with *-ed/-ing*		
The feeling	Tasha is tired	adjective + *-ed*
Reason or source of the feeling	The flight was tiring	adjective + *-ing*

Here's another example:

How does John feel?	Interested	Internal Feeling + *-ed*
Why?	His book is interesting	Source of feeling + *-ing*

→ Complete the dialogue below.
→ Choose the correct form of the adjective in the brackets ( ).
→ Use your dictionary if necessary.

A I feel a bit ________1 (tired/tiring) actually – it was a very long journey. And the plane was completely full!

B Oh! That's ________2 (surprised/surprising) at this time of year. When I travel, I go to sleep if I'm ________3 (bored/boring) on a plane. But sometimes it's ________4 (interested/interesting) to talk to the person next to you.

A Oh, the man next to me on this flight was really ________5 (bored/boring). The conversation was all about his business trips – I wasn't very ________6 (interested/interesting) at all, really.

A Yes, but it is ________7 (fascinating/fascinated) to travel and visit different countries, isn't it?

B Absolutely! I just find it ________8 (frustrated/frustrating) if I can't speak the language at all.

A Yes, I was a bit ________9 (disappointed/disappointing) with our last holiday because of that.

☑ Check your answers

1 tired **2** surprising **3** bored **4** interesting **5** boring **6** interested **7** fascinating **8** frustrating **9** disappointed

→ Correct the *-ed/-ing* adjectives in these sentences, if necessary.

1 The journey was very tired.
2 I'm very exciting about my trip.
3 I was really surprising about the new job.
4 The film was bored.
5 It's a fascinating story.

Check your answers

1 tiring – source **2** excited – feeling **3** surprised – feeling **4** boring – source
5 *Correct*

Grammar and communication 3

Saying *Thank you*

Example from *The Story*:

Tasha is happy that Helen is at the airport to meet her.
She says, 'Thanks **for** pick**ing** me up.'

Summary – saying *Thank you*		
	Preposition '*for*'	**Verb + *-ing* – gerund**
Neutral Thank you Thank you very much **Formal** Thank you very much indeed **Informal** Thanks Many thanks	for	picking me up

Q ***Can I also say***

a ***'Thank you to meet me?'*** ✗

b ***'Thank you for meet me?'*** ✗ OR

c ***'Thank you for to meet me?'*** ✗

A No, 'Thank you for meeting me' } is the only correct expression.
Thank you + *for* + verb *-ing*.

→ Complete these sentences.

1 Thanks _____/ _____ (help) me.
2 Thanks ____ /________(come) to pick us up.
3 Thank you very much _____/______ (wait) for me.
4 Thank you _____/ ______ (meet) us.
5 Thanks _____/ _____ (calling). (on the telephone)

Check your answers

1 Thanks for helping me. **2** Thanks for coming to pick us up. **3** Thank you very much for waiting for me. **4** Thank you for meeting us. **5** Thanks for calling.

Saying *Thank you*

→ Use the verbs in the box to say *thank you* in the situations below.

let me know	go	tell	come	help	call	invite	wait	ask

Example:

A friend tells you something very important.
You ***Thank you for telling me.***

1 A friend in another country invites you for a holiday.
You ________________________________

2 You arrange to meet a friend at 2 o'clock. You arrive at 2.20.
You ________________________________

3 Your colleague shows you how to use the new computer in the office.
You ________________________________

4 You've got an appointment for tomorrow – but something happens and you can't go. You telephone and tell them. The other person says,

____

5 Your colleague's partner was ill yesterday. Today you ask about her. Your friend says, 'She's much better today.' ____________________

6 Your friend goes to the doctor's. You go with her. Later, at home she says,

____

7 You call a business friend. At the end of the conversation he/she says,

____

8 You invite some friends to your house. When they leave you can say,

____

Check your answers

1 Thanks for inviting me. **2** Thanks for waiting for me. **3** Thank you for helping me. **4** Thanks for letting me know. **5** Thank you for asking. **6** Thanks for going with me. **7** Thanks for calling. **8** Thanks for coming.

Responding to *Thank you*

→Read the formal, neutral and informal expressions in the box.
→Choose an appropriate expression for the situations **1–6** below.

Formal – *You're welcome*	OR	*Not at all*
Neutral – *That's O.K.*	OR	*That's alright*
Informal – *No problem*	OR	*Any time*

1 Your friend says, 'Thank you for helping me with my English.'
You respond, ____________________

2 On the bus, you give your seat to an old lady.
She says 'Thank you so much. You're very kind!'
You respond, ____________________

3 A young person talks to you in the street. He says 'Excuse me, where's the station, please?' You say, 'Just there.' He says, 'Thank you.'
You respond, ____________________

4 The bus is at the bus stop. A woman is getting on the bus with three young children. You help her. She says, 'Thank you ever so much.' You respond, ________________________

5 In a class you lend your dictionary to a friend. S/he says, 'Thanks.' You respond, ________________________

6 You're in a shopping centre. You open the door for someone. The person says, 'Thank you.' You respond, ________________________

Check your answers

1 Informal: Either *No problem* or *Any time* **2** Formal: Either, *You're welcome* or *Not at all* **3** Neutral: *That's O.K.* or *That's alright* **4** Neutral: *That's O.K.* or *That's alright* **5** Informal: *No problem* or *Any time* **6** Formal: *You're welcome* or *Not at all*

British culture – meeting people at the end of a journey

- **Clothes**
  In your country, do you wear formal clothes to meet a friend or family member at the end of a journey? In Britain, it is usual to wear everyday clothes.
- **Saying *Hello***
  When we meet a family member or friend, it is common to **kiss them on the cheek (1)** and sometimes **hug them (2)**.
  Men often **shake hands (3)** or just say *Hello*. Good friends or family members sometimes shake hands and **hold the other person's arm (4)**, or **pat each other on the back (5)**. When we meet a business friend, it is common to shake hands.

Adults often hug and/or kiss children.

- In Britain, some friends and families touch each other. Others don't. Touching isn't always the norm.

About your country: meeting people you know

→Read the questions below.
→Either write your answers or prepare to tell a friend.

What do you do when you meet someone after a journey?

a a family member? ______________________
b a friend? ______________________
c business friend? ______________________
d child? ______________________

What's the right word?

Saying large numbers – *and*

i **British culture – London Heathrow Airport**

- London Heathrow Airport is the busiest international airport in the world with around 63 million passengers a year. There are 1,255 flights a day, with over 90 airlines flying to 160 destinations world-wide. 68,000 people work at the airport. Every day over 26,000 cups of tea, 6,500 pints of beer and 6,500 sandwiches are sold to the public at Heathrow.

→ How do we say the numbers below? Choose the correct expression from the box.

10 100 1,000 10,000

100,000 1,000,000 1,000,000,000

a million	a hundred	ten thousand	ten	a billion
	a hundred thousand	a thousand		

Check your answers

10 – ten
100 – a hundred
1,000 – a thousand
10,000 – ten thousand
100,000 – a hundred thousand
1,000,000 – a million
1,000,000,000 – a billion

→ Now look at these numbers – where's the ***and***?

120
A hundred
and twenty

1,358
One thousand
three hundred
and fifty-eight

10,579
Ten thousand
five hundred
and seventy-nine

150,550
One hundred
and fifty thousand,
five hundred
and fifty

1,350,425
One million, three
hundred
and fifty thousand,
four hundred
and twenty-five

→ Read the sentence about *and* and choose True or False.

With big numbers we say *and* before the 'tens'.
('Tens' are twenty, thirty, forty, etc.) True/False

Check your answer

True

Saying large numbers

→ Write these numbers in words – don't forget the *and*.

1 594,000 ______________________________
2 611,420 ______________________________
3 4,601 ______________________________
4 827 ______________________________
5 32,158 ______________________________
6 24, 250,000 ______________________________
7 6,368 ______________________________
8 923,750 ______________________________

Check your answers

1 Five hundred **and** ninety-four thousand. **2** Six hundred **and** eleven thousand, four hundred **and** twenty. **3** Four thousand, six hundred **and** one. **4** Eight hundred **and** twenty-seven. **5** Thirty-two thousand, one hundred **and** fifty-eight. **6** Twenty-four million, two hundred **and** fifty thousand. **7** Six thousand, three hundred **and** sixty-eight. **8** Nine hundred **and** twenty-three thousand, seven hundred **and** fifty.

→ Read aloud the numbers in the text about Heathrow Airport on page 272.

Check your answers

sixty-three million passengers, one thousand two hundred and fifty-five flights, ninety airlines, one hundred and sixty destinations, sixty-eight thousand people, twenty-six thousand cups of tea, six thousand five hundred pints of beer, six thousand five hundred sandwiches.

About your country: large numbers

→ Read the questions below.
→ Either write your answers or prepare to tell a friend.

1 What is the population of your country/the capital/your town/village, etc.?

____

2 If you work, how much do you earn a year?

____

3 How much does a room/flat/house cost in your area? – to rent a month/to buy?

____

4 How much does a new car cost in your country?

____

Our story continues ... Helen and Tasha go to the airport car park to get Helen's car

Understanding the important information

→ Read the sentences below.
→ Listen to the Recording 4, *The Story* and choose *True/False/ We don't know*.

1 Tasha pays for the car park. True/False/We don't know
2 They can't find the car. True/False/We don't know
3 They ask a man for help with the suitcase. True/False/We don't know

Recording 4 – The Story

Helen	The car's on level 4. We can take the trolley in the lift. But first, I have to pay at the machine just here. Now, where's the ticket? Wait a minute… Oh, here it is, in my pocket. How much do I need? One hour – £2.60. Let me see if I've got the right money.
Tasha	I'm afraid I haven't got any change. I've only got notes.
Helen	No, don't worry. I'm getting this. Look, the machine gives change. Right, let's find the car. The lift is this way.
Helen	Here we are – it's the green Ford. Now, let's get your luggage in the boot. Can I help you with your suitcase?
Tasha	No, really, it's alright thanks – I can manage. Could you just hold this bag for a minute while I get the suitcase in, then we can put the bag on top.
Helen	Come on! Let me help. Don't lift that suitcase on your own.
Tasha	O.K. – Thanks – it is quite heavy… Ready? One, two, three…
Helen	We can put our coats on the back seat.
Tasha	I think I'll keep mine on. I'm really cold.
Helen	I expect that's because you're tired after your long journey. Let's get home and you can have a rest.

Check your answers

a False **b** False **c** False

Understanding more

→Cover the text of Recording 4.
→Read the sentences on page 277. Some are True , some are False.
→Listen and tick ✓ the True sentences.

1 The car is on level 2.
2 First they pay, then they get the car.
3 The car park costs £3.60.
4 They take the lift.
5 They leave the trolley on the ground floor.
6 Helen's got a red Honda.
7 Tasha's suitcase is heavy.
8 They put the luggage on the back seat.
9 Helen helps Tasha with her luggage.
10 They put their coats in the boot.
11 They're going straight to Helen's house.

Check your answers

1 False 2 True **3** False **4** True **5** False **6** False **7** True **8** False **9** True **10** False **11** True

→ Now listen again and correct the wrong information in **1, 3, 5, 6, 8, 10**.

Check your answers

1 The car is on level 4. **3** The car park costs £2.60. **5** They take the trolley in the lift. **6** Helen's got a green Ford. **8** They put the suitcase in the boot. **10** Helen puts her coat in the back but Tasha keeps her coat on.

What do they say?

→ Read the sentences below
→ Listen to Recording 4 again and try to complete the words.
→ Then read the text of the recording to help you if necessary.

1 The Car Park isn't free. Helen says,
'But first, I / h _ _ _ / t _ / pay at the machine.'

2 Helen needs time to find the car park ticket. She says,
'W _ _ _ / a / m _ _ _ _ _.'

3 Helen needs time to see if she's got £2.60 in change. She says,
'L _ _ / m _ / s _ _ / i _ / I've got the / r _ _ _ _ / m _ _ _ y.'

4 **a** Tasha is sorry she hasn't got change. She says,
'I' _ / a _ _ _ _ _ / I haven't got any change.'
b Helen tells her it isn't a problem.
She says, 'D _ _ ' t / w _ _ _ _ .'

5 Helen tells Tasha she's paying. She says,
'I' _ / g _ _ _ _ _ g / t _ _ _.'

6 **a** Helen offers to help with Tasha's suitcase twice. The first time, she says,
'C _ _ / I / h _ _ _ / y _ _ with your suitcase?'
b Tasha says no. She says,
'No, / r _ _ _ _ _ , / it's / a _ _ _ _ _ t / thanks./ I / c _ _ / m _ _ _ _ e .'
c Helen insists. She offers Tasha help again. She says,
'C _ _ _ / _ n! / L _ _ / m _ / help. D _ _ ' _ / l _ _ t / that big suitcase…'
d Tasha accepts. She says,
'O. _. / T _ _ _ _ _ /. It / _ _ / q _ _ _ _ / h _ _ _ y.'

Check your answers

1 But first, I have to pay at the machine. **2** Wait a minute. **3** Let me see if I've got the right money. **4 a** I'm afraid I haven't got any change. **b** Don't worry. **5** I'm getting this. **6 a** Can I help you with your suitcase? **b** No, really, it's alright, thanks. I can manage. **c** Come on! Let me help. **d** O.K. Thanks. It is quite heavy.

Find the words and phrases

→Read the sentences below.
→Read the text of Recording 4 and complete the words and phrases.

1 Helen finds the car park ticket.
She says, 'H _ _ _ / i _ / i _/, in my p _ _ _ _ _.'

2 It's not necessary to pay the exact money because the machine gives / c _ _ _ _ _ /. You can pay with /n _ _ _ _ .

3 Tasha needs help with the bag. She says,
'C _ _ _ _ / you / j _ _ _/ h _ _ _ / this bag for a minute?'

4 Helen holds the bag /w _ _ _ _ / Tasha puts the suitcase in.

5 They put the suitcase in the boot first.
Then they put the bag / o _ / t _ _ / t _ _ .

6 Helen wants to help Tasha with the suitcase. She says, 'Don't lift it / o _ / y _ _ _ / o _ _.'

7 Is the suitcase very heavy? No, but it's q _ _ _ _ heavy.

8 Tasha decides not to take her coat off. She's cold. She says, 'I / think / I ' _ _ / k _ _ _ / m _ _ _ / o _.'

9 Tasha's tired. When they get to the house she can go to her room and relax – she can h _ _ _ / a / r _ _ t.

10 Verb *get*. In the sentences below *get* means **a** go/ arrive
b put – with difficulty
c pay

i Let's **get** your luggage in the car.
ii Don't worry! I'm **getting** this.
iii Let's **get** home.

Check your answers

1 Here it is, *in* my pocket. (preposition!) **2** change/notes **3** Could you just hold this bag for a minute? **4** while. **5** *on* the top (preposition!). **6** on your own. **7** quite. **8** I think I'll keep mine *on*. (preposition!) **9** have a rest. **10** Get **i b ii c iii a.**

Using these words and phrases

→ Match the following **1–10** with **a–j**.

1 Why don't you take your jacket off?
2 Where's John?
3 Don't go on your own.
4 The boot is full.
5 I'll pay for the drinks.
6 I love vanilla ice cream.
7 Have you got change for £20?
8 Is that a good T.V. programme?
9 While Tasha is going to Helen's,
10 Do you need help with that?

a Yes, it's quite interesting, actually.
b I can give you two ten pound notes
c with chocolate sauce on the top.
d Oliver is going to the centre by bus.
e I'll go with you.
f I'll put the bag on the back seat then.
g No, thanks, it's alright. I can manage.
h He's upstairs, having a rest.
i I prefer to keep it on, thanks. I'm a bit cold.
j No, it's my turn. I'll get them.

Check your answers

1 i **2** h **3** e **4** f **5** j **6** c **7** b **8** a **9** d **10** g

Q ***What's the difference between 'car park' and 'parking'?***

A *Car park* is a noun. It's a public place to leave a car.

For example: 'When I go to London, I leave the car in the car park at the station.'

Not: '~~I leave the car in the parking~~'.

Park is a verb, for example, 'You can't park here'.

The phrase *No parking* means 'You can't park here'. This is a **verbal noun** (a verb used as a noun).

Grammar and communication 4

Obligation and necessity – *Have to*

Example from *The Story*:

The car park isn't free. Helen says,
'But first, **I have to** pay at the machine just here.'

Meaning

Is it necessary to pay? Yes, it is a regulation of the car park.
And if Helen doesn't pay? She'll have a problem – she is obliged to pay.

Grammar Summary – *have to* – obligation and necessity						
Affirmative			**Negative**		**Questions**	
I	have	to + verb	I don't	have to + verb	Do I	have to + verb
S/he	has		S/he doesn't		Does s/he	

Look at these examples:

1 **I don't have to** go now. I can stay until 1.00.
Meaning It's not necessary for me to go now.

2 **Do I have to** enrol before the next course or can I just come on the first day?
Meaning Is it an obligation to enrol before the next course or is it possible to just go to the class on the first day?

> **Tip:** Learners of English often say, *Is it necessary for me to…?* ☹
> ★ This isn't wrong but *Do I have to….?* is more common.

Q ***What's the difference between 'Where <u>do I have to go</u> now?' and 'Where <u>do I go</u> now?'?*** (Topic 8)

A The difference is small:

a asks more about obligation – rules and regulations
b asks more about systems – what is the custom/norm?

★ In some situations both are appropriate.

Examples:

1 You are filling in a form:
'Where do I sign?' and
'Where do I have to sign?' are both correct and appropriate.

2 You are using a new photocopier:
'Which way do I put the paper?' and
'Which way do I have to put the paper?' are both correct and appropriate.

Obligation and necessity – *have to*

→ Complete these sentences with the correct form of *have to.*

1 My husband ____________travel a lot for his job. He's always away.
2 How many times a day _____________ take this medicine, doctor?
3 We _______________go if you don't want to. I really don't mind.
4 **Mother** Come on Tommy – it's time for bed.
Tommy Oh, Mum ______________? I'm not tired.
5 You _______________ say 'yes' or 'no' now. You can tell me later.
6 I __________ come back again tomorrow, do I? Can't we finish all the work today?

7 **A** What time ___________ be at the airport for your flight?
B Half past ten.
8 I'm sorry but I really ___________ go now, or I'll miss my train.
9 **A** Could you please tell me why I __________ fill this form in?
B I'm sorry, sir. It's a company regulation.
10 Which number ___________ phone to confirm my return flight?

Check your answers

1 has to. **2** do I have to. **3** We don't have to. **4** Do I have to? **5** you don't have to. **6** I don't have to. **7** do you have to. **8** have to. **9** have to. **10** do I have to.

Grammar and communication 5

The imperative

Examples from *The Story*:

1 Helen needs time to find the car park ticket.
She says, '**Wait** a minute.'
2 Tasha wants to help with the money. Helen says it isn't a problem.
She says, '**Don't worry**.'

Meanings

1 '*Wait.*' Helen is telling Tasha to do something.
2 '*Don't worry.*' Helen is telling Tasha not to do something.

'*Wait*' is the imperative. '*Don't worry*' is the negative imperative.

Grammar Summary – the imperative		
		Examples
Positive imperative	Verb without *to*	Stop!
Negative imperative	*Don't* + verb without *to*	Don't forget!

The negative imperative – Prohibition – *don't*

→ Use the correct form of the verbs in the box below to complete the sentences.

write	wait	forget	worry

1 ___________ for me. I'll be home late tonight.
2 ___________ it's Mum's birthday tomorrow.
3 ___________! Everything will be alright.
4 ___________to me. It takes too long. Can't you e-mail me instead?

Check your answers

1 Don't wait. **2** Don't forget. **3** Don't worry! **4** Don't write.

The positive imperative

★ Be careful! The imperative is a **danger zone** for communication in English. In many languages it is very common to use the imperative in many situations.

★ In English we use the imperative in some situations. In other situations it is impolite.

When do we use the positive imperative?

→ Look at the examples **1–6** below and match with **a–f** from the box on page 284.

→ Use your dictionary if necessary.

1 **A doctor** 'Stay in bed for two days.' ___________________
2 'Come in!' ___________________
3 'Have a good weekend!' ___________________
4 'Be careful!' ___________________
5 'Stay in touch.' ___________________
6 'Go to the end of the road and turn right.'

a invitations and offers
b instructions – telling someone to do something
c giving street directions
d asking for contact
e hopes and wishes
f warnings

Check your answers

1 b **2** a **3** e **4** f **5** d **6** c

What are they saying? What are they communicating?

→ Match the situations (**A–E**) on page 285 with the correct imperative phrase from **Box 1** and the correct communication from **Box 2** on page 286.

Example: 'Have a good holiday'
Hopes and wishes

Situation A

Situation B

Situation C

Situation D

Situation E

Situation F

Box 1

1 'Take the second on the left'
2 'Go ahead. Help yourself!'
3 'Put the cup here and press that button'
4 'Write to me'
5 'Enjoy yourselves!'
6 'Look out!'

Box 2

a Instructions
c Street directions
c Offers and invitations
d Hopes and wishes
e Warnings
f Asking for contact

Check your answers

Situation A	**2** 'Go ahead. Help yourself!	**c**	Offers and invitations
Situation B	**6** 'Look out!'	**e**	Warning
Situation C	**4** 'Please write to me'	**f**	Asking for contact
Situation D	**5** 'Enjoy yourselves!'	**d**	Hopes and wishes
Situation E	**3** 'Put the cup here and press that button.'	**a**	Instructions
Situation F	**1** 'Take the second on the left'	**b**	Street directions

★ For instructions and street directions, you can also use *you* + verb (the present simple, Topic 8).
This form is also very common.
Examples:
A Instructions
1 You put your cup here then you press that button.
2 First you fill this form in, then you pay over there.
B Street Directions:
1 You take the second on the left.
2 You go as far as the station and then you turn right.

Be careful with the positive imperative

Q ***When is the positive imperative impolite?***

A When we ask people to do things.

→ Look at these examples.

Situation You are eating with friends or colleagues. A person at the table says,

a 'Give me some bread.' ☹
'Can you give me some bread, please?' ☺
b 'Put this on the table.' ☹
'Could you put this on the table, please?' ☺

(See Topic 7 for more practice with *Can you...?*, *Could you...?* for asking people to do things.)

Telling people to do things – The imperative

★ The positive imperative is appropriate in some situations.

→ Match sentences (**1–4**) below with situations **a–d**.

1 Do your homework first.	**a** with a close friend
2 Empty your pockets onto the table.	**b** an adult to a child
3 Sit, Jack, sit.	**c** a policeman
4 Don't go home yet! Stay a bit longer.	**d** to an animal

Check your answers

1 b **2** c **3** d **4** a

★ To make an imperative more polite, add *please*.
For example, 'Please tell me' or 'Tell me please'.

Summary – The use of the imperative – spoken English

→ Read these sentences about the use of the imperative.
→ Choose true or false.

1 The negative imperative is appropriate in many situations, e.g. 'Don't say that!' True/False
2 The positive imperative can be impolite, e.g. 'Sit here.' True/False
3 We use the positive imperative for wishes, e.g. 'Have a good journey!' True/False

4 We use the positive imperative for invitations and offers, e.g. 'Come and join us.' True/False

5 We use the imperative with good friends and children. True/False

Check your answers

1 – 5 are all True.

What's the right word?

Public signs – the imperative

The positive imperative

★ The positive imperative is common in written instructions and warnings.

→ Look at the pictures below and the imperative phrases in the box on page 289.

→ Write the correct imperative phrase for each picture.

→ Use your dictionary if necessary.

Example:

1

2

3

4

5

6

7

8

9

10

Book your tickets here   Please drive slowly   Give way
Mind your head   Stop   Look right   Beware of the dog
Cut along the dotted line   Insert your card here   Queue here
~~Pay here~~

Check your answers

1 Mind your head **2** Insert your card here **3** Queue here **4** Look right **5** Please drive slowly **6** Cut along the dotted line **7** Beware of the dog **8** Book your tickets here **9** Stop **10** Give way

Verb *mind*

★ In the exercise above, *mind* means 'be careful of...' This verb is common for warning people.

You can use the verb 'mind' with both

a the person or thing in danger:
For example, 'Mind your head'.

b the dangerous thing:
For example, 'Mind the door'.

→ Write an expression with the verb *mind* for the following situations.

1 You are crossing the road. A bus is coming. Warn your friend.
2 There's a step. Warn your friend.
3 A child is sitting in a car, his legs outside the car. You want to shut the car door.
4 Your friend is in the car with the door open. Another car is coming.

Check your answers

1 Mind the bus! **2** Mind the step! **3** Mind your legs! **4** Mind your door! OR Mind the car!

Find the right word

Public signs – Negative imperative

★ The negative imperative is not common in signs.
★ '*No* + verb + *ing*' or '*No* + noun' is more common.

→ Label the signs below with the correct expression from the box.
→ Use your dictionary if necessary.

No entry	No parking	No photography	No left turn
No bathing	No smoking		

1

2

3

4

5

6

Check your answers

1 No smoking **2** No parking **3** No bathing **4** No entry **5** No left turn **6** No photography

Grammar and communication 6

Offering, rejecting, insisting, accepting

Examples from *The Story*:

a Helen offers to help Tasha with her suitcase.
She says, 'I'll help you with that suitcase.'

b Tasha says no.
She says, 'No, really, it's alright thanks. I can manage.'

c Helen insists. She offers Tasha help again.
She says, 'Come on! Let me help.'

d Tasha accepts.
She says, 'O.K. Thanks. It is quite heavy.'

a Offers

For more practice with *I'll*, see Topic 6.

b Rejecting an offer

Example from *The Story*: 'No really, it's alright. I can manage.'

★ We use *manage* when the action is difficult but possible.
Manage is about effort and success.

In the sentence above, 'manage' means 'It's difficult to lift the suitcase because it's heavy, but I can lift it with effort.'

→Listen to these mini-dialogues on Recording 5.
→Repeat B's responses in the spaces.

Recording 5

1 **A** Can I help you with that?
B Thanks very much, but I think I can manage it on my own.

2 **A** Let me do that.
B No, honestly, I can manage thanks.

3 **A** I'll take that if you like.
B No, really, I'm fine thanks. I can manage.

4 **A** Shall I do that?
B It's O.K. I can manage, thanks.

5 **A** Would you like me to carry that for you?
B Thanks for the offer but I think I can manage it.

Verb *manage*

→ Complete the mini-dialogues below with the correct sentence from the box.

Example: How often do you go home to see your parents?
B ***I usually manage to go about once a month.***

1 A The meeting is now at three o'clock and not four. Can you manage to get here one hour earlier?
B ______________________________

2 A That's a big box! Mind your back!
B ______________________________

3 A I'm sorry I can't help.
B ______________________________

4 A I've got no idea how to do this.
B ______________________________

5 A Tom worries so much about exams.
B ______________________________

6 A How much do you understand when you watch a film in English now?
B ______________________________

7 A Do you do any sport?
B ______________________________

8 A Do you see your children in the evenings?
B ______________________________

a I try to get to the gym twice a week but I don't always manage it.
b Don't worry! I'll manage on my own.
c It's alright. I think I can manage it. Where shall I put it?
d If we work together, we'll manage something.
e Yes, I usually manage to spend an hour or so with them before they go to bed
f ~~I usually manage to go about once a month~~.
g I can try.
h Yes, but he always manages to get good marks.
i I manage to understand quite a lot, actually.

Check your answers

1 g **2** c **3** b **4** d **5** h **6** i **7** a **8** e

c Offering again – insisting

Example from *The Story*:

Helen insists. She offers Tasha help again.
She says, 'Come on! Let me help.'

Verb *let*

Form:

Verb *let*, imperative form	person	verb.

★ The expressions 'Come on!' and 'Go on!' make the phrase stronger.

→ Look at the situations 1–7 below. You are the person
→ Complete the dialogues with sentences from the box.

Let me call an ambulance.
No, it's heavy. Let me take it!
Wait a second. Let me open the door for you.
Come on! It's my turn. Let me pay this time.
Come on! Let me have a look at it.
No, really. Let me do something to help.
Come on, its late! Let me take you.

1 **A** Can I carry that for you?
B I'm alright thanks.
A ____________________
B Thank you. It is very heavy, actually.

2 **A** I'll get this.
B ____________________
A O.K. Thanks.

3 **A** Can I take some of those for you?
B No, it's alright. I can manage.
A ______________________
B Thanks.

4 **A** Can I just sit down for a minute?
B Of course. Would you like me to get you anything?
A No, I'm… oh, the baby…
B ______________________

5 **A** Do you know where the nearest bus stop is?
B It's O.K. I've got the car. I can drive you home.
A No, I can get the bus. It's no problem.
B ______________________
A Thanks. It's really nice of you to offer but I can get the bus.

6 **A** Can I do anything?
B No, you go and sit down.
A ______________________
B Thanks, could you peel the vegetables?

7 **A** Oh! My eye!
B What's the matter?
A I think I've got something in it.
B ______________________

Check your answers

1 No, it's heavy. Let me take it! **2** Come on! It's my turn. Let me pay this time. **3** Wait a second. Let me open the door for you. **4** Let me call an ambulance. **5** Come on, it's late! Let me take you. **6** No really. Let me do something to help. **7** Come on! Let me have a look at it.

Grammar and communication 7

Introducing something negative in a polite way – *I'm afraid*

Example from *The Story*:
Tasha is sorry she hasn't got change. She says,
'**I'm afraid** I haven't got any change.'

★ Use *I'm afraid* to introduce something negative in a polite way.

→ Match **1–8** below with the correct response **a–h**.

1	Excuse me, are you the manager?	**a**	I'm afraid I can't. I'm driving.
2	Could you tell me the time please?	**b**	I'm afraid I don't know. I'm not from here.
3	Excuse me, where I can get a taxi?	**c**	I'm afraid I've got some bad news.
4	Could I borrow your dictionary?	**d**	I'm afraid we can't. We're going to my mother's.
5	Come on! Have another glass of wine.	**e**	No, actually I'm not. I'm afraid he's not here at the moment.
6	Would you like to come to dinner on Saturday?	**f**	I'm afraid I can't eat another thing!
7	Do have some more cake	**g**	I'm afraid I haven't got a watch.
8	What's the matter?	**h**	I'm afraid I haven't got one.

Check your answers

1 e **2** g **3** b **4** h **5** a **6** d **7** f **8** c

Short answers – *I'm afraid so, I'm afraid not*

★ To respond to questions with *Yes* or *No* alone can sound rude.
★ To express that you are sorry about a situation, use *I'm afraid so* and *I'm afraid not.*

I'm afraid so

Meaning

I'm sorry but yes.

Examples:

He's drunk, isn't he?
He isn't ill, is he?
It's a big problem, isn't it?
It's too expensive, isn't it?

} **Response:** I'm afraid so.

I'm afraid not

Meaning

I'm sorry but no.

Examples:

Is he here?
You haven't got a car, have you?
Have you got any change?
Can you help me?

} **Response:** I'm afraid not.

→ Respond with *I'm afraid so* or *I'm afraid not.*

1 **A** It's a bad accident, isn't it? **B** ____________________
2 **A** This isn't right, is it? **B** ____________________
3 **A** Do you know where he lives? **B** ____________________
4 **A** You don't like this, do you? **B** ____________________
5 **A** You can't swim, can you? **B** ____________________
6 **A** Do we have to pay? **B** ____________________

☑ Check your answers

1 I'm afraid so. **2** I'm afraid not. **3** I'm afraid not. **4** I'm afraid not. **5** I'm afraid not. **6** I'm afraid so.

Using these words and phrases

Get for *pay* or *buy*

Example from *The Story*:
Helen tells Tasha she's paying. She says,
'I'm **getting** this.'

★ *Get* is an indirect verb for *pay*.
→ Put the words in the right order to make sentences.

1 ____________________
this/get/I'll
2 No, I insist!____________
getting/I'm/these
3 __________________________ It was your turn last week.
me/ice creams/the/get/today/let
4 __________________________
card/get/I'll/on/credit/this/my

Check your answers

1 I'll get this. **2** I'm getting these. **3** Let me get the ice creams today. **4** I'll get this on my credit card.

Q ***What's the difference between 'I'll get this' and 'I'm getting this'?***

A *I'll get this* is an offer
I'm getting this insists more.

What would you say?

1 You come to England to stay with an English family. You don't know whether to use their first names or their surnames. You ask.

____

2 Your friend hasn't got any change for the car park. You have.

____

Possible answers
1 What shall I call you? Advanced alternative: What would you like me to call you? **2** I've got some change. Here you are.

Revision

How do you say it in your language?

Here are some examples of the important points in this topic.

→ Translate the sentences below into your language in the spaces.
→ Remember – translate the idea, not the words.

1 It's lovely to see you again.

___

2 How was your journey?

___

3 I'm tired! My job is very tiring!

___

4 Thank you for inviting me.

___

5 Don't wait for me. I have to finish this.

___

6 **A** Shall I do that?
B Thanks but I think I can manage.

___

C Come on! Let me help you.

___

7 I'm afraid the manager's not here.

___

8 Have a good weekend!

___

Join the conversation

→ Look at Recording 1 (page 258) again.
→ Listen to Recording 6.
→ Read **Tasha's** words in the spaces.

TEST 9

Which one is right?

→ Choose **a** or **b**.

1 **a** It's nice to have a holiday.
b Is nice to have a holiday.

2 **a** How was your day?
b How were your day?

3 **a** I'm very interesting in football.
b I'm very interested in football.

4 **a** Thank you for to ask me to go with you.
b Thank you for asking me to go with you.

5 **a** I'm have to leave now.
b I have to leave now.

6 **a** I'll pay this.
b I'll get this.

7 **a** Please come with us today.
b Please to come with us today.

8 **a** Let me to do that.
b Let me do that.

9 Can you come with us?
a I afraid no.
b I'm afraid not.

10 Can I help with that?
a Thanks but I can manage.
b Thanks but I manage.

Write a dialogue

Meeting someone after a journey

Situation You travel to visit a friend. Your friend is at the station to meet you.

1 **Your friend**
greets you. She is happy to see you.

You
greet your friend. You are happy to see her.

3 Your friend asks about your journey

4 Say something positive
You ask about her life in general

5 Your friend replies and shows you the way to the taxis

6 You thank your friend for meeting you

7 Your friend responds and then says

__________ Look, here's a taxi. Go on! You get in first.

8 You arrive. Your friend asks the driver how much it is.

9 You decide to pay

10 Your friend says she's paying

Check your answers

1 a **2** a **3** b **4** b **5** b **6** b **7** a **8** b **9** b **10** a

Dialogue: model answers

1	**Your friend**	Hello, X. It's great to see you again.
2	**You**	Hi, X. It's lovely to see you too.
3	**Your friend**	How was your journey?
4	**You**	It was good thanks. How are things with you?
5	**Your friend**	I'm fine. The taxis are this way.
6	**You**	Thank you for picking me up, by the way.
7	**Your friend**	That's O.K. Look, here's a taxi. Go on! You get in first.
8	**Your friend**	How much is it, please?
9	**You**	Let me pay.
10	**Your friend**	No, I'm getting this.

10 FINDING ACCOMMODATION

Grammar and communication	Vocabulary
◆ Asking *Who?* + short answers	◆ Hotel language
◆ Talking about the number of people	◆ Ordinal numbers
◆ Talking about the same thing – *one, ones*	**Pronunciation**
◆ Asking for an alternative	◆ *Schwa* / ə /
◆ Negative comparisons	
◆ Decisions – buying things	
◆ Verb *hope*	
◆ Talking about the past – past simple	
◆ Past experience – present perfect	

Oliver is at the hotel reservations desk in the tourist information centre at Victoria station in central London. He needs a room.

Understanding the important information

→ Read the sentences on page 302.

→ Listen to Recording 1 *The Story* and answer *Yes* or *No* to the sentences.

1 Oliver books a hotel room.	Yes/No
2 They talk about	
– type of room	Yes/No
– hotel facilities	Yes/No
– prices	Yes/No
– one particular hotel	Yes/No

Recording 1 (and 9) – The Story

Assistant	Who's next, please?
Oliver	I think I am. I'd like to book a room, please.
Assistant	Yes, how many of you are there?
Oliver	It's just for me.
Assistant	And how long is it for?
Oliver	I need a room from tonight until the end of next week.
Assistant	O.K. So that's a single room for 14 nights altogether.
Oliver	Yes, that's right.
Assistant	In any specific area?
Oliver	I don't mind, as long as it's central.
Assistant	What sort of price are you looking to pay?
Oliver	Between £50 and £60 a night.
Assistant	There's the Trafalgar Hotel. It's very near here.
Oliver	How much is that one?
Assistant	£55 a night.
Oliver	That would be fine.
Assistant	I'll just see if they have any vacancies. Would you like to take a seat for a moment?
Oliver	Thanks.

Check your answers

1 No **2 a** Type of room	Yes
b Hotel facilities	No
c Prices	Yes
d One particular hotel	Yes

Understanding more

Finding a room

→ Cover the text of Recording 1.
→ Read the table below.
→ Listen to the recording and complete the table.

Number of nights	Oliver's price range	Location (where?)	Name of hotel	Price
	£..... – £.....			

Check your answers

Number of nights: 14; Price range: £50 – £60 a night; Location: central; Name of hotel: Trafalgar; Price: £55

What do they say?

→ Read the sentences below.
→ Listen to Recording 1 again and try to complete the words.
→ Then read the text to help you if necessary.

1 A The assistant starts the conversation.
She asks, 'W _ _ 's / n _ _ _?'
B Oliver responds, 'I think _ / _ m.'
2 A The assistant asks about the number of people.
She says, 'H_ _ / m _ _ y / o _ / y _ _ / a _ e / t _ _ r _?'
B Oliver responds, 'J _ _ _ / m _.'
3 A The assistant suggests the Trafalgar and Oliver asks the price.
He says, 'How much is /t _ _ _ / o _ _?'
B The assistant responds, '£55 / _ / n _ _ _ t.'

Check your answers

1 a Who's next? **b** I think I am.
2 a How many of you are there? **b** Just me.
3 a How much is that one? **b** £55 a night.

Find the words and phrases

→ Read the sentences below.
→ Read the text of Recording 1 and complete the words and phrases.

1 Oliver is looking for a room.
He says, 'I'd like to / b _ _ k / a room, please.'

2 a The assistant asks about the number of nights.
She says, 'H _ _ / l _ _ g / _ s / i _ / f _ r?'
b Oliver responds, 'F _ _ _ / tonight / u _ _ _ _ / the end of the week.'

3 Oliver needs a room for one person. He needs a /s _ _ _ _ _ / room.

4 The location of the hotel isn't very important to Oliver, but he wants to be in the centre. He says, 'I don't mind, / a _ / l _ _ _ / a _ / it's central.'

5 a The assistant asks how much Oliver wants to pay.
She says, 'W _ _ _ / s _ _ _ / o _ / price / are / you / l _ _ _ _ _ g / t _ / p _ _ ?'
b Oliver's minimum is £50 and his maximum £60.
He says, 'B _ _ _ _ _ n / £50 and £60 / _ / n _ _ _ t.'

6 When you need a room, you can say,
'Have you got any rooms free?' or
'Have you got any v _ _ _ _ _ _ _ _?'

7 The assistant asks Oliver to sit down.
She says, 'Would you like to t _ _ _ / a / s _ _ _ / for a moment?'

Check your answers

1 I'd like to book a room, please. **2 a** How long is it for? **b** From tonight until the end of next week. **3** He needs a single room. **4** I don't mind, as long as it's central. **5 a** What sort of price are you looking to pay? **b** Between £50 and £60 a night. **6** Have you got any vacancies? **7** Would you like to take a seat for a moment?

Using these words and phrases

1 Questions with *for* at the end

Example from *The Story*:
The assistant asks about the number of nights.
She says, '**How long** is it **for**?'

How long asks about the number of days.
It refers to 'the room'.

She can also say, *How long for?* but this is more direct. It can sound abrupt.

Summary – Questions with *for* at the end

How many How long When Who	is are	it/this/that they/these/those	for?

→ Complete these dialogues. Make questions from the words in the table above.

1 **A** Good evening, sir.
_____________________?
B There are four of us.
A If you would like to follow me, I'll show you to your table.

2 **A** Here are our tickets to New York.
B _____________________?
A Next Wednesday.

3 **A** Here's the bill.
B Let's pay half each.
_____________?
A £20.50.

4 **A** They're beautiful.
_______________?
B Oh, that's my little secret.

5 **A** If you want to go out on the lake you can hire a boat. It costs £10.

B ______________________?

A One hour.

Check your answers

1 How many is it for? (it' refers to 'table') **2** When are they for? **3** How much is it for? **4** Who are they for? **5** How long is that for?

2 As long as

The location of the hotel isn't very important to Oliver, but he wants to be in the centre.

The assistant asks, 'In any specific area?'
Oliver says, 'I don't mind, as long as it's central.'

As long as talks about condition. It means 'if' but we use *as long as* when the condition is important to us.

→ Complete the mini-dialogues on page 307.
→ Use *as long as* + the correct phrase from the box.
→ Change the verb if necessary.

as long as …	be in a non-smoking area get there by twenty past be back before 11 o'clock go to London find me a room rain take me home afterwards ~~be careful~~

Example:

A Dad, can I borrow the car?

B Yes, ***as long as you're careful.***

1 **A** Can we go on a trip to England?
B Why not, __________we___________

2 **A** Could you baby-sit for us on Saturday evening?
B Of course,________ you __________

3 **A** We're going to the open-air theatre this evening.
B That can be really good, _____________it___________

4 **A** The train leaves at half past three.
B So, _________we____________ we'll be O.K.

5 **A** Would you like a table by the window, sir?
B I don't mind, __________it______________

6 **A** Mum, can I go out?
B Yes , ____________you______________

7 **A** I'm sorry sir, but the hotel is full. I understand you've got a booking but...
B I don't mind how long I have to wait, ________you
____

Check your answers

1		we go to London.
2		you take me home afterwards.
3		it doesn't rain.
4	as long as	we get there by twenty past.
5		it is in a non-smoking area.
6		you are back by 11 o'clock.
7		you find me a room.

3 Talking about how much you want to spend

Example from *The Story:*
The assistant asks Oliver how much he wants to pay.
She says, 'What sort of price are you looking to pay?'

Q ***What's the difference between***
a ***'How much do you want to pay?'***
and
b ***'What sort of price are you looking to pay?'***

A The grammar is correct in both questions. The meaning is the same.

a 'How much do you want to pay?' is more direct.
b 'What sort of price are you looking to pay?' is indirect.

Question **b** is common in shops and when you are buying a service.

Q ***Can I say, 'What kind of price...?' instead of 'sort'.***

A Yes, *What kind of ...?* and *What sort of ...?* are the same.

Responses – The price

Oliver's minimum is £50 and his maximum is £60.
He says, 'Between £50 and £60.'

Other possible responses:

Anything up to £20 is alright Anything under £20 is O.K. As long as it's less than £20	These expressions mean £20 is your maximum
About £20 Around £20	It can be a little more or a little less than £20

Prices, quantities and time

How much is a room at the Trafalgar? '£55 **a** night.'

★ We use *a/an* for measurements of time, units of quantity etc. For example, 50p **a** packet.

→ Complete the mini-dialogues below. Use one picture from the top of page 309 and one word from the box under the pictures.
→ Use your dictionary if necessary.

Example: **A** He's very good at his job. How much does he charge?
B ***£25 an hour***

1 **A** How much does it cost to have a car?
B About__________________.
Expensive, isn't it?

2 **A** Can you tell me how much those flowers cost, please?
B Yes,__________________

3 **A** How much are these bananas, please?
B Yes,__________________

month kilo bunch packet bottle box ~~hour~~

4 **A** Those strawberries look nice. How much are they, please?
B ____________________

5 **A** Can you tell me the price of these biscuits, please?
B ____________________

6 **A** Let's get some more of that wine, shall we? How much is it?
B ______________________

Check your answers

1 £90 a month. **2** £3 a bunch. **3** 90p. a kilo. **4** £1.49 a box. **5** 65p. a packet. **6** £3.99 a bottle.

Q ***Can I also say 'per', for example, '£20 per hour'?***

A *A/an* is normal in spoken English.
Per is formal. It is more common in written English.

How do you pronounce it?

Schwa / ə /

★ This is the most common sound in English.
★ Why? The vowel in unstressed syllables is often pronounced *schwa.*
★ In the words and phrases on the next page, all the letters with the *schwa* symbol / ə / on the top have the same sound *schwa.*

→ Listen to Recording 2 and repeat the words and phrases. The stress is underlined in each phrase.
→ Pay special attention to the pronunciation of the *schwa* / ə /.

Recording 2

1 to, to book, a, a room, to book a room,

I'd like to book a room

2 for, for me, it's just for me

3 tonight, from, from tonight

4 of, the end of, the end of next week

5 as, as long as, as long as it's central

6 sort of, sort of price, what sort of price are you, to pay,

What sort of price are you looking to pay?

7 a night, £55 a night

8 vacancies

9 to take, to take a seat, for a moment,

Would you like to take a seat for a moment?

What's the right word?

In a hotel

→ Complete these mini-dialogues with the correct response from the box on page 311.
→ Use your dictionary if necessary.

1 **A** There are two of us.
B ______________________________

2 **A** Does the room have a private bathroom?
B ______________________________

3 **A** Is it half board?
B ______________________________

4 **A** Do you do full board?
B ______________________________

5 **A** I see B & B signs everywhere. What does B & B mean?
B ______________________________

6 **A** What does 'No vacancies' mean?
B ______________________________

7 **A** I'm very sorry but the lift isn't working.
B ______________________________

8 **A** Don't I need a key to open the door of my room?
B ______________________________

9 **A** Where could I have a business meeting, please?
B ______________________________

10 **A** We're really thirsty and I'd like something to eat, too.
B ______________________________

a No, sir. Just put this card in the machine on the door.
b Yes, the price includes dinner.
c Do you prefer a double or twin room?
d Yes, all our rooms have ensuite facilities, madam.
e It means there are no rooms free. The hotel is fully booked.
f The lounge is always open to visitors, madam.
g Yes, that price includes a light lunch and a 3-course dinner.
h It stands for 'bed and breakfast'. It's very common in Britain.
i The bar is open all day for refreshments, sir.
j Oh, dear ! We'll have to go up the stairs.

☑ Check your answers

1 c **2** d **3** b **4** g **5** h **6** e **7** j **8** a **9** f **10** i

Grammar and communication 1

Asking *Who?* + short answers

Example from *The Story*:

The assistant asks, 'Who's next?' Oliver responds, 'I think I am.'

★ Short answers are very common in English.

Who works in this office?	→	I do
Who likes coffee?	→	Peter does
Who can drive?	→	David and Sally can
Who hasn't got a sister?	→	Tom hasn't
Who's hungry?	→	We are
Who's going to Italy?	→	I am

Look at the examples below.

→ Complete the short answers in these mini-dialogues.
→ Choose from

am/am not	*is/isn't*	*are/aren't*
do/don't	*does/doesn't*	
have/haven't	*has/hasn't*	
can/can't	*could/couldn't*	

1 A Who lives at No. 12?
B John and Sheila ________. You don't remember them, do you?

2 A Who's coming to the cinema with us tonight?
B I ______. Have you got my ticket?

3 A Who's not here yet?
B Sue ______ – she's always late.

4 A Who's got a watch?
B I ______. It's six o'clock.

5 A Who can cook tonight?
B We _______, if you like.

6 A Do you all like pizza?
I'm afraid Mike _________. He can't eat cheese.

7 A Who has to go to work tomorrow?
B I ________ but my partner ________
Isn't she lucky?

8 A Who's using the computer?
B Robert _____, as usual.

9 A Who thinks it's a good idea?
B I ________ – I think it's great!

10 A Who understands her?
B No-one ________ . She talks so fast.

11 A Who's got a car?
B Kate ______
A Good! Perhaps she can take us there.

12 A Who watches T.V. in your house?
B We all _______

Check your answers

1 John and Sheila do. **2** I am. **3** Sue isn't. **4** I have. **5** We can. **6** I'm afraid Mike doesn't. **7** I do but my partner doesn't. **8** Robert is. **9** I do. **10** No-one does. **11** Kate has. **12** We all do.

Grammar and communication 2

Talking about the number of people – *How many?*

Example from *The Story*:
The assistant asks about the number of people.
She says, '**How many of you are there?**'
Oliver responds 'Just me.'

How many of you are there?

→ Answer the following questions about you.

1 How many of you are there in your family?
There are _____ of us.

2 How many of you are there in the room at this moment?
T _____/ are / _____/ o _/ u _
OR
J_____/ m_____

3 If you are a student – how many of you are there in your class?

____

4 If you work – how many of you are there in the company?

____

Check your answers

All answers: 'There are XXX of us.' If you're alone, the answer to question **2** is: 'Just me.'

Grammar and communication 3

Talking about the same thing – *one/ones*

Example from *The Story:*

The assistant suggests the Trafalgar Hotel and Oliver asks the price.

He says 'How much is that one?'

★ Don't repeat the noun. Use 'one' or 'ones' instead.

→ Complete the speech bubbles.

→ Choose from the sentences in the box on page 315.

1

2

3

4

5

a I think I'll take this one.	**b** Have you got any smaller ones?
c I prefer the white one.	**d** A large one, please.
e Excuse me, can you tell me how much the small one is, please?	

Check your answers

1 e **2** d **3** c **4** a **5** b

Common mistake – *One/Ones*

Example from the exercise above:
'A small or a large Coke?'

Answer: 'A large, please.' ✗
'A large one, please.' ✓

→ Look at these examples.

1 A Would you like a large Coke? **B** No, can I have a small one?

2 I like the green car but I prefer the white one.

3 This bag is too big. Can I see that one, please?

4 A Peter's out on his new bike. **B** A new bike? Who's got his old one?

5 A I like green apples. **B** Do you? I prefer red ones.

Example sentence	Grammar Summary – *One/Ones*		
1	*a*	adjective	*one*
2 4	*the* *my* etc.	adjective	*one* or *ones*
3	*this/that*	(adjective)	*one*
5	*these/those* no article	adjective	*ones*

Let's look at sentence **4** on page 315, about the bike.

Q ***Can't I say, 'The old is in the garage?'*** ✗

A No, with *the* + adjective, say *one* or *ones*.
'The old one is in the garage'

→ Complete the mini-dialogues below. Use *a*, *the*, *my* etc. + *one*, *ones*.

1 A Would you like a hot or a cold drink?
B Could I have /_____/ cold_____, please?
2 A Which umbrella is yours?
B _____black_____
3 A Do you like your new computer?
B Not really, I prefer _____/ old /_____
4 A Do you like that blue hat?
B It's too expensive. How about _____ red _____?
5 A Are you going on a long trip?
B No, it's just _____ short _____ this time.
6 A Which shoes shall I wear?
B Why don't you wear _____new _____?
7 A Can I borrow a pen?
B I've only got _____ red _____
8 A Where do I put the clean plates?
B Here.
A And _____ dirty _____?
B They go over there.
9 A How many children have you got?
B Two. They're both girls. The oldest one's called Marie and _____ other ____'s name's Danielle.

☑ Check your answers

1 a cold one. **2** the black one. **3** the/my old one. **4** the/this/that red one. **5** a short one. **6** the/your new ones. **7** a red one. **8** the dirty ones. **9** the/my other one's.

Q ***Where's the stress in the sentences above?***

A Stress is always on the important or new information.

So, in these sentences, the stress is on the adjectives, for example, cold, black, old, etc. A cold one, the black one, my old one etc.

Our story continues... the assistant telephones the Trafalgar Hotel and talks to Oliver again

Understanding the important information

→ Cover the text of Recording 3.
→ Read the sentences below.
→ Listen to the recording and answer the questions.

1 Oliver books a room at the Trafalgar Hotel? Yes/No.
2 They talk about two, three, four or five hotels?

Recording 3 – The Story

Assistant Sorry to keep you waiting sir. I'm afraid the Trafalgar is fully booked. There are no vacancies until next week.
Oliver Have you got anything else?
Assistant How about these two? The Park Hotel is in the Holland Park area and the Royal is very central, near Oxford Street.
Oliver Are they about the same price?
Assistant Let me see. The Royal is £60 a night and the Park is a bit cheaper, £55. They're both 3-*** (3-star) hotels so the facilities are about the same. Breakfast is included, of course, and both have ensuite bathrooms, television, direct-dial telephones and tea and coffee facilities in the room.
Oliver Which one is more central?
Assistant The Royal, but the Park is smaller, it's in a quieter street and is perhaps a little more comfortable. It's more traditional, a family-run hotel. Breakfast at the Royal is Continental, buffet style, where you help yourself but at the Park they also do a full, traditional English breakfast.
Oliver I think I'll take the room at the Park. I prefer smaller, quieter hotels and it's better for me because it's nearer the office where I'm working for the next two weeks.

Check your answers

1 No **2** three

Understanding more

→ Cover the text of Recording 3 again.
→ Read the grid below.
→ Listen to Recording 3 again and complete the grid.

Name of Hotel	The Park Hotel	The Royal Hotel
Price per night	£	£
Ensuite bathrooms		
Direct-dial telephones		
Tea and coffee facilities		
Breakfast included	Yes/No	Yes/No
Type of breakfast	Continental/English	Continental/English
Oliver chooses		

☑ Check your answers

Name of Hotel	The Park Hotel	The Royal Hotel
Price per night	£55	£60
Ensuite bathrooms	✓	✓
Direct-dial telephones	✓	✓
Tea and coffee facilities	✓	✓
Breakfast included	Yes	Yes
Type of breakfast	Continental/English	English
Oliver chooses	✓	

What's the right word?

Hotels

→ Choose words from the box below to complete the sentences below.
→ Use your dictionary if necessary.

1 My hotel is very _______ because it's ___ a park. There's not much traffic.

2 **A** How much is that hotel?
B I don't know but it's in the centre of town. That means it's __________
A I prefer to pay a bit more and be ________ so I can walk to the museums, shops and all the other places I want to visit. I also need a hotel that is __________ – being a tourist is tiring.

3 I really like my hotel. Everything looks so ________ and the staff are very _______ – they always talk to me.

small	modern	traditional	big	comfortable	friendly
clean	central	expensive	quiet	near	

Check your answers

1 quiet… near **2** expensive…central…comfortable **3** clean...friendly

What do they say?

→ Read the sentences below.
→ Listen to Recording 3 again and try to complete the words.
→ Then read the text of the recording to help you if necessary.

1 Oliver waits and the assistant comes back. She starts the conversation. She says, 'S _ _ _ y / t _ / k _ _ p / y _ _ / w _ _ _ _ _ g.'

2 When she says the Trafalgar is full Oliver asks about other possibilities. He says, 'H _ _ _/ y _ _ / g _ t / a _ _ t h _ _ g / e _ s _?'

3 The assistant compares the Royal and the Park. What does she say about the Park Hotel? She says, 'The Park is s _ _ _ _ _ r, it's in a q _ _ _ _ street and is perhaps a little m _ _ _ / c _ _ _ _ _ _ _ _ _ e./ It's m_ _ _ / t r _ _ _ _ _ _ _ _ l/'

4 Oliver decides on the Park.
He says ' I ' _ _ / t _ _ _ / the room at the Park.'

How do they pronounce it?

Schwa (Part 2)

→ Listen to Recording 4 and repeat these words and phrases from the conversation above.
→ Remember *schwa* / ə / is common in unstressed syllables.
→ Pay special attention to the letters with the *schwa* symbol / ə / on the top. The pronunciation is always *schwa* / ə / – they are unstressed.
→ Stressed syllables are underlined.

Recording 4

1	Royal	7	continental
2	Holland Park	8	cheaper
3	Oxford Street	9	smaller
4	facilities	10	quieter
5	traditional	11	nearer
6	breakfast	12	better

Grammar and communication 4

Asking for an alternative

1 A general alternative

Example from *The Story*:
The Trafalgar Hotel is full. Oliver asks about other possibilities.
He says, 'Have you got **anything else**?'

★ This question is very general.
★ You can use it to ask about everything.

2 A more specific alternative

→ Look at this example.

Receptionist: I've got one room at £100 a night.
Client: Have you got **anything cheaper?**

★ We can use the **comparative** with this question.

→ Ask questions in these situations. Use the comparative.

1 In a shop
You ____________________?

2 In a shop
You ____________________?

3 Your travel agent suggests a flight at 22.00. It's too late.
You ____________________?

4 You book a hotel room in London. Your friend tells you it's far from the centre. You phone your travel agent.
You ____________________?

Check your answers

1 Have you got anything smaller? **2** Have you got anything longer? **3** Have you got anything earlier? **4** Have you got anything /nearer the centre? / more central?

Grammar and communication 5

Negative comparisons

Oliver chooses The Park because it's **smaller**, **quieter**, **more comfortable**, it is **more traditional** and it's **nearer** the office than the Royal.

Why doesn't Oliver choose the Royal?

The Royal's **not as quiet** (as The Park) OR
The Royal **isn't as quiet** (as The Park).
The pronunciation of 'as' is also with *schwa* / ə /.

→ Complete the sentences below. Use adjectives from the box.

quiet	comfortable	big	traditional	good	near	expensive

1 The Royal's not___/_____. It's in a really busy street.

2 The Royal's ______as________/___ the Park. The beds are hard.

3 The Royal's _____/____ traditional. The style is more modern.

4 The Royal's ___/___ good ____ the Park for Oliver because it isn't /____/n_____his office.

Check your answers

1 not as quiet. **2** not as comfortable as. **3** not as traditional. **4** not as good as, as near.

British culture – accommodation for visitors

Where to stay

- In Britain you can stay in a hotel, a guest house or a 'bed and breakfast'.
  - Hotels have 1* (star), to 5*****. It depends on the facilities.
  - A guest house is a small hotel. It can be part of a private house. Visitors have breakfast and sometimes an evening meal in a guest house. Guest houses are cheaper than big hotels.
  - A Bed and Breakfast is also a private house. Sometimes it is just one or two rooms in a family home.
- Tax (V.A.T. – Value Added Tax – currently 17.5%): It is common to include V.A.T. in hotel prices.

→ Read the text and label the pictures below.
→ Use your dictionary to help you if necessary.

Breakfast

Breakfast is usually included in the price of hotels in the U.K.

- Continental breakfast can include cereals, yoghurt, rolls, croissants, toast, butter, cheese, jam, coffee, tea and hot chocolate.
- English breakfast includes fruit juice, cereals, eggs, bacon (sometimes tomatoes, sausages, mushrooms), toast, butter, marmalade, tea and coffee.
  – Nowadays not many people in Britain eat a traditional full English breakfast at home. Sometimes it's a treat (something special) for weekends.

Continental breakfast

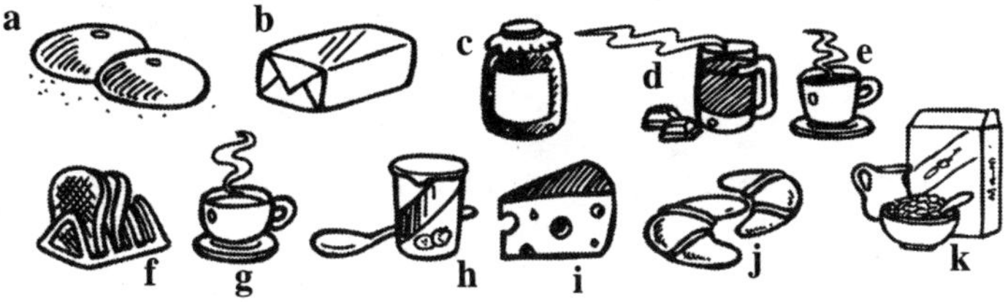

English breakfast

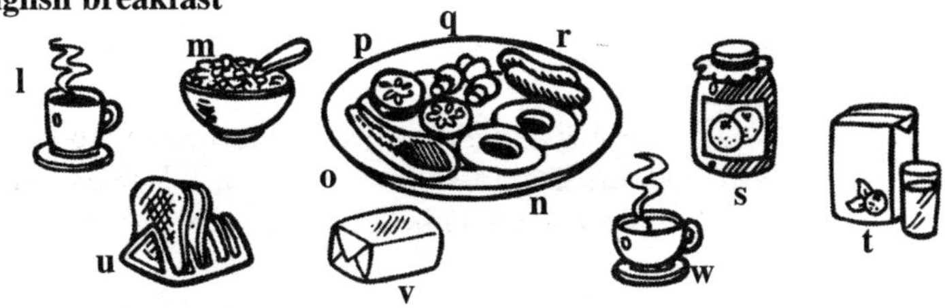

Check your answers

a rolls **b** butter **c** jam **d** hot chocolate **e** coffee **f** toast **g** tea **h** yoghurt **i** cheese **j** croissants **k** cereal **l** coffee **m** cereal **n** eggs **o** bacon **p** tomatoes **q** mushrooms **r** sausages **s** marmalade **t** fruit juice **u** toast **v** butter **w** tea

→ Now read about this London hotel.

The Royal Scot Hotel, London

→ Look at the map below. Where is the Royal Scot Hotel?

→ Read the text from a London Tourist brochure and choose **A, B, C, D,** or **E**.

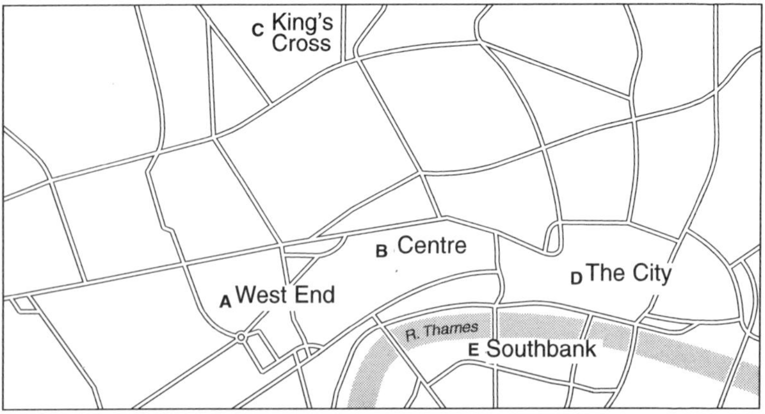

Situated between the West End and the City of London, close to Kings Cross station, this modern hotel with 87 refurbished deluxe rooms, provides the ideal base for a shopping and sightseeing visit to the capital. London Zoo and Madame Tussaud's famous waxworks are within easy reach and local attractions include the British Museum and Sadler's Wells.

Check your answer

C – Close to (near) King's Cross Station.

→ Read the questions below.
→ Read the text again and tick ✓ all the right answers.

The Royal Scot is:
- ☐ small
- ☐ large
- ☐ traditional
- ☐ modern
- ☐ good for visiting London's shops
- ☐ good for tourists
- ☐ good for sports enthusiasts
- ☐ hot in the summer
- ☐ air-conditioned

It has got:
- ☐ a swimming pool
- ☐ a big car park
- ☐ limited car parking
- ☐ three restaurants
- ☐ views of the park
- ☐ more than 80 rooms

Check your answers

The Royal Scot is:
large
modern
good for visiting London's shops
good for tourists (sightseeing)
air-conditioned

It has got:
limited parking
more than 80 rooms

Grammar and communication 6

Decisions – buying things

Example from *The Story*: Oliver decides on The Park Hotel.
He says, '**I'll take** the Park.'

★ Say *I'll take* when you decide to buy.

Situation You are in a shop and you decide to buy.

1 You look at two boxes of chocolates, a big one and a small one.
You decide to buy the small one.
You ______________________________

2 You look at two pictures – one in black and white, one in colour.
You decide to buy the one in black and white.
You ______________________________

3 You look at two watches – a more expensive one and a cheaper one.
You decide to buy the more expensive one.
You ______________________________

Check your answers

1 I'll take the small one, please. **2** I'll take the black and white one please.
3 I'll take the more expensive one, please.

Our story continues. Oliver arrives at the Park Hotel. He checks in

Understanding the important information

→ Cover the text of Recording 5.
→ Read the sentences below.
→ Listen to the recording and choose *Yes* or *No*.

They talk about

a Oliver's passport	Yes/No
b his room number	Yes/No
c the restaurant	Yes/No
d the breakfast room	Yes/No
e the cost of the room	Yes/No
f Oliver's luggage?	Yes/No

Recording 5 – The Story

Receptionist	Good afternoon. Can I help you?
Oliver	Yes, I've got a room booked.
Receptionist	In what name, sir?
Oliver	Rees, R – double E – S, Oliver.
Receptionist	Yes, here it is, a single room for 14 nights.
Oliver	That's right.
Receptionist	Could you sign this registration card, please?
[Oliver signs]	
Oliver	There you are.
Receptionist	Thank you. Here's your key. Room 508's on the fifth floor. Breakfast is served in the breakfast room downstairs from 7 to 10 o'clock and the lift is round the corner to your right. Do you need help with your luggage?
Oliver	No thanks, I'm fine.
Receptionist	I hope you enjoy your stay with us, Mr Rees.
Oliver	Thank you.

Check your answers

a passport – no **b** room number – yes **c** restaurant – no **d** breakfast room – yes **e** cost – no **f** luggage – yes

Understanding more

→ Cover the text of Recording 5 again.
→ Read the questions below.
→ Listen to the recording and write short answers.

1 What does Oliver sign? ________________
2 What's his room number? ________________
3 Where's the breakfast room? ________________
4 What time's breakfast? ________________
5 How much luggage has Oliver got? ________________

Check your answers

1 the registration card. **2** 508. **3** downstairs. **4** 7.00 – 10.00. **5** Not much.

What do they say?

→ Read the sentences below.
→ Listen to Recording 5 again and try to complete the words.
→ Then read the text of the recording to help you if necessary

1 Oliver says he has a reservation.
He says: 'I've / g _ _ / a / _ _ _ _ / b _ _ _ _ d.'

2 The receptionist asks his name.
She says, ' I _ / w _ _ _ / n _ _ e / sir?'

3 Where is room 508?
'....../ _ n / the / f _ _ t _ / floor.'

4 Where can Oliver have breakfast?
She says, ' Breakfast / i _ / s _ _ _ _ d /
in the breakfast room.'

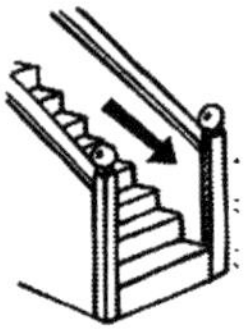

5 Where's the breakfast room?
'D _ _ _ _ _ _ _ _s.'

6 Where's the lift?
'R _ _ _ _ / the / c _ _ _ _ _ / t _/
y _ _ _ / r _ _ _ t.'

7 The receptionist wants Oliver to enjoy his stay.
She says: 'I / h _ _ _ / you enjoy your stay with us, Mr Rees.'

Check your answers

1 I've got a room booked. **2** In what name? **3** … on the fifth floor. **4** Breakfast is served in the breakfast room. **5** Downstairs. **6** Round the corner to your right. **7** I hope you enjoy your stay.

Common mistake

'**On** the first floor'

Not: ~~In the first floor~~
or ~~At the first floor?~~

To say 'where', *on* is the only correct preposition with *floor*.

What's the right word?

Ordinal numbers

Example from *The Story*:
'Room 508 is on the **fifth** floor.'

→ Look at this lift notice and complete the words on the right.

■ 12th	← twelfth
■ 11th	eleventh
■ 10th	_ _ _ th
■ 9th	_ _ _ _ h
■ 8th	e _ g _ _ _
■ 7th	_ _ _ _ _ _ _
■ 6th	_ _ _ t _
■ 5th	_ _ f _ _
■ 4th	_ o _ _ _ h
■ 3rd	third
■ 2nd – Restaurant	second
■ 1st – Bar/Lounge	first
■ G – Reception	ground floor
■ LG – Breakfast room	lower ground

Check your answers

10th – tenth; 9th – ninth; 8th – eighth; 7th – seventh; 6th – sixth; 5th – fifth; 4th – fourth

→ Look at the lift notice above and complete these mini-dialogues.

Example: 617 Where's your room? ***I'm on the sixth floor.***

1 A Excuse me, where's reception?
B It's / _ _ / t _ _/ g _ _ _ _ _ _ / f _ _ _ _ .

2 **A** Can you tell me where the restaurant is, please?
B Yes, / i _ ' _ / o_ / t _ _ / s _ _ _ _ _ _ / floor.

3 **A** Where do we go for breakfast?
B Downstairs. The breakfast room's /_ n / t _ _ / l _ _ _ _ _ / g _ _ _ _ _ _/ floor.

4 **A** Excuse me, where can I get a drink?
B The bar's / on / t _ _ /f _ _ _ _ _ / f _ _ _ _ _.

Check your answers

1 It's on the ground floor. **2** Yes, it's on the second floor. **3** Downstairs, the breakfast room's on the lower ground floor. **4** The bar's on the first floor.

→ Complete the rule below.

For ordinal numbers in English, add the letters _ _ to the number.

The ordinals f _ _ _ _, s _ _ _ _ _ _ and _ _ _ _ d are irregular.

Check your answer

For ordinal numbers, add the letter 'th' to the number.
The ordinals *first*, *second*, and *third* are irregular.

On which floor?

→ Answer these questions.

1 If you live in a flat – where is your flat? On which floor?
You ______________________________

2 If you live in a house – where is your bedroom? On which floor?
You ______________________________

3 Where do you work or study – on which floor?
You ______________________________

4 Where are you now?
You ______________________________

Grammar and communication 7

Verb *Hope*

Example from *The Story*:

The receptionist wants Oliver to enjoy his stay.
She says, 'I **hope** you enjoy your stay.'

→ Write sentences for these situations. Use the verb *hope*...

1 It's the end of the week.
What do you say to your colleagues when you leave work?
I hope ____________________

2 Your friend is going out for the evening.
You ____________________

3 Your friend is going on holiday.
You ____________________

4 Your friend is going on a journey.
You ____________________

5 Your friend is taking an exam/having a baby/taking a driving test etc.
You ____________________

✓ Check your answers

1 I hope you have a good weekend. **2** I hope you have a nice evening. **3** I hope you enjoy your holiday. **4** I hope you have a good journey. **5** I hope everything goes well.

Q ***What's the difference between 'I hope you have a good weekend' and 'Have a good weekend'? (Topic 9)***

A They are very similar. Both are appropriate in most situations. *I hope* can be more formal.

How do you pronounce it?

Schwa (Part 3)

→ Listen to Recording 6 and repeat the words and phrases from Oliver's conversation in the hotel.

→ Pay special attention to the letters with the *schwa* symbol / ə / on the top. The pronunciation is always *schwa* / ə /. Stressed syllables are underlined.

Recording 6

1 Can I help you?

2 Oliver

3 single

4 registration

5 of course

6 signature

7 just here

8 to your right

9 round the corner

10 Do you need help?

Our story continues ... Oliver is in his hotel room in London. He phones his mother in Edinburgh.

Understanding the important information

→ Cover the text of Recording 7.

→ Read the sentences below.

→ Listen to the recording and choose *Yes* or *No*.

Oliver and his mother talk about

a	the weather	Yes/No
b	Oliver's hotel	Yes/No
c	his trip	Yes/No
d	his work in London	Yes/No
e	Tasha	Yes/No
f	Oliver's father	Yes/No
g	a message	Yes/No

Recording 7 – The Story

Oliver	Hi! Mum, it's Oliver. How are you?
Mother	Hello, dear. Where are you?
Oliver	I'm in a hotel in London, the Park. I haven't stayed here before. It's quite nice – small but comfortable and quiet. I've just got here from the airport.
Mother	How was your trip?
Oliver	It went quite well, actually. First, I visited our new representative in Chile, and then on Tuesday, Wednesday and Thursday I went to the Computer Fair in Buenos Aires. I talked to a lot of people there and had lots of meetings. And then on the flight on the way back I met a very interesting girl.
Mother	Oh, did you?
Oliver	Yes, she's an English teacher in South America. She's on holiday here, staying with friends, just outside London. I've got her number there so I can contact her again. I'm going to call her one day next week. We might have dinner together, or something. Anyway, how are you?
Mother	Did you get my message?
Oliver	What message?
Mother	I left a message at your hotel in Argentina two days ago.
Oliver	What was it about, Mum? Come on! What's happened?

Check your answers

a No **b** Yes **c** Yes **d** No **e** Yes **f** No **g** No

Understanding more

→ Cover the text of Recording 7 again.
→ Read the sentences below.
→ Listen to the recording and choose the correct answer.

1 The name of Oliver's hotel is
a the Palmer
b the Park
c the Plaza
d the Spa.

2 **a** This is Oliver's first visit to this hotel.
b This isn't Oliver's first visit to this hotel.
c Oliver always stays at this hotel.

3 Oliver thinks the hotel is
a excellent
b good
c poor.

4 Oliver's business trip was
d good
e not very good
f terrible.

5 Oliver is thinking about inviting Tasha
a for lunch
b for a drink
c for dinner
d to the cinema.

6 Oliver doesn't know about …
a a letter
b a problem
c a ticket
d an invitation.

Check your answers

1 b **2** b **3** b **4** d **5** c **6** b

What do they say?

→ Read the sentences below.
→ Listen to Recording 7 again and try to complete the words.
→ Read the text to help you, if necessary.

1 This is Oliver's first visit to the Park Hotel.
He says, '/ I / h _ _ _ n ' _ / s _ _ _ _ d / here before.'

2 Oliver talks about this trip.

a He says, 'First / I / v _ _ _ _ _ d / our new representative…'

b … then on Tuesday, Wednesday and Thursday I / w _ _ _ / to the Computer Fair…'

c He talks about his activities there.
He says, 'I / t _ _ _ _ d / t _ / a / l _ _ / o _ people there and h _ _ / l _ _ _ / o _ / meetings.'

3 a Oliver tells his mother about Tasha.
He says, 'On the flight on the way back / I / m _ _ / a very interesting girl.'

b His mother is interested. She says, 'Oh, d _ _ / y _ _?'

4 Oliver plans to phone Tasha next week.
He says, 'I ' _ / g _ _ _ _ / t _ / call her one day next week.'

5 Oliver talks about the possibility of dinner with Tasha.
He says, 'We / m _ _ _ _ / h _ _ _ / dinner together.'

6 a Verb *get*: Oliver's mother asks him about her message.
She says, 'Did you get my message?
Here, 'get' means *find*, *buy*, *receive*?

b Oliver says no. His mother gives more information about the message. She says, 'I / l _ _ _ / a message at your hotel two days / a _ _ /.

c Oliver asks about the message.
He says, 'W _ _ _ / w _ _ / _ _ / a _ _ _ _?'

7 He wants to know what the situation is.
He says, 'W _ _ _ ' _ / h _ _ p _ _ e _ ?'

Check your answers

1 I haven't stayed here before. **2 a** First I visited our new representative… **b** then on Tuesday, Wednesday and Thursday I went to the Computer Fair. **c** I talked to a lot of people there and had lots of meetings **3 a** On the flight on the way back I met a very interesting girl. **b** Oh, did you? **4** I'm going to call her one day next week. **5** We might have dinner together. **6 a** Here, *get* means *receive* **b** I left a message at your hotel two days ago. **c** What was it about? (preposition!) **7** What's happened?

Find the words and phrases

→ Read the sentences below.
→ Read the text of Recording 7 again and complete the words and phrases.

1 When Oliver's mother starts the conversation, she says, ' Hello, / d _ _ _ /' to her son.

2 **a** What's the hotel like? It's q _ _ _ _ / n _ _ _ .
b Is there a lot of traffic noise? No it's a /q _ _ _ _ / hotel.

Check your answers

1 Hello dear.
(Older people often say *dear* to be friendly.)
2 a quite nice **b** No, it's a quiet hotel.

Q ***What's the difference in pronunciation between 'quite' and 'quiet'?***

A *Quite* has one syllable / kwaɪt /.
Quiet has two. (qui-et) / kwaɪət /

Grammar and communication 8

Talking about the past – Past simple

Example from *The Story*:

Oliver talks about his trip.
He says, 'First I **visited** our new representative.
Then on Tuesday, Wednesday and Thursday I **went** to the Computer Fair.
I talked to a lot of people there and I **had** a lot of meetings
On the flight on the way back, I **met** a very interesting girl.'

All the verbs in **bold** are in the **past simple tense**.

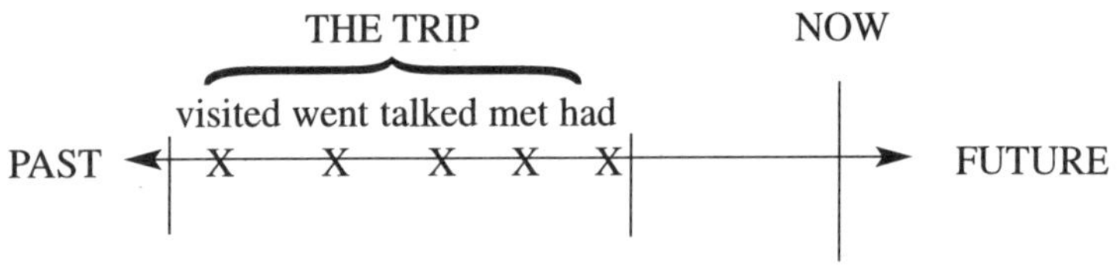

→ Read these questions and answers about the past simple.

Meaning:

Q Is the trip **a** in the past?
b in the present?
c in the future?

A In the past.

Q Oliver **visited** the new representative. Do we know when?

A Yes, during his trip. His trip is in the past.

Q Oliver **went** to the Computer Fair. Do we know when?

A Yes, on Tuesday, Wednesday and Thursday.

Q Oliver **talked** to lots of people and **had** lots of meetings. When?

A During the Computer Fair. The Computer Fair is in the past.

Q Oliver **met** Tasha. When?

A On the way back to England.

All these activities were during his trip. His trip is in the past.

Is there a connection with the present? No. The trip is finished.

Form – past simple

Regular verbs – verb + *-ed*	**Irregular verbs**
visit – **visited** talk – **talked**	go – **went** have – **had** meet – **met**

Note: The verbs in **bold** are the past simple.

Summary – Past Simple		
Affirmative I, you, he, she, it we, they	talked (verb + -ed or irregular verb)	
Negative I, you, he, she, it we, they	didn't	talk (verb)
Questions Did	I, you, he, she, it we, they	talk? (verb)
Tag questions, echo questions and short answers I talked, didn't I? Yes, I did, etc.		

Past simple

→ Complete the dialogue below.

Situation It's Monday morning. Two colleagues, Natalie and Dan are talking about the weekend.

Is the weekend in the past? Yes
Is it finished? Yes
So, the verbs are in the past simple.

Natalie Hi, Dan, ____ you ______(have/had) a good weekend?

Dan Yes, I _____ thanks. It ______ (be/was) really nice, actually. On Saturday, I ______ (wash) the car. Then in the afternoon I ____(take/took) the children to the park. Yesterday I ____ (play) tennis in the morning and for lunch we ____ (have/had) a barbecue in the garden.

Natalie Great!

Dan How about you? What _____ you _____ ?(do/did)

Natalie I _____ (be/was) so tired after last week. I really ____ / ____ (do/did) much at all. I ____ (see/saw) a good film on the T.V. on Saturday night and yesterday I just ______ (relax) at home. My husband's sister ____ (come/came) to see us. We ____/ ___ (want) to cook so we ____ (get/got/got) an Indian takeaway. Later, in the evening we _____ (go/went) out for a drink and then we _____ (drive/drove) her home.

Check your answers

Natalie Hi, Dan, **did you have** a good weekend?

Dan Yes, I did thanks. It **was** really nice, actually. On Saturday, I **washed** the car. Then in the afternoon I **took** the children to the park. Yesterday I **played** tennis in the morning and for lunch we **had** a barbecue in the garden.

Natalie Great!

Dan How about you? What **did** you **do**?

Natalie **I was** so tired after last week. I really **didn't do** much at all. I **saw** a good film on the T.V. on Saturday night and yesterday I just **relaxed** at home. My husband's sister **came** to see us. We **didn't want** to cook so we got an Indian takeaway. Later, in the evening we **went** out for a drink and then we **drove** her home.

Grammar and communication 9

Experience up to now – present perfect

Examples from *The Story*:

1 This is Oliver's first visit to the Park Hotel.
He says, 'I **haven't stayed** here before.'

2 Oliver asks what was in the message.
He says, 'What'**s happened**?'
has

Now look at this example:

'I've **stayed** in this hotel three times.'

Meaning

→ Read these questions and answers about '*I have stayed.*'

1 Is the action in the past? Yes.
2 Do we know when? No. When is not the focus.
We use the present perfect to connect past actions with the present.
3 Is there a connection between staying in the hotel and now? Yes. I know the hotel now because of my three visits in the past.

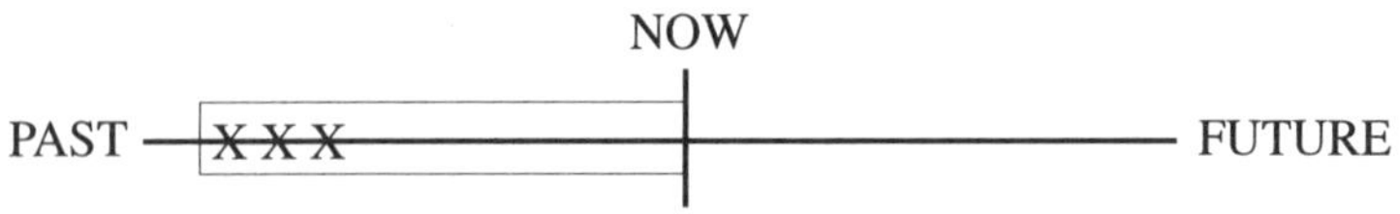

Form

The name of this tense is **present perfect**.

Q ***Why is it called the present perfect?***

A Let's look at another example.

I	**have**	**lived**	**in France**
subject	*have* in present	past participle	

Half the verb is present (*have*) and half is the past participle (*lived*).
This tense connects the past and the present.
My time in France is in the past, but the experience is with me today.

Grammar Summary – Present Perfect		
I/you/we/they	+ have ('ve)	+ past participle
He/she/it	has ('s)	(regular verb + 'ed') or irregular
Negative		
I/you/we/they	haven't	+ past participle
He/she/it	hasn't	
Question		
Have	I/you/we/they	+ past participle
Has	he/she/it	
Tag questions, echo questions and short answers		
Have(n't)	I/you/we/they?	
Has(n't)	He/she/it?	

The past and the present are connected = present perfect.

★ Asking questions with the **present perfect**:
The **present perfect** is the same as all other two-word verbs in English. To make questions you change the word order.

For example: (1) *He* → (2) *has* → (3) *visited*
For questions, say (2) *Has* → (1) *he* → (3) *visited*?
(2) auxiliary, *Has* (1) the subject, *he* (3) the past participle, *visited*.

★ The past participle is the third in a list of irregular verbs.
For example: see – saw – **seen**
write – wrote – **written**

'I have **seen** this film before.'
'She has **written** three books.'

→ Put the words in the right order to make sentences about Oliver.

1 __________ at his hotel.
arrived/Oliver/has/

2 ___________to his mother.
spoken/has/he

3 ______________ Tasha? No, not yet. He's going to call her next week.
called/he/has

4 _________________ the office. He's going there later.
contacted/hasn't/he

5 How many times __________ to South America? About six times.
he/been/has

Check your answers

1 Oliver has arrived. **2** He has spoken. **3** Has he called. **4** He hasn't contacted. **5** has he been.

→ Use the verbs in brackets in the present perfect to complete these mini-dialogues.

1 **A** ____ you ______(see/saw/seen) the film 'Titanic'?
B Yes I ___.

2 **A** How many times ____ you ______ (go/went/been) to France?
B I '__ / ___ lots of times.

3 **A** How many countries ____ you ______ (visit)?
B Me? I' ___/_____ to the States but I _____/_____ anywhere else.

4 **A** How many jobs ____ your brother ____(have/had/had)?
B He ______n't / ____ many, actually.

5 **A** How many English books ___ you ______ (read/read/read)?
B I' ___ / ______ hundreds!

6 **A** ____ they _______ (finish)?
B No, not yet.

7 **A** You ____ _______ (forget/forgot/forgotten), have you?
B No, of course not.

8 **A** My sister '__ / ______ (buy/bought/bought) a new house.
B Oh! _____ she? Whereabouts?

Check your answers

1 A Have you seen the film 'Titanic'?
B Yes, I have.
2 A How many times have you been to France?
B I've been lots of times.
3 A How many countries have you visited?
B Me? I've been to the States but I haven't been anywhere else.
4 A How many jobs has your brother had?
B He hasn't had many actually.
5 A How many English books have you read?
B I've read hundreds.
6 A Have you finished?
B No, not yet.
7 A You haven't forgotten, have you?
B No, of course not.
8 A My sister's (has) bought a new house.
B Oh! Has she? Whereabouts?

> **Tip:** If you can't answer the question *when* about the past, use the present perfect.

Goodbye!

Leaving the hotel

→ Put this conversation in the right order. Use the letters.

______ **A** Certainly. What room number is it, please?
______ **B** Good morning. Can I help you?
______ **C** Room 201.
______ **D** Of course. If you wait at the front door, one will be here in a few moments. Goodbye. I hope you have a good flight.
______ **E** Let me see... Here's your bill. How would you like to pay?
______ **F** Thanks. Goodbye.
______ **G** Morning. Yes, I'd like to check out, please.
______ **H** There you are. Could you possibly call me a taxi to go to the airport?
_____ **I** If I could ask you to just sign here then, please.
_____ **J** By card, if that's O.K.

→ Listen to Recording 8 and check your answers.

Check your answers *(Recording 8)*

Receptionist	**B**	Good morning. Can I help you?
Guest	**G**	Morning. Yes, I'd like to check out, please.
Receptionist	**A**	Certainly. What room number is it, please?
Guest	**C**	Room 201.
Receptionist	**E**	Let me see… Here's your bill. How would you like to pay?
Guest	**J**	By card, if that's O.K.
Receptionist	**I**	If I could ask you to just sign here then, please.
Guest	**H**	There you are. Could you possibly call me a taxi to go to the airport?
Receptionist	**D**	Of course. If you wait at the front door, one will be here in a few moments. Goodbye. I hope you have a good flight.
Guest	**F**	Thanks. Goodbye.

About your country: hotels

→ Write answers to these questions or prepare to tell a friend.

1 When was the last time you stayed in a hotel?

____

2 Talk or write about **a** the place
b how long you stayed
c who you went with
d why you went there.

____

____

____

3 What was the hotel like? Describe it and talk or write about the facilities.

____

____

4 How much did you enjoy your stay there?

____

What would you say?

1 You are in a hotel. You would like to watch T.V. You turn the T.V. on and nothing happens. You call reception.

____

2 You can't find your hotel key. You look everywhere but you can't find it. You're at reception.

____

Possible answers

1 The television in my room doesn't work. **2** I'm very sorry but I can't find my key. Advanced alternative: I'm terribly sorry but I think I've lost my key.

Revision

How do you say it in your language?

Here are some examples of the important points in this topic.

→ Translate the sentences below into your language.
→ Remember – translate the idea, not the words.

1 A Who's next? **B** I think I am.

____

2 A How many of you are there? **B** There are four of us.

____

3 A How much is this one?

____

4 £3 a packet.

____

5 I don't mind where we go as long as you come too.

____

6 Have you got anything cheaper?

____

7 On the 6th floor.

____

8 I haven't been to Singapore.

____

9 He telephoned last week.

____

10 I got the letter yesterday.

____

Join the conversation

→ Look at the text of Recording 1 (page 302) again.
→ Listen to Recording 9 and say **Oliver's** words in the spaces.

TEST 10

Which one is right?

→ Choose **a** or **b**.

1 I've seen that film on video.
a Did you? What's it like?
b Have you? What's it like?

2 **a** My room is in the 1st floor.
b My room is on the 1st floor.

3 **a** This ice cream costs £2 a box.
b This ice cream costs £2 the box.

4 **a** Could I see the red one, please?
b Could I see the red, please?

5 **a** I hope you to enjoy your trip.
b I hope you enjoy your trip.

6 **a** Yesterday I went to the cinema.
b Yesterday I was to the cinema.

7 **a** Where you met my brother?
b Where did you meet my brother?

8 **a** How would you like to pay?
b How would you like to paying?

9 **a** With card, please.
b By card, please.

10 **a** The bar is in the downstairs.
b The bar is downstairs.

11 a What did you at the weekend?
b What did you do at the weekend?

12 a When have you arrived?
b When did you arrive?

13 a I'll take this one, please.
b I buy this one, please.

14 a In which floor is the restaurant, please?
b What floor is the restaurant on, please?

Write two dialogues

1 **A In the travel agency**
The travel agent asks about the type of hotel you want.

You

2 The only thing you don't like is noise

3 She asks about the number of people

4 You and your partner

5 She asks you about price you want to pay

6 Your maximum is £70

7 She suggests the Plaza Hotel – £65

8 You say yes

9 She asks about method of payment

10 In cash, please

B You pay and then you go to the shop next door to buy a suitcase. You are looking at a small suitcase

1 Shop assistant

2 You want the same suitcase but bigger

3 The shop assistant says yes and shows it to you

4 You decide to buy it

☑ Check your answers

1 b **2** b **3** a **4** a **5** b **6** a **7** b **8** a **9** b **10** b **11** b **12** b **13** a **14** b

Dialogues: model answers

A	**1**	**Travel agent**	What sort of hotel are you looking for?
	2	**You**	I don't mind, as long as it's quiet.
	3	**Travel agent**	How many of you are there?
	4	**You**	There are two of us.
	5	**Travel agent**	What sort of price are you looking to pay?
	6	**You**	Anything up to £70.
	7	**Travel agent**	How about the Plaza Hotel? It's £65 a night.
	8	**You**	O.K.
	9	**Travel agent**	How would you like to pay?
	10	**You**	In cash, please.
B	**1**	**Shop assistant**	Can I help you?
	2	**You**	Yes, have you got a bigger one like this?
	3	**Shop assistant**	Yes, I have – this one.
	4	**You**	I'll take that one, please.

To the learner

We hope you have enjoyed learning with *Teach Yourself English* and that you are happy with the progress you have made. We enjoyed finding a method to help you learn English in English, without a teacher, and writing this course for you.

We wonder what will happen to Oliver and Tasha in the future?
Will Tasha enjoy her holiday?
Will Oliver and Tasha meet again?
What do you think?
We'll see!

With best wishes

Sandra Stevens

Sandra Stevens

GLOSSARY

Auxiliary (verb) A verb used with another verb. The auxiliary (verb) shows tense etc. For example:

*She **is** reading*	Present progressive
*He **can** drive*	Modal auxiliary/ability
*I **have** finished*	Present perfect

Reading, *drive* and *finished* are the main verbs – they give the meaning. ***Is***, ***can't***, ***have*** are the auxiliaries.

- The auxiliary for the present simple is ***do/does***
- The auxiliary for the past simple is ***did***
- Auxiliaries are always part of the verb in all other tenses

We use auxiliaries to make questions. We change the word order: the auxiliary goes *before* the person. For example:

*She **is** reading*
***Is** she reading?*
She likes Coke
***Does** she like Coke?*

To make the verb negative, we add '*n't*' (*not*) to the auxiliary. For example:

*He **can't** drive*
*She **doesn't** like Coke*

Some auxiliaries have a short form or contraction (see **Contraction**), for example *he's*, *they**'re***, *we**'ve***. Contractions are common in spoken English and informal written English.

Auxiliaries are very important in English because we use them a lot to make conversation: **Question tags** and **short answers** both use **auxiliaries**.

Some examples of **auxiliaries** in **question tags** are:

*He's working, **isn't** he?*
*They**'re** married, **aren't** they?*
*She**'s** got a cat, **hasn't** she?*

And here are some examples of **auxiliaries** in **short answers**:

A *He's here*	**B** *Oh, **is** he?*
A *They can't come*	**B** ***Can't** they? Why not?*
A *She's had the baby*	**B** ***Has** she? Is it a boy or a girl?*

Comparative Comparing two things. For example:

*Peter is old**er than** his brother.* Short adjective *old* + *er* (*than*)
*A house is **more** expensive **than** a flat.* Longer adjective, *more* + adjective (+ *than*)

Contraction A short form of verbs *be* and *have*, some auxiliary verbs and *us* in *let's*. We write an apostrophe (') in the place of the missing letters. For example:

I am = ***I'm***
It is and *it has* = ***it's***
He would not = ***He wouldn't***

Contractions are very common in spoken and informal written English.

Direct language Can be impolite in English. For example: *Give me a glass of water* is often impolite. It is more polite to use indirect language, for example, *Could you give me a glass of water, please?*

Echo questions Help conversation. They show you are interested and want to continue the conversation. Echo questions have two words: the auxiliary + subject. For example:

A *I live in Paris*	**B** ***Do you?***
A *He hasn't got a car*	**B** ***Hasn't he?***

Formal language Is appropriate with people you don't know, people in authority and official situations and documents. (see **Informal language** and **Neutral language**). For example: *Thanks* is informal language. *Thank you very much indeed* is formal.

Gerund The verb + *ing*, used like a noun. For example:

*I enjoy **travelling**.*

Imperative The verb without *to*, for example, ***Wait** a minute.*

Remember the imperative is a danger zone for learners of English. We often use other forms of the verb to ask/tell someone to do something.

The imperative is common for:

Wishes:	***Have** a nice day!*
Instructions:	***Take** this train*
Directions:	***Turn** left at the end of the road*
Warnings:	***Be** careful!*

Informal language Appropriate with family, friends and children. For example, *Hi!* is informal, *Hello* is neutral/formal.

Intonation Is the music or movement of the voice on the syllable with stress. English expresses different meanings through intonation. For example:

Yes →

Flat intonation. The person isn't interested.

Yes ↘

A big movement in the pitch of the voice. The person is interested.

Less direct language – English uses indirect language a lot. It helps conversation and communication. Direct language with flat intonation can sound rude. For example:

Dialogue 1 – direct	**Dialogue 2 – less direct**
A *Where's John?*	***Do you know where John is?***
B *I've got no idea*	***I'm afraid I've got no idea***

The words in Dialogue 1, with flat intonation, can sound rude. The words in Dialogue 2 are less direct.

Neutral language Appropriate in most situations. For example, *Hello* is appropriate with people you know, people you don't know, people in authority and children (see **Formal language** and **Informal language**).

Past participle The verb + *ed*. The third part of an irregular verb, for example *see/saw/**seen** – **seen***, is the past participle. We use the verb *have* + past participle to form the perfect tenses. For example, *I have eaten* – present perfect.

Plural More than one. For example, *sandwiches*, *grapes*.

Preposition Little words that connect nouns, etc., with other words. For example, ***to** the station* (direction), ***at** the restaurant* (place), ***before** two o'clock* (time).

The preposition is sometimes part of a phrase. For example, *interested **in**, I'm interested **in** sport* or *to be married **to**, She's married **to** a Frenchman.*

There are lots of prepositions in English. They are a problem zone for learners because it's often difficult to know which preposition to use. To help you:

- Try to learn the meanings of the prepositions (for example direction = *to*)
- When you learn a phrase with a preposition, remember to learn the preposition, too!

Question tag A short question form at the end of a sentence. This question form with falling intonation isn't really a question. It *is* a way of starting or making conversation. For example:

A *Terrible weather, **isn't it**?* **B** *Yes. It's not very good, **is it**?*

The speakers know that the weather is terrible. They are not really asking questions. They are using question tags to start/continue the conversation.

Schwa – The vowel sound / ə /, as in *a* book. It is the only sound in English with a name!

Short answers *Yes* and *No* alone can often sound rude in English. Short answers are: *Yes/No* + person + auxiliary. For example:

A *Is Sue here?* **B** ***Yes, she is.***
A *Can you drive?* **B** ***No, I can't.***

Singular One only, for example, a *bus*, a *biscuit*.

Stress Emphasis or force on a syllable or word. In all words with two syllables or more in English, one syllable has stress. Example, *<u>Eng</u> - lish, fan – <u>tas</u> – tic.*

In sentences, the stress is on the important words, the words with a lot of meaning. For example, *I've bought some <u>bread</u>, some <u>cheese</u> and some <u>fruit</u>.*

In English we also use stress to give a particular meaning or emphasis: *Could I have a cold drink?* (meaning not a *hot* one).

We also use it to correct people. For example, *The books on the desk, not under it.*

Syllable Part of a word with a vowel sound. For example, the word *question* has two syllables, ***ques – tion***. And the word *popular* has three, ***pop – u – lar***.

Uncountable Nouns that you can't count – mass nouns. For example, *rice* and *money* are uncountable nouns. You can't say one, two, three + noun.

Weak form In some short, common words (for example *but, for, from, to, was, does*), the vowel has two pronunciations: one strong (when the word has stress), for example, *who is it for?*; and one weak (when the word doesn't have stress), for example, *it's **for** you, **but** not now, **from** Tom, **to** Paris, **Was** it good? **Does** she know?* In all these words, the pronunciation of the vowel is *schwa* – it is very short and weak. *Schwa* is the most common weak form vowel sound.

QUICK REFERENCE: COMMUNICATIVE FUNCTIONS

The figure in brackets ( ) is the topic number.

Ability (3)
Questions: *Can you* + verb?
Do you + verb?
Responses: *No, not at all*
Yes, but not very well
Yes, not too badly

Asking about the same topic (3)
And you?
How about you?

Asking for an alternative – general (10)
Have you got anything else?

Asking for an alternative - specific
Can I/ Could I have X instead, please? **(2)**
Have you got anything... (+ short adjective + *er*?)
Example: *Have you got anything cheaper?* **(10)**
(+ more + long adjective)
Example: *Have you got anything more suitable?*

Asking for help – Indirect questions (7)
Can you tell me where X is, please?
Do you know how much X costs, please?
Could you tell me if ...

Asking for help, systems – Present simple (8)
What/Where/When/How do I ... + verb?
Example: *Where do I sign?*

Asking for information (6)
Could you tell me ...? I'd like (to know) ... What's the ...?

Could you tell me }
I'd like (to know) } *the time of the next train, please?*
What's }

Asking for opinions (9)

How is/was ...?

Example: *How was your meal?*

Asking for things (2)

Could I have ...?

Example: *Could I have a glass of water, please?*

Asking someone to do something

Can you ..., Could you ..., Would you mind + verb -ing **(7)**

Examples: *Can you* } *wait a moment, please?*
Could you }
Would you mind waiting a moment?

If you would like to ... (very indirect) (7)

Example: *If you would like to call again tomorrow ...*

Attracting attention (1)

Excuse me ...

Example: *Excuse me, could I have the bill, please?*

Buying things, decisions (10)

I'll take ...

Example: *I'll take this one*

Choosing – responding to offers (2)

X, please
X for me, please
I'd like X, please
Could I have X, please?
I'll have X, please

Decisions (2)

I'll ...

Negative decisions – I don't think I will **(2)**

Decisions, buying (10)

I'll take ...

Negative decision – *I think I'll leave it*

Insisting, offering help (9)

Come on! Let me ... + verb

Example: *Come on. Let me do that!*

Response: Yes: *Thank you/ Thanks*

No: *No thank you/thanks. I can manage*

Invitations and offers

Question: *Would you like a ...?* **(1)**

Example: *Would you like an ice cream?*

Responses: Yes: *Yes, please. That would be nice*

Yes, please. I'd love one/some

No: *No, thank you*

No, thanks. I'm fine

Question: *Would you like to...?* **(7)**

Response: Yes: *Yes, that would be nice*

No: *I'm sorry, I'm ...* (reason)

Question: *If you would like to ...* (a very indirect way of asking someone to do something)

Responses: Yes: *Thank you*

Yes, of course

Yes, that's fine

Yes, I'll...

No: *I'm sorry but I can't*

Likes and dislikes – *like, enjoy, mind, be keen on* (4)

Question: *Do you like/enjoy X*/verb + ing?

Do you like your job?

Do you enjoy being a mother/father?

Responses:	Very positive:	*Yes, I really enjoy it*
	Yes:	*Yes, I quite like it*
	Neutral:	*I don't mind it*
	No:	*I'm not very keen on it, actually*
	Very negative:	*Actually, I don't like it at all*

Making conversation

actually **(3)**

Actually, I + verb or *I* + verb, *actually*

Example: *I live in London, actually*

echo questions **(3)**

auxiliary + person

Do you? / Have you? / Can she? / Aren't they? etc.

Number of people, talking about the (10)

Question: *How many of you are there?*
Response: *There are X of us*

Offers (see **Invitations and offers**)

Offering help (6)

Offers: *I can...*
I could...
I'll...
Shall I...?
Would you like me to...?

Example: *I can* / *I could* / *I'll* } *do that for you,* (if you like)

Example: *Shall I* / *Would you like me to* } *do that for you?*

Responses: Yes: *Thanks*
Thank you
That's very kind of you
Can you? Could you? Would you?
No: *Thanks for the offer but it's alright*
Thanks but I can manage

Offering more

(some) more, another **(1)**
Question: *Would you like some more coffee?*
Would you like another sandwich?
Responses:(see **Invitations**)

Permission, asking for (2)

Questions: *Is it alright if I ,...?*
Could I...?
Can I...?

Example: *Is it alright if I* / *Could I* / *Can I* } *use your phone?*

Responses: Yes: *Of course*
Go ahead
No: *I'm sorry but...* + reason

Possibilities and suggestions (6)

We could...
Example: *We could go to the cinema*
You can...
Example: *You can tell me tomorrow*

Possibilities, suggestions and offers (see **Offering help**)

Price, talking about the (10)

Question: *What sort of price are you looking to pay?*
Response: Maximum: *Anything up to XXX*
Anything under XXX
As long as it's less than XXX
Approximately: *About XXX*
Around XXX

Rejecting an offer of help (9)

No, really. It's alright thanks
No, really. I can manage

Requests (see **Asking for things/Asking people to do things**)

Same, asking for the (2)

The same for me, please
I'll have X, too, please

Starting a conversation – Question tags (1)

Adjective +, *isn't it?*
Example: *Nice, isn't it?*
Not very + adjective +, *is it?*
Example: *Not very interesting, is it?*
Sentence + question tag
Example: *He isn't playing very well, is he?*
It was a good film, wasn't it?

Suggesting doing something together (7)

Let's ... + verb
Example: *Let's go to the cinema*
Responses: Yes: *OK*
Alright
Yes, why not?
That's a good idea
Yes, why don't we?

No: *Do you really want to?*
I'm not too sure
Perhaps not
Actually, I'm not too keen

Negative suggestion: *Let's not ...*
Example: *Let's not go to the party. I'm too tired*

Suggestions, possibilities and offers (see **Offering help**)

Thanking (9)

Neutral:	*Thank you*	*for* + verb *-ing* e.g. *for inviting me*
	Thank you very much	
Formal:	*Thank you very much indeed*	
Informal:	*Thanks*	
	Many thanks	
	Thanks a lot	

Responses:
Neutral: *That's OK*
That's alright
Formal: *You're welcome*
Not at all
Informal: *No problem*
Any time

Why, saying (5)

Question: Why are you…?
Responses: *to...* + verb
because I want to...
because I need to...
because I like to...
so (that) (I can)
because...
because of... + noun

Example: **A** *Why are you going to Italy?*
B *To*
Because I want to
Because I need to
Because I like to
So (that) (I can)
} *visit my Italian friends*
Because of my friends – they're Italian
Because I'm going to visit my Italian friends

INDEX